Pneumatology and Union

Pneumatology and Union

John Calvin and the Pentecostals

Peter Ross

⟨PICKWICK *Publications* · Eugene, Oregon

PNEUMATOLOGY AND UNION
John Calvin and the Pentecostals

Copyright © 2019 Peter Ross. All rights reserved. Except for brief quotations in critical publications or reviews, no part of this book may be reproduced in any manner without prior written permission from the publisher. Write: Permissions, Wipf and Stock Publishers, 199 W. 8th Ave., Suite 3, Eugene, OR 97401.

Pickwick Publications
An Imprint of Wipf and Stock Publishers
199 W. 8th Ave., Suite 3
Eugene, OR 97401

www.wipfandstock.com

PAPERBACK ISBN: 978-1-5326-5051-2
HARDCOVER ISBN: 978-1-5326-5052-9
EBOOK ISBN: 978-1-5326-5053-6

Cataloguing-in-Publication data:

Names: Ross, Peter Graham.

Title: Pneumatology and union : John Calvin and the pentecostals / by Peter Ross.

Description: Eugene, OR : Pickwick Publications, 2019 | Includes bibliographical references.

Identifiers: ISBN 978-1-5326-5051-2 (paperback) | ISBN 978-1-5326-5052-9 (hardcover) | ISBN 978-1-5326-5053-6 (ebook)

Subjects: LCSH: Calvin, Jean,—1509–1564. | Pentecostalism—Relations—Reformed Church. | Reformed Church—Relations—Pentecostalism.

Classification: BT121.3 .R82 2019 (print) | BT121.3 .R82 (ebook)

Manufactured in the U.S.A.   07/09/19

Notes

Gender Neutral Language

In order to be gender neutral in this work, I have adopted a practice of referring either to "him" or "her," or equivalent pronouns, in a roughly alternate manner. I have chosen this in preference to other constructions (such as "him/her" or making all references impersonal) as I consider it considerably less clumsy, thereby assisting the clarity of the argument.

Biblical Quotations

Unless otherwise specified, Scripture quotations are taken from New Revised Standard Version Bible, copyright © 1989 National Council of the Churches of Christ in the United States of America. Used by permission. All rights reserved worldwide.

Contents

Preface | ix

1 Pneumatology and Union: John Calvin | 1
2 Pneumatology and Union: The Pentecostals | 49
3 The Assurance of Faith | 107
4 Providence and Guidance | 136
5 Justification | 173
6 From Calvin to Pentecostals | 211

Bibliography | 249

Preface

When I began work on my doctoral dissertation, from which this book has developed, I was a Pentecostal minister sharing ministry in a Pentecostal church. As well as my personal interest in the topic, my aim in pursuing this work was to show that Pentecostalism could access the long history of Christian thought in a way which would be beneficial to it as it seeks to develop its own theology. I had long considered that Pentecostalism, within which I had worshipped and ministered for twenty years, had a pressing need to deepen its theology in order to remain strong and healthy for the future. My hope was that this work, and my ministry beyond its completion, would make some small contribution in that regard. Now that this work is complete, I find myself, somewhat to my surprise, an Anglican priest, ministering and worshipping within that tradition. My contribution to Pentecostalism through this work may be somewhat more muted than I initially hoped as a result, but my observation concerning Pentecostalism and its theology remains the same. Accordingly, I think that what I have shown in this work does make a useful contribution to the development of a global Pentecostal theology.

I have addressed my task by setting up a conversation with a major Protestant theologian in an effort to show where affinities might exist between his thought and Pentecostalism. I settled on John Calvin as the theologian because in my first reading of him I was struck by his pastoral concern for his readers and the intimate way he described the relation between God and the believer, incorporating a strong divine influence on the believer's life. These echoed what I perceived as Pentecostal viewpoints, so there appeared to be potential for a fruitful exchange.

I chose to investigate pneumatology as it is the claims surrounding the work of the Spirit, particularly in the context of Spirit baptism (or Spirit release, as I prefer), which sets Pentecostalism apart from the Protestantism from which it sprang. Alongside this, I also selected the union between the believer and Christ as a focus because of its importance in Calvin's thought and the fact that, for him, it is the work of the Spirit. There is thus a close relation between the Spirit and the union for Calvin and I considered it most likely that I would find touch points between the two systems in these areas. It would be these touch points, or affinities, which I anticipated could provide a basis for a deepening of Pentecostal theology in these areas.

In pursuing this work, I have focused on the individual and their relationship with God, their union with Christ in Calvin's terms. I acknowledge that there is much more to the union and pneumatology to be found in Calvin's ecclesiology than what I examine here concerning each believer's personal union with Christ, and that the influence of that cannot be dismissed. However, I have limited the discussion to the personal union, with reference to the church as necessary, because that is my personal interest and it makes for a better match with Pentecostal thought.

This better match points to how I have approached the task. In identifying affinities, it is not necessary to give a complete account of each theology only to pick a small corresponding part from each to look at in detail. It is only necessary to ensure that the description of each small part is complete and accurate in the context of the whole. I do not attempt to give a full and rounded account of either theology, but I have given enough attention to the aspects I look at that the reader can be confident that what I describe is true to each.

I begin with a discussion of Calvin's pneumatology and the union between the believer and Christ, followed by the same for Pentecostal theology. The latter cannot hope to be complete in the way the former is because there is no global Pentecostal theology at present, so any review would necessarily have to be very large to begin to capture something of the totality of Pentecostal views. Space obviously prevents such a review, but this is not disadvantageous to my task. I have chosen to follow a direction which gives prominence to Spirit release and the work of the Spirit in salvation. By doing so, I have retained a close focus on Spirit release, which is at the core of Pentecostal testimony, so the outline I have given is representative of the core aspect of Pentecostal thought. In any event, if the outcome is to show that affinities exist between the Pentecostal position outlined and Calvin which are sufficient to allow some grounding in Calvin for Pentecostals, then it will have been shown that the deepening of Pentecostal theology by appeal to such as Calvin is possible.

These outlines establish the positions which can be used to evaluate whether some relation can be established between the two systems of thought. This evaluation is done by examining the assurance of faith, providence, and justification respectively, looking at the respective theologies in more depth in order to tease out affinities. Each of these topics was chosen because of the substantial influence of the Spirit in the union in the particular areas, as will be seen. Justification was also chosen because it represents a major doctrine and one such needs consideration. Together, these doctrines represent a substantial enough sample of thought to establish links which are not simply isolated coincidences. That is, if successful, the analysis will show that a deepening of Pentecostal theology is possible through engagement with Calvin, at least.

In the final chapter, I give some extended consideration to Spirit release in order to examine whether a concept of it can be developed which could be called "Calvinist," in the sense that it could sit well with his thought (not within his thought, note), not that it accords with later thought identified as Calvinism. I then consider whether this can give rise to significant touch points and review those identified in the earlier discussion in order to demonstrate whether a relation can be established between Calvin and the Pentecostals. That is, can Pentecostal thought on pneumatology and union be so cast as to be an extension from Calvin's thought? Or, to put it another way, and one within the scope of this study, can Pentecostals usefully look to Calvin on pneumatology and union to deepen their own theology and so aid the move towards a global Pentecostal theology? My aim is that the following discussion and its conclusions will make the answers to these questions clear.

1

Pneumatology and Union
John Calvin

The Person and Work of the Spirit

Calvin maintains an orthodox[1] doctrine of the Trinity and the place of the Spirit within it. Thus, God is one essence which contains three persons,[2] terms which Calvin expands upon. "The essence of God is simple and undivided,"[3] he says, by which he attempts to capture a oneness in God whereby God is a unity, yet his being is of a nature which allows distinction within. Within this unity there are three "subsistences," a term he prefers to "person." These three are in close relation with each other but each has an individual quality or qualities which cannot be communicated to the others. Thus, while inseparable from the essence, each subsistence can be distinguished, and the distinguishing qualities are what set apart the Father, Son, and Holy Spirit.[4] Note that God is not the essence and neither is the essence something separate from God, rather it is a quality of God in which all three subsistences share; they are all equally divine.[5]

The Spirit is therefore fully divine, and Calvin demonstrates this specifically by examining the work the Spirit does and scriptural references to the fact.[6] It is the Spirit who sustains all of creation; who does the work of

---

1. By "orthodox" in this context I mean the classical doctrine such as that summarized in the so-called *Nicene-Constantinopolitan Creed* adopted at the Council of Constantinople in 381.

2. Calvin, *Institutes*, I.13, chapter heading. Hereafter I will refer to this work as *Institutes* but in references follow the convention of only referring to Book, Chapter and Section numbers, except where the reference is to the prefatory articles.

3. I.13.2.

4. I.13.6.

5. I.13.25.

6. I.13.14 and 15 respectively.

regeneration; and brings believers into "communion with God,"[7] all tasks requiring a divine hand. It is the understanding of these functions, and others, which comprise Calvin's pneumatology which will be described. Because of the ontological status of the Spirit, it is a pneumatology by which we are to understand that it is God who is directly involved and at work when the Spirit acts. The Spirit is not a tool or anything less than God which God uses in these acts; they are clearly direct divine work.

We are also to understand that one, at least, of the qualities which distinguishes the Spirit from the Father and the Son is how the Spirit functions in the world, in humans, and particularly in the elect. God comes to humans through the activity of the Spirit as it is by the Spirit alone that God dwells in believers.[8] Calvin acknowledges that God can operate in the world and with humans in any way and through any agency he chooses, even Satan,[9] but it is the Spirit who works with believers, and even a "lower working" of the Spirit is possible in the reprobate.[10] Any illumination believers have about God is a work of the Spirit;[11] any faith believers have is a work of the Spirit;[12] anything good in believers is the result of the work of the Spirit,[13] and so on. However, while the Spirit permeates every part of the believer's life and is hugely active, almost at times to the exclusion of the individual it seems, he is nonetheless an invisible and secret influence.

For Calvin, this secrecy is a deliberate act of God. When the Spirit appeared as a dove at Jesus' baptism (Matt 3:16), he then immediately disappeared in order that humans might understand "the Spirit to be invisible" and so refrain from seeking a representation of him.[14] Not infrequently, Calvin refers to the work of the Spirit being secret, thus the testimony of the Spirit in showing believers the truth of Scripture is secret; the virtue of the Spirit which nourishes the church is secret; believers receive the benefits of Christ by the secret operation of the Spirit; the efficacy of the sacraments is secret and a work of the Spirit; and so forth.[15] Mere invisibility does not, by itself, prevent believers experiencing the Spirit in ways not dependent on

---

7. I.13.14.
8. I.13.14.
9. I.18.2.
10. III.2.13.
11. II.2.19–21, III.1.3.
12. III.1.4, III.2.7, III.2.35.
13. III.17.5.
14. I.11.3.
15. I.7.4, II.12.7, III.1.1, IV.14.9.

sight and so becoming directly aware of his presence, but the secrecy Calvin claims does mean that such awareness is not possible.

The Spirit is an active influence in every part of a believer's life (as will be seen), teaching, directing, correcting, and regenerating, yet the believer cannot be aware of his presence other than by seeing his effects. In the absence of any obvious effects, the only way the believer can know the Spirit is present, therefore, is by faith, itself an effect or work of the Spirit in the believer.[16] The Spirit is, of course, active in the sacraments, but this also is a matter of faith as it is the outward witness of the elements or water and the actions of the believer which make the Spirit's presence evident.[17] It is true that the Christian "rejoices in the indwelling of the Spirit" and that Calvin notes that believers can have no hope of resurrection "unless we feel the Spirit dwelling within us," and that one is reprobate unless one knows that Christ dwells within, something demonstrated by the Spirit.[18] But in these instances Calvin is not contemplating some direct experience of the Spirit which produces an awareness of a presence within apart from anything else. Rather, the "feeling" is still *via* the indirect experience of the Spirit's effects. First, it is the illumination believers receive: the conviction of the truth and value of Scripture that demonstrates the Spirit's presence. Second, and in a related and less circular manner, it is the faith which believers have and experience, a faith which is inseparable from the Spirit and the Spirit's "peculiar" work. Thus, experiencing faith is a work of the Spirit. It is in these ways that believers feel the Spirit within.[19]

This anonymity is necessary for Calvin's conception as he rejects any notion that the Spirit teaches directly apart from Scripture—there can be no new revelation which is neither unsupported nor untested by Scripture.[20] If the Spirit was not anonymous, then believers could experience his presence directly, and interact with him directly without the need for any moderating influence of Scripture. But Calvin wants Scripture to be the sole authority, the only place to receive the revelation of the Word, so the Spirit cannot be experienced directly and must be self-effacing. Of course, it must be emphasized that there is no sense of absence in this anonymity; the influence

16. III.2.8, III.2.35, IV.14.8, 9, etc.

17. IV.14.9, 17, 22, etc.

18. III.2.39.

19. Randall Zachman comments that Calvin thinks humans can "feel the life of God within" themselves. Zachman, *Reconsidering John Calvin*, 13–14. While this is real, this comes about from the contemplation of creation and observing God's works in making it all function, including ourselves. This is an indirect apprehension of God and so is consistent with the above.

20. I.9.

and activity of the Spirit is absolutely necessary for Scripture to be the word of God to any believer reading it, but to the believer the revelation resides in Scripture, not in the Spirit. The Spirit "must ever remain just as he once revealed himself" in Scripture.[21]

Care needs to be taken here to ensure clarity is maintained when discussing Calvin's pneumatology. For him, the content of God's revelation is Jesus Christ, and how this is made clear to humans is through the Spirit, whom Christ sends and empowers. Thus, Christ is the revelation residing in Scripture and the giver of the Spirit who reveals him. The progressive regeneration of the believer is not progressive revelation or an adding to the revelation but is rather an increasing knowledge or understanding of the revelation, which remains undivided. In no sense is the Spirit the revelation; instead, the Spirit is always the one who points to Christ who is the revelation. In the discussion which follows it must always be remembered that the work of the Spirit is christological in both origin and focus.

It is legitimate to object here that it is possible for the Spirit to give independent knowledge which is consistent with Scripture but experienced by the believer separately from reading Scripture or listening to it being preached. Calvin rejects this,[22] and in support of him it can be observed that it is only through knowledge of Scripture that the believer may judge the consistency of any understanding with it. This knowledge may be gained beforehand, so the believer recognizes the consistency on perceiving what the Spirit is giving, or it could come afterwards when the consistency is recognized upon reading Scripture or hearing it being expounded. In either case, it could be said that it is Scripture which is illuminated in a way no different in quality from a discovery coincident with hearing it preached or reading it. The only difference is that there is a separation in time between receiving true knowledge of Scripture and direct contact with it. At its core, the realization is the believer perceiving the truth he sees in Scripture. This is certainly an action of the Spirit, but to preserve the anonymity Calvin claims for him, this secure link to Scripture must be preserved.

While Calvin's concern is naturally theological, he does make it clear that the Spirit works everywhere outside of faith. In fact, the source of all truth and gifts, whether they be of a religious nature or not is the Spirit.[23] The discoveries of science[24] are revealed by the Spirit and all talents, whether

21. I.9.2.
22. I.9.1; III.3.14.
23. II.2.13–17.
24. By which, of course, Calvin does not mean the modern understanding of science and scientific method.

artistic or the manual abilities of each human, are given by the Spirit.[25] The Spirit "fills, moves, and quickens all things"[26] so that what they do or produce is a result of God's grace, is a work of God. The Spirit acts in conformity with the character of who or what is acted upon, so that what is produced is what might be expected from whatever creature it is. Here, of course, the Spirit remains anonymous in a more definitive way than in the religious life of the believer, as the results are distinctly owned by the individual.

While Calvin is willing to talk of the Spirit filling all things, he is careful to point out that this is of a different character from the presence and activity of the Spirit in believers. The difference is in the operation of the Spirit. In believers, the Spirit dwells and sanctifies so that they become temples of God.[27] The purpose and object of this indwelling is to increase godliness. At the same time, a filling to give talent and natural truth is occurring, so within believers there must be two activities of the Spirit: one for sanctification and one for general activity. In non-believers, there is only the latter. Therefore, Calvin understands that the Spirit is the source of all truth, but that there are two levels at which the Spirit works. There is a lower level of natural or general truth and a higher level of revelatory truth which is manifested in the call of the elect and their sanctification. The former is surely the way in which the Spirit can work at a lower level in the reprobate.[28]

The Spirit and Scripture

Scripture is paramount for Calvin. It is in Scripture that knowledge of God is found, and it is only in Scripture. It is from Scripture that believers learn right and sound doctrine, and any straying from it in seeking knowledge of God is bound to lead to error.[29] God by the Holy Spirit is the author of Scripture and, also by the Spirit, God confirms it.[30] It was authored by men in whom God placed certainty concerning doctrine and also the idea to record it for posterity. What they recorded was what they had learned and understood to be true.[31] By putting it in this way, Calvin makes it clear that while Scripture was initiated and inspired in its writing by God, it has not been dictated verbatim by God. It is what its human authors understood

25. II.2.15, 16.
26. II.2.16.
27. II.2.16.
28. III.2.13.
29. I.6.1, 2.
30. I.9.2.
31. I.6.2.

about God and his ways which has been preserved.[32] However, despite its divine origins, Scripture is dead in and of itself—if left to itself it is a collection of words which does not bring life, which teaches nothing.[33]

To fulfil its purpose, Scripture requires divine assistance when it is read or heard. It requires the Spirit to confirm it, to make it true for us.[34] Calvin emphasizes this point repeatedly: the Word is given serious effect only by the Spirit;[35] it requires the inward persuasion of the Spirit so as to be true for believers;[36] its readers and hearers receive inward conviction from the "secret testimony" of the Spirit;[37] and by the Spirit it penetrates into the hearts of believers.[38]

Here we see a close intertwining of the work of the Spirit and Scripture, an interdependence between them which is necessary for Scripture to be properly apprehended as truth about God. The words of Scripture are given to believers, but for the individual believer, there is no certain knowledge of God in her unless the Spirit shows it to be so. This is true whether Scripture is read or heard—it is the Spirit who ministers in preaching, not the preacher.[39] While Scripture is the source of knowledge of God, the true knowledge is only available when the Spirit works with or in the believer to make it so. Faith itself is given in this process: as the Spirit gives understanding and knowledge of Scripture, faith is kindled within the believer.[40] This process must be understood even to the extent that knowledge of the Spirit's person and work comes from Scripture.[41]

It has been suggested that Calvin is being contradictory here. The Spirit needs to give authority to Scripture on the one hand, but this can only be so if the authority given agrees with the words of Scripture.[42] Alternatively, it also seems a circular proposition: the Spirit teaches about Scripture, but Scripture is the only source of teaching on the Spirit. However, this apparent difficulty is expressed, Niesel resolves it by noting that in the whole process God is being self-revelatory. The Spirit, being also the Spirit of Christ, brings

---

32. I.6.2, and n5. See also Niesel, *The Theology of Calvin*, 30–37.
33. I.9.3.
34. I.9.1–3.
35. I.7.5.
36. I.8.13.
37. I.7.4.
38. I.7.4.
39. IV.1.6.
40. III.2.33.
41. III.3.14.
42. Niesel, *The Theology of Calvin*, 38.

the incarnate Word to us as God's self-revelation, testifying to Jesus Christ by illuminating the biblical witness to him.[43] Inevitably, in such self-revelation circularity or seeming contradiction will exist, but it must be remembered that God is both subject and object in this revelatory activity and is, after all, God, and therefore need not be measured otherwise. In any event, the triune nature of God means that self-revelation by God does include the revealing by one person of another. For Calvin, the Spirit is the revealer and Jesus Christ is the revealed.

The interdependence of Scripture and the Spirit is more than an attribute of each among others. It is the core or foundation of the operation of each within the human condition. Each is necessary for the other to function according to God's intent. Without the Spirit, Scripture is isolated and any reading or interpretation can only accord with the revelation of Jesus Christ by chance; it cannot be the Word of revelation itself. Without Scripture, the Spirit is, of course, not powerless, but the Spirit's work in the sanctification of believers is not possible as knowledge cannot arise to inform them about the reality of their situation. This has at least three implications which are important in Calvin's pneumatology.

One is that a cessationist view of the activity of the Spirit is inevitable. By this I mean the view that the miraculous or supernatural activities of the Spirit recorded or referred to in the New Testament, particularly in the book of Acts, ceased after the initial establishment period of the church.[44] This is the period during which, as Calvin sees it, Scripture in part consisted of the teaching of the apostles,[45] not yet recorded, or in the process of being recorded. In such an environment, the Spirit must be inspiring or teaching directly for the new parts of Scripture to be formed,[46] and there is freedom for the Spirit to work directly to the benefit of the disciples and Apostles so that they might be taught and be able to record the growing knowledge of the revelation of the Word for the benefit of those to follow. But this teaching or communication is not continuous; rather, it pleased God to give Scripture "to hallow his truth to everlasting remembrance."[47] Now, therefore, we are left with a closed canon. There is no room in this conception[48] for the

---

43. Ibid., 38–39.

44. Elbert, "Calvin and the Spiritual Gifts," 319 and Sweetman, "The Gifts of the Spirit," 280–82 both note this does not mean gifts have ceased for Calvin, rather that visible supernatural gifts have ceased, but they can still operate in a secret way through the unseen activity of the Spirit in the life and witness of the church.

45. I.7.2.

46. I.8.11.

47. I.7.1.

48. Not that Calvin would consider this a conception. He would consider it truth revealed which has been "discovered".

later operation of the Spirit in any open supernatural way unconnected with Scripture. Of course, the Spirit operates in a lower way in the world and with the reprobate (and believers are not excluded from this), but this operation is "natural"; it is in accord with the "natural" character and operation of the world and its inhabitants. On the other hand, the Spirit's operation with believers is certainly supernatural, but it consists in the illumination of Scripture so it becomes the Word of God for the believer, or in the secret work within the Sacraments and the lives of believers. All this is not in accord with "natural" character, but all is in close accord with Scripture.

The second is that interpretations of Scripture can change: it is safe and appropriate to view any interpretations as always provisional. This is not to say that eternal truths cannot be found there, but the very fact that Scripture must be operated on by the Spirit to reveal Jesus Christ for the reader contains within it the possibility that a subsequent reading, or interpretation, can be different from an earlier one. This must be understood as a broadening or addition to the earlier interpretation (the earlier interpretation cannot be wrong, as it would then not have been true knowledge), not a complete change. This process can be illustrated by a now non-controversial example.

Joshua 10:12–14 records that Joshua petitioned God to stop the Sun and the Moon to extend the day and allow his complete victory. This petition was granted, so that the day was about twice as long as usual. The church understood this to mean that the Sun revolved around the Earth, quite apart from its demonstration of God's power over nature. However, in the early seventeenth century it was shown that the Earth revolves around the Sun, so the interpretation of the verses must change to take account of this fact. If a fixed view is taken of Scripture, this is highly problematical, to say the least. However, Calvin's view easily accommodates the change.

It is not a matter of saying that the earlier interpretation is wrong, so the knowledge gleaned was wrong, but it is a matter of saying that the new facts need to be taken into account. Thus, a new interpretation accommodates new natural knowledge, so realizing that to interpret the verse as teaching about physical realities is incorrect: what was previously thought of as revealed knowledge by some is not the reality at all. This accommodation does not take anything away from God who, after all, causes the physical realities, but actually has a major positive impact as it emphasizes the purpose of Scripture and the character of what the Spirit will reveal. It does this by eliminating interpretations which are not possible, so directing the reader towards those which are intended by the Spirit and perhaps by the original author. So, in the above example, no longer is the reader distracted by the impossible physical interpretation, now she must contemplate others, such as the powerful statement made about the sovereignty and authority of the God who can lengthen the day to allow his people to accomplish his purpose.

The third is that no completely new activity of the Spirit can occur. It is not sufficient that any claimed activity be merely consistent with Scripture, such activity must be revealed in Scripture. Scripture, in a sense, is the lens through which the believer perceives reality, but it is a lens which is dark and obscure without the Spirit. It requires the Spirit to illuminate the subject, or clear the lens, so that things can be perceived correctly. The Spirit illuminates or clears only this lens; there is no other lens and, without a lens, the Spirit does not reveal anything. This is not to say that God is not able to speak apart from Scripture, but it is to say that God chooses not to in dealing supernaturally with believers. Saying that mere consistency with Scripture is all that is required for the work of the Spirit means that the scriptural lens need not be applied—whatever occurs need only to be *like* what Scripture declares, not be *identified* with it. If this position is reached, we have departed from Calvin's conception because we have "untangled" the intertwining and interdependence of the Spirit and Scripture he asserts.

This position certainly serves Calvin's opposition to the Roman view of church authority and the place of church teaching and tradition. But it also has the great strength of always pointing to Scripture, always reminding believers that this is the source and norm of God's revelation and that this is where they must look to find God. Calvin makes this clear in his introduction to *Institutes* where he views his work as being only an aid to the believer as he reads Scripture for himself.[49] By excluding independent action by the Spirit in relation to Christ and the written Word, Calvin also excludes the possibility of purely human conceptions being viewed as religious truth and thus closely guards what he views as attesting to God's revelation. It can be protested that this is an unnecessary limitation on God's activity by the Spirit but, if so, this is nonetheless Calvin's position.

The Spirit and the Sacraments

The Spirit is also active in the sacraments: baptism and the Lord's Supper. They are "vessels of the Spirit,"[50] Christ's presence in them is brought about by the Spirit[51] and the inconceivably great "secret power" of the Spirit ensures life is transferred to the believer in the Supper and unites Christ to

49. Calvin, "John Calvin to the Reader," in *Institutes*, 4.
50. IV.19.1.
51. IV.17.26.

us.[52] Calvin is at pains to point out that there is work done by the Spirit within the sacraments with the believer such that there is a real benefit conferred on the believer. He carefully explains that this work is connected with, or associated with, the elements and the ritual, but only that: the elements and the acts themselves carry no intrinsic benefit at all.[53] This benefit is solely the guarantee of God's promises to the believer,[54] something which incorporates confirmation and increase of faith within the believer,[55] but it is a guarantee sealed by the Spirit. Read in isolation, it might be thought that Calvin is either linking the activity of the Spirit to the acts of the sacraments in a similar manner to his view on Scripture, or suggesting some independent activity of the Spirit, but neither is the case.

The guarantee which the Spirit gives is the conviction that what is understood in Scripture (by the illumination offered by the Spirit) is true. Nothing beyond what is contained in Scripture is conferred in the sacraments,[56] and, indeed, there is a close relation between the Spirit's activity in the sacraments and Scripture. Calvin sets this out clearly.

> For first, the Lord teaches and instructs us by his Word. Secondly, he confirms it by the sacraments. Finally, he illumines our minds by the light of his Holy Spirit and opens our hearts for the Word and sacraments to enter in, which would otherwise only strike our ears and appear before our eyes, but not at all affect us within.[57]

Calvin is not reciting a sequence here—it is not a progression from the Word to the sacraments and then the light of the Spirit. Rather, what others see as one,[58] he clearly sees as three things. Believers are taught and instructed by Scripture and this teaching is confirmed by the sacraments. But each of these operations occurs only by the activity of the Spirit; without the Spirit believers could perceive the words and acts but have no hope of them having any impact within. That is, there is only the inner conviction of true faith conveyed by Scripture and the sacraments when the Spirit operates with them and the believer.

---

52. IV.17.10, 31.
53. IV.14.17.
54. IV.14.12.
55. IV.14.9.
56. IV.14.14.
57. IV.14.8.
58. As he notes immediately prior to the passage above.

Remembering that the sacraments confirm and increase faith,[59] it is important to show that, for Calvin, this is not independent of Scripture, a claim which is dependent on his understanding of faith.[60] He gives his "right definition of faith" as "a firm and certain knowledge of God's benevolence towards us, founded upon the truth of the freely given promises in Christ, both revealed to our minds and sealed upon our hearts through the Holy Spirit."[61] This is a very full definition which conveniently comprises three components. The first is that faith consists of knowledge of God's good favor towards Christians.[62] This knowledge is not simply intellectual assent or agreement, but assurance.[63] That is, it is not deciding that certain propositions are true; or choosing to believe them because that provides the highest probability of a good outcome for the individual; or choosing to act as if they are true because it seems likely that they are right. Rather, it is a concrete assurance, a *knowing* that God and God's promises in Christ are right. This is a difficult concept to grasp, not easy to demonstrate to the western, scientifically inclined mind. Perhaps a helpful analogy is that of Sir Edmund Hillary's ascent of Everest. Sir Edmund experienced the ascent himself and knew he made it to the summit—he has his experience, the testimony of his companion, Tensing, and photographs of Tensing to convince him that he made it to the summit. He *knew* in the faith sense that he accomplished it. Others, except for Tensing, have only his testimony on which to base their view. They can have knowledge of his ascent, and even claim to know that it is true knowledge, but they have not had Sir Edmund's experience: they cannot relive the experience in their minds in the same way Sir Edmund could. This is the essential nature of Christian faith, that it is an experience which can be lived and relived repeatedly including, and in fact most importantly, in the present, in contrast to the Everest ascent which the participants could only relive as something which occurred in the past. Thus, Christian faith is something which gives certainty and confidence, something by which believers make God's promises of mercy theirs by "inwardly embracing them."[64] This faith is absolutely necessary for the believer as, without it, God and God's mercy cannot be comprehended.

---

59. IV.14.12

60. See Ross, "New Life for Old," 30–35, from which the following discussion on Calvin's definition of faith is largely taken.

61. III.2.7.

62. Faith is the "internalized understanding of divine goodness" (Charry, *By the Renewing of Your Minds*, 213).

63. III.2.14.

64. III.2.16.

There is thus an intimacy about Christian faith: it speaks of encounter, of God's Word and promises being "revealed to our minds and sealed upon our hearts,"[65] it is not something mediated by the Church. That is, it is not a set of propositions set out by the church which Christians must choose to believe: Calvin dismisses this as "implicit faith" which cannot provide what God requires.[66]

Second, faith is founded on the promises of Christ, and thus is intimately related to the Word. It is knowledge perceived from the Word of God;[67] it is founded in the Word itself,[68] and it leans on God's mercy.[69] Niesel sums up Calvin's view as faith being aroused by the preaching of the Gospel.[70] What faith does is give proper understanding of the Word, so that it is illuminated to the Christian.[71]

Third, these actions or results are through the Spirit, who forms the bond by which Christ binds himself to believers.[72] "Through the Spirit" does not mean the Spirit is to be thought of as a conduit or cable through which the believer is able to access Christ as if making a telephone call. No, "through" means that faith comes by an act of the Spirit.[73] It is a work, and in Calvin's view the principal work, of the Spirit.[74] But it is a work of the Spirit which does involve the believer. As Niesel summarizes, there is a human response which the Spirit engenders: the Spirit inspires the "yes" which enables the believer to become a participator in the life of Christ.[75] Faith is not Christian self-effort, but is something which occurs because of, and is directly due to, the action of the Spirit.[76] Without the Spirit, there can be no faith, ever. As Calvin points out, people of faith call out to God for help; it never occurs to people without faith to do so.[77] God has

65. III.2.7.
66. III.2.2.
67. III.2.6.
68. IV.14.6.
69. IV.14.7.
70. Niesel, *The Theology of Calvin*, 183.
71. III.2.33.
72. III.1.1.
73. Van Buren, *Christ in Our Place*, 100.
74. III.1.4.
75. Niesel, *The Theology of Calvin*, 123.
76. Faith is a human response, but "not a work that merits payment or reward, since it does not accomplish anything" (Matera, *New Testament Theology*, 189). On the same lines, "Faith is a 'gift', but faith is also a participation in a covenant, which requires voluntary consent" (Billings, *Calvin, Participation and the Gift*, 189).
77. III.2.21.

identified Godself by faith to the believer who knows God is there and so can appeal to God; there is nothing to appeal to for those to whom God has not revealed Godself.

These three parts of Calvin's definition described are all necessary. It is insufficient to truncate the definition and say that faith is a certain knowledge revealed and sealed through the Spirit. The certain knowledge that the Spirit reveals is that contained in the Word, in Scripture, and no other. So, faith is at all times inextricably linked with the incarnate Word and Scripture—what is held in faith is what is expressed in Scripture as illuminated by the Spirit. Therefore, when the sacraments confirm and increase faith, they are (of course, through the work of the Spirit) establishing and putting flesh[78] upon the promises of Scripture. The promises which the sacraments guarantee are therefore the promises contained in Scripture, so it can be said that the sacraments confirm the promises contained in Scripture. In saying this, Calvin is not setting up the sacraments as independent affirmation; rather, he is acknowledging his understanding that there is a dependent linkage between the sacraments and Scripture—the confirmation can only occur if the believer is aware that the promises of Scripture apply to her, and it arises from that knowledge by the action of the Spirit. It is not something which the believer is shown by the Spirit through the sacraments which she can then take to Scripture to confirm—this can never occur.[79] Rather, it is always that in participating in the sacraments the understanding already grasped and then encountered at the table (in the case of the Lord's Supper) is confirmed to be true.

This linkage means that nothing is done within the sacraments apart from the Word, revealed in Scripture by the Spirit, so the involvement of the Spirit in the sacraments is also closely linked to Scripture. What is seen and understood in the sacraments are the promises in Scripture, so it again functions as a lens through which the Spirit reveals the incarnate Word, even in the operation of the sacraments. The character of this linkage means that the sacraments are subordinate to Scripture: while the Spirit illuminates so the Word is apprehended in Scripture, in the sacraments what has been seen is confirmed. The Word of God can be discerned through the Spirit if Scripture alone is read, but it cannot be discerned through the sacraments alone. Hence the work of the Spirit within the sacraments differs from his work with Scripture because it cannot stand alone in the way it does with Scripture. But it is also crucial in the life of the believer as God, through the Spirit, uses the ministry of the sacraments to come close to the believer so

---

78. Not literally, for Calvin!
79. In this specific instance; it is not necessarily the general case.

that "hearts are penetrated and affections moved and our souls opened"[80] to effectively build faith.

The Spirit and Union[81]

The union between the believer and Christ is dealt with in detail later, but it is appropriate here to discuss some, at least, of the activity of the Spirit within it and the importance of the Spirit to the very existence of the union.[82] It is basic to the ontology of the union that Calvin envisages that Christ establishes it through the Spirit[83] in a way which allows the Spirit to work to regenerate the justified believer.

Calvin notes that "the whole Christ is everywhere ... ever present with his own people,"[84] and his discussion around his description of the mystical union makes it clear that it is not some desiccated Christ portioned out he is referring to, but Christ himself, sovereign and undiminished.[85] The union is with this undiminished Christ, but it is the Spirit who establishes the bond, who makes entry in the believer for Christ.[86] There are two in union, a new creation established within the very being of one by the divine action of the other, but this action is by the Spirit, rather than by Christ. Christ can be said to dwell within the believer, and the Spirit also dwells within,[87] but the respective "dwellings" are of a different character. Calvin makes it clear that, to share the benefits which have been bestowed on Christ, he has to become the believer's and dwell within her. There is thus an indwelling, but it is one in which the believer puts on Christ (Gal 3:27) and grows "into one body with him."[88] It is an indwelling which allows a participation[89] in the

80. IV.14.9.

81. See Ross, "New Life for Old," 45–50. The following discussion owes much to this source.

82. I will refer to the union with Christ in this section without any consideration concerning the two natures of Christ and the role each might play. Here, the discussion is not to be taken as indicating the function of one nature compared to the other. See note 125 in this chapter.

83. Hence the union is a work of the Spirit, but "equally and completely the work of Christ" (Edmondson, *Calvin's Christology*, 137).

84. IV.17.30.

85. III.11.10.

86. II.13.2; III.1.1, 3; III.2.34.

87. I.13.14.

88. III.1.1.

89. Billings, *Participation and the Gift*, 52; Zachman, *Reconsidering John Calvin*, 122.

benefits of Christ by the believer. The Spirit, on the other hand, "*is* the bond by which Christ effectually unites himself to us."[90] Christ dwells within in a way which allows the believer to contemplate him and his ways, and join in with them, but the Spirit dwells within as the means by which this is made possible for the believer. Without the Spirit, there could be no indwelling,[91] but the Spirit, through this indwelling, reveals only Christ and gives access only to Christ and his benefits.[92]

The presence of the Spirit in this union transforms the believer—"the Lord, by his Spirit directs, bends, and governs, our heart and reigns in it as in his own possession."[93] The Spirit works to sanctify the believer, making him teachable and obedient, leads him to do good works and restrains him from evil ones, causing him to advance in godliness.[94] It is the Spirit who puts the law in the believer's heart and who gives vigor.[95] In fact, the desire to do good, to obey God, to live a pious life and the energy to do so all come from the Spirit. It is right to understand this as an intimate and deeply personal activity which is worked out on an ontological level within the believer. However, this does not imply that there is a direct awareness of the Spirit on the part of the believer; in fact, there is none as all this occurs by the secret power of the Spirit.[96] The Spirit is a real *pneuma*, the effects of which are obvious and directly felt, but which is unseen itself. As will be seen below in the extended discussion of the union, there is no limit to the extent of God's work in the believer by the Spirit, so that the Spirit's work and presence is encountered in every aspect of the believer's life. However, it is by faith that the believer can declare all that to be the result of the indwelling Spirit.

The influence of Christ, through the Spirit, in this union is such that any thought or action of the believer which is "godly" has its source in Christ and not the believer. The believer by himself is capable only of sin, so any godly act cannot be sourced in him, but must be sourced in God.[97] There is no intrinsic ability of the believer to do *anything* godly by himself. Nevertheless, the believer is involved.[98] As the Spirit works within the union, it is true to say that the believer encounters God through the Word and Spirit, but

---

90. III.1.1 (emphasis mine).
91. And, equally, without Christ there could be no indwelling of the Spirit.
92. II.15.5; II.16.19.
93. II.3.10.
94. II.5.11, 14; III.5.13, 24.13; IV.16.21.
95. II.8.57; III.15.5.
96. III.11.5; III.24.13.
97. III.11.16.
98. Billings, *Participation and the Gift*, 49.

the Spirit works on or through the believer in such a way that the believer is personally involved. From the believer's perspective, all his actions appear to be his own, but in reality anything "godly" is not his own as it has its source in every respect in the Spirit, including even the ability to do it. His every response is a work of the Spirit. There is a real livening of the believer by the Spirit but just how this is so is a mystery, yet nevertheless a mystery in which believers can live by the power of the Spirit, a mystery in which believers encounter and experience the real God in Christ through the Spirit. Calvin recognized this in calling the growth of godliness the "secret work of the Spirit,"[99] and its echo (or perhaps its genesis) can be seen in his frank admission that the elect, to whom the growth of godliness is restricted, are chosen for reasons denied to humans.[100] The mystery is deepened by the fact that it is the Spirit *in toto* who exists and operates in the union, not merely some influence or power of the Spirit.

This can be seen in Calvin's treatment of Osiander's position. According to Calvin, righteousness for Osiander is the "holiness and uprightness that the essence of God" inspires in believers, or that believers "are made partakers in God's righteousness when God is united to us in essence," an essence of the Father, Son, and the Spirit severally.[101] That is, it is the inherent divine righteousness of God which justifies, and believers receive this when the essence of God is somehow poured into them. In this scheme, what the believer becomes is a being containing some mixture of God and human which enables him to be righteous by what appears as his own decision and effort, although actually assisted by the essence of God.

If Osiander is right, much of the mystery is removed, because no longer is a godly act the result of the secret, mysterious activity of the Spirit in the believer, but is an act arising from the capabilities of the believer who has the essence of God infused. It is little different from a person putting skills to use which have been acquired. In addition, believers would be correct to understand that they can use this infused essence and are expected to use what it gives in living righteous lives. Equally, the infusion of this essence is not an indwelling of God *in toto*, but is something of God which the believer obtains for her benefit.

Calvin objects to Osiander on several grounds, of which one will be mentioned here. Through "the power of the Holy Spirit . . . we grow together with Christ, and he becomes our Head, and we his members,"[102] something

99. III.24.13.
100. III.21.7; III.23.1, 2, 4.
101. III.11.5, 6.
102. III.11.5.

which is no intermingling of something of God with the believer,[103] but rather her coming, or more properly for Calvin, being drawn, to God and being united to God in a way allowing her to share the benefits God provides. In this coming, there is an indwelling of Christ in the believer, and in her "the fullness of deity dwells . . . so in him we possess the whole of deity."[104] Calvin means here for the reader to understand that the fullness of deity in Christ includes the Father and the Spirit, so it is the fullness of the Spirit who operates in the union and so in the life of the believer.[105] There is none of the "gross mingling" which Osiander forces.[106]

In this work of the Spirit within the union there is still a link to scripture. While close and intimate and pervasive in action, the Spirit does not stand alone within the believer, the Spirit reveals Christ and does the work of Christ. Christ and his work, of course, are revealed in scripture, so it is to be expected that what the Spirit does is illuminated by scripture. The union and the work of the Spirit within it must be understood in the light of this link. Calvin says that "God works in his elect in two ways: within, through his Spirit; without, through his Word,"[107] but these are not separate, independent operations. The reprobate are also addressed by his Word, but for them it is to show what is right and render them without excuse; this is the result for any without the Spirit dwelling within. The same Word for the elect with the indwelling Spirit arouses a desire for righteousness and sanctification. The independent operation of the Word leads to judgment; the interdependent operation of the Spirit and the Word leads to life.[108]

The Spirit—Indwelling, Filling, and Gifts

It is important at this point to identify what Calvin means by the terms *dwell*, *fill*, and *gift* when he uses them in relation to the Spirit as they are important terms to understand within Pentecostal theology.

Dwelling is a real occupation by the Spirit of the believer. Just as God dwelt in the Jerusalem temple, occupying the holy of holies, to say that believers are temples of God means that the Spirit dwells within each believer,[109] so

103. I.15.5.

104. III.11.5.

105. Calvin takes "fullness" to mean having "everything necessary for perfection in God," not that all of God dwells within or the individual becomes God in any sense. Calvin, *Galatians, Ephesians, Philippians and Colossians*, 169.

106. III.11.10.

107. II.5.5.

108. II.5.5.

109. I.13.15.

we are to understand that the character of the indwelling of the Spirit is that of one divine, undivided being occupying each believer in the same way. This does not mean that the indwelling has an identical impact: from an indwelling of the same character, different outcomes result for different believers. Greater or lesser effects are produced through the indwelling from one believer to the other, although always under the sovereignty of Christ. There is no infusion or mixing of the beings, as each remains separate from the other. However, the dwelling is also an occupation of the believer in a fashion which allows the Spirit to have an impact on the believer, to work on her in sanctifying her, where the believer can actually yield to the Spirit and allow the Spirit to rule her.[110] This indwelling can be identified, not by any direct sensing of the Spirit by the believer, but by the presence of faith and the "fruits of regeneration,"[111] the latter being good works.

Being filled with the Spirit is not synonymous with the Spirit dwelling within, for Calvin, but is rather a way of saying one is influenced by the Spirit. To be sure, this is not some vague impact affecting how a person may think or act, but is a real application of real power to produce definitive results. It is the action of God which produces life and vigor in not only people, but all things in accordance with the character of each thing.[112] Filling can therefore occur for anything, but certainly occurs for believers alongside the indwelling of the Spirit. Hence, believers need the power, vigor or energy of the Spirit to win in warring with Satan because only in this way are they free from the weakness of the flesh. In short, believers need to be filled with the Spirit to succeed here.[113] In contrast, non-believers are also filled with the Spirit, in that they are influenced, but not being indwelt by the Spirit as believers are in the mystical union, they may be used by God but are lost in the battle with Satan.

The Spirit also certainly brings gifts to believers, but Calvin means gifts in a very general sense. The gifts of the Spirit are whatever the Spirit brings, or all that the Spirit does,[114] which produce good works and sanctification in believers.[115] They are certainly not distributed uniformly across the church, but all this means is that the church has members of differing abilities and an accompanying responsibility to share those with others,[116] not that there

---

110. III.14.9; II.3.10.
111. III.1.4; III.14.16.
112. I.14.18; II.2.16.
113. III.20.46.
114. II.15.5; II.16.9.
115. III.17.5.
116. IV.1.3.

are specific gifts which God chooses from to confer on believers according to God's grace. However, there are limits to the gifts God now bestows. Calvin certainly accepts the miraculous (or supernatural) gifts (e.g., 1 Cor 12:4–10) as being genuine gifts of the Spirit, but he considers they were given for the specific time of the apostolic age only. Hence the gift of tongues is confined to that earlier time as he has no doubt that in his time prayer with words but without thought displeases God.[117] He is more specific when he states that healing and other miraculous powers disappeared as they had only been given for a time, then moving aside so that the "preaching of the gospel [might be] marvelous forever."[118] It seems he regards the miraculous as having the potential to distract people from the gospel, to draw their attention away from Christ and his gospel.

The Union of the Believer with Christ

Calvin is aware that it is one thing to identify the benefits which Christ has brought for humanity and another to show how those benefits can be effectually made available to humanity. "How do we receive those benefits which the Father bestowed on his only-begotten Son—not for Christ's own private use, but that he might enrich poor and needy men?"[119] he asks. He goes on to say that Christ cannot bestow these benefits from outside humans because this still means humans are separated from him. Therefore, for the benefits to be of use to humans, Christ "had to become ours and dwell within us," and "all that he possesses is nothing to us until we grow into one body with him." It is the "secret energy of the Spirit" by which humans can "come to enjoy Christ and all his benefits."[120] This coming to dwell and growth into one body describes the uniting of Christ and humans, a union which is the means by which humans receive the benefits of Christ.[121] This union is a work of the Spirit, who "is the bond by which Christ effectually unites us to himself."[122] It is in no sense a metaphorical union, but a true union in a body whereby the Spirit joins the elect to Christ to bring about a union of head and members,[123] brought about by Christ "cleaving to us

117. III.20.33.
118. IV.19.18.
119. III.1.1.
120. Ibid.
121. Evans, "Calvin's Doctrine," 6, points out the importance of the union to Calvin by describing it as the "overarching reality in which all the benefits of salvation are received."
122. Ibid.
123. McDonnell, *The Church, and the Eucharist*, 182.

wholly in spirit and body."[124] The union is as concretely real as the actual bread and wine are real in the Lord's Supper.[125]

Calvin says, "that joining together of Head and members, that indwelling of Christ in our hearts—in short, that mystical union—are accorded by us the highest degree of importance, so that Christ, having been made ours, makes us sharers with him in the gifts with which he has been endowed."[126] Having stated such, it is perhaps remarkable that the term "mystical union" only occurs at one other place in the *Institutes*,[127] although as the discussion below will show, the interaction it implies between believer and God is certainly a key factor in Calvin's account. Before proceeding further, it is worthwhile examining this quote as it provides some foundation for what follows.

It comes in the middle of a passage where Calvin is refuting Osiander and at this point he acknowledges, with Osiander, that whatever good believers get from Christ is unavailable unless Christ is somehow made

---

124. IV.17.9. See also Tamburello, *Union with Christ*, 87, who says Calvin stresses the "Holy Spirit as the bond of a spiritual (yet absolutely real) union with Christ."

125. Calvin makes it clear that the union is with Christ's human nature. Humans are too lowly to reach God without a mediator, and so God has to become "God with us" so that "his divinity and our human nature might by mutual connection grow together" (II.12.1). Calvin continues: "Ungrudgingly he took our nature upon himself to impart to us what was his" (II.12.2). It is not only that he shared the human condition so as to save humans, but he reaches humans and imparts to them what is his through his humanity; that is, the union is with Christ, yes, but with his human nature. Calvin later makes this explicit when he says of Christ that "as God he is the destination to which we move; as man, the path by which we go" (III.2.1. He is taking this from Augustine, *City of God* XI.ii (MPL. 41.318; tr NPNF II.227)). Dennis Tamburello comments that "Calvin is emphatic that our union with Christ is with his humanity," citing just this section in *Institutes* (Tamburello, *Union with Christ*, 92.) See also Zachman, *Teacher, Pastor and Theologian*, 251. By this union with Christ's human nature, believers have access to Christ's divine nature through the hypostatic union of the two natures within the one person, Jesus Christ. It is therefore quite correct to talk of union with Christ and understand that this means intimate connection with God. On this point, Tamburello gives a helpful summary on the variety of ways Calvin refers to the union between the believer and Christ. It is mostly characteristic of Calvin for him to speak of union with Christ, but he also speaks of union with the Father and union in the power of the Spirit. Calvin's discussion of the union thus contains a trinitarian element. Equally, he "is not opposed to speaking of union with God" which occurs both in *Institutes* and in his commentaries. In fact, Tamburello suggests that the terminology may have made no difference to Calvin; he quotes from a comment on 1 John 4:15: "We are united to God by Christ and . . . we can only be joined to Christ if God abides in us." Also "men are so engrafted into Christ by faith that Christ joins them to God" (Tamburello, *Union with Christ*, 93). The citations are from Calvin, *The Gospel According to St John 11–21 and the First Epistle of John*, 293–94).

126. III.11.10.

127. At II.12.7.

theirs. The "mystical union" is the mechanism by which Christ is available to the believer and so is of the highest importance, although note that this is not a claim that it is the central tenet of his theology, but only a statement of its importance in his thought, occupying a place which it shares with others. Earlier in the same chapter, justification by faith is said to be the "main hinge on which religion turns,"[128] so it is difficult to accord some other, albeit related, factor a higher place in Calvin's thought. The union itself comprises here the joining of head and members in the church and the dwelling of Christ in the heart of each believer. The way Battles renders the sentence ("are") implies that the union incorporates these two things which are separate attributes of it, rather than simply two ways of saying the same thing. Whether or not Battles is correct, it is clear that the union has two aspects to it. First, it has a corporate aspect in the context of the church, where Christ as head is in union with its members so as to establish and maintain the nature of the church as the body of Christ. Second, it clearly involves a personal aspect with Christ indwelling the believer in an obviously close relation. That is, the believer is in a personal union with Christ, but this is always within the church, which is Christ's body, the sum of those with which he is in union. It is difficult to overstate how intimate this union is, as it consists of a joining of Christ with the members of the church, as a head is joined to a body, both physically and functionally, to direct the body in its activity. It also consists of an indwelling, of a real presence within the believer by which one being, Christ, can direct and transform the deepest convictions held by the other being, the believer.

By this union, Christ is "made ours." No possessive sense is implied here, but rather there is an availability of Christ created for the believer so that he can share in the benefits with which Christ is endowed. An immediacy of Christ is certainly created by the union, but there is no sense of the believer obtaining something he can use to his advantage or for his purposes. Indeed, it is emphatically the other way around—the availability allows the believer to share in the gifts of Christ, to share in what Christ desires, to share in what Christ directs. It is an availability which consists in making it possible for the believer to participate in what Christ is and does,[129] not to enhance himself intrinsically.

128. III.11.1.
129. III.2.24; 11.1, 23.

Union and the Body of Christ

The union with Christ is primarily a union in the church, for Calvin. In saying "a union in the church," Calvin's image of the union being an engrafting is helpful to a correct understanding. On the one hand, it is not that union is simply joining the church. If this were so then the reprobate would be in union with Christ as well as the elect.[130] On the other hand, union is not with each believer one by one so that the church is individual believers gathered in community. Mere participation in the life of the institutional church does not constitute a true engrafting because there is no link to Christ, the source of sustenance for the church. Neither is a one-by-one union apart from the church a true engrafting because it ignores how Christ has chosen to sustain his members—by being the source of their nourishment through the church. In the botanical sense, this would mean what is engrafted is expected to obtain its sustenance direct from the leaves and roots without any intervening structure.

What occurs is a middle way between these two positions. The establishment of the union is a true engrafting because, by it, the new believer is united with Christ in a very real and direct way so that she will now be sustained by him. But this link is through the stem and branches which form his body, so at the same time the believer is firmly united to him in the church. The union of the believer and Christ cannot be separated from the church and always occurs through a real connection *via* the church. Thus, for Calvin, the primary form of union is that of the church. Believers are united to Christ as members of his body, as Niesel says.[131]

Union and the Marks of the Church

For Calvin, the marks of the church are preaching and the sacraments.[132] Each of these marks bears a close relation to union with Christ.

It is through the preaching of the Word that people come to faith in Christ and are nourished by its teaching,[133] both works of the Spirit. Scripture is illuminated by the Spirit through preaching,[134] so allowing believers

---

130. III.24.8; IV.1.2.

131. Niesel, *The Theology of Calvin*, 122. See Also McDonnell, *The Church, and the Eucharist*, 185.

132. IV.1.9: "Wherever we see the Word of God purely preached and heard, and the sacraments administered according to Christ's institution, there, it is not to be doubted, a church of God exists."

133. IV.1.1, 5.

134. Calvin does not exclude illumination directly to the believer as Scripture is read, something he clearly expects of his readers. See pp. 5–9.

to grow to maturity "under the education of the church" by "the preaching of the heavenly doctrine."[135] This growing to maturity is the process of regeneration,[136] starting at conversion when the believer is united with Christ and continuing in the life of the believer.

Knowledge of God is found in the glory of creation and in Scripture, where Scripture "clearly shows us the true God," that is reveals clearly what is only, at best, muted as creation is contemplated.[137] The believer has access to that clear knowledge in Scripture and receives the greater part of it through preaching. Such knowledge is to be sought nowhere else, so it follows that as growing in maturity is a development of the believer's understanding of God and God's demands on her and so a function of knowledge, then regeneration is closely linked to knowledge of God. Calvin defines it as "a departing from ourselves, [in which] we turn to God, and having put off our former mind, we put on a new."[138] This captures well the occurrence at conversion, but also points to the ongoing aspect of regeneration being of the same ilk: an ongoing turning to God and putting on of the new mind. The believer must look to God for regeneration, but the place in which the believer learns to look to God is the church, by listening to the proclamation of the Word.

The second of the marks is the sacraments.[139] Baptism, for its part, is "the sign of the initiation by which we are received into the society of the church, in order that, engrafted in Christ, we may be reckoned among God's children"[140]—we are his by adoption. It is not a mere sign, but is a "token and proof" of the believer's cleansing for the whole of life; of mortification and renewal in Christ; and of her union with Christ.[141] Along with the adoption motif, Calvin's further ground for saying the latter is that Christ "dedicated and sanctified baptism in his own body in order that he might have it in

---

135. IV.1.5.

136. Calvin's treatment of regeneration in *Institutes* begins under the heading of "Repentance." He equates repentance with regeneration (III.3.9) but does not consistently use either term or restrict himself to just these. Other terms that he uses are sanctification (e.g., III.3.14, 19, 23) and renewal (III.17.5). However, what he identifies here as repentance occurs at conversion (III.3.11) and continues through life (III.3.9). I consider "regeneration" as better capturing this sense of something which starts and is continuous than the other terms so will use it consistently in this part of the work.

137. I.5.6. The quotation is from I.6.1.

138. III.3.5.

139. Evans, "Calvin's Doctrine," 8, shows the importance of this mark by noting that the sacraments are the seal of the divine promise, which is Christ, so offer and convey Christ to the believer.

140. IV.16.1.

141. IV.16.1–6.

common with us as the firmest bond of the union and fellowship which he has deigned to form with us."[142] That is, baptism is an event grounded in the believer's union with Christ and it is an experience shared by each.

The second sacrament, the Lord's Supper, is given to nourish believers throughout life, as "a spiritual banquet, wherein Christ attests himself to be the life-giving bread, upon which our souls feed unto true and blessed immortality."[143] Believers are formed by the visible signs which are given by God as best adapted to human capacity, but are not to ascribe to them anything of themselves; at core the Supper is about Christ's secret union with believers, not at all about the substance of bread and wine.[144]

However, the bread and wine are not *only* symbols; there is some way in which the elements *are* the body and blood of Christ to the partakers. In his institution of the Supper, Christ taught that what was his is now the believers' and that they, in partaking of his body and blood, are made one substance with him.[145] Believers are not "partakers of the Spirit only, omitting mention of flesh and blood."[146] In the elements, Christ is truly shown, "his very body and blood."[147] This is a difficult concept to grasp, and Calvin admits that he doesn't have the thoughts or words to explain it, so must simply give way in wonder to the mystery it is.

The ingesting of the elements, then, is a genuine real-time participation in Christ.[148] The union with Christ is not only being expressed, but is actually operating through partaking in the sacrament. The Supper is a tangible means by which God assures believers of God's promises[149] and it brings believers "into relationship with Christ and [binds them] to him."[150] It functions "to interpret more precisely and more concretely the union we have with Christ."[151]

---

142. IV.16.6.

143. IV.17.1.

144. Ibid. See Evans, "Calvin's Doctrine," 5, and Nevin, *The Mystical Presence*, 54, cited in Cunnington, "Calvin's Doctrine of the Lord's Supper," 73, 215, who both note that a person's theology of the Supper will accord with their view of the union between the believer and Christ.

145. IV.17.3.

146. IV.17.7.

147. IV.17.11. See also Zachman, *Teacher, Pastor and Theologian*, 186, who notes the signs "actually offer the reality they represent."

148. Redding, *Prayer and the Priesthood of Christ*, 86, points out that the Supper, as this participation, is only possible because of the union between the believer and Christ. See also McDonnell, *The Church, and the Eucharist*, 184–85.

149. Niesel, *The Theology of Calvin*, 213–14.

150. Ibid., 217. Niesel here refers to both sacraments.

151. McDonnell, *The Church, and the Eucharist*, 179.

In sum, the Lord's Supper plays a prominent and vital role in the life of the believer and the union he enjoys with Christ.[152]

Despite the importance of the Lord's Supper, it is a mistake to give it primacy in the union of the believer and Christ. There is nothing given in the Supper, for Calvin, "which is not given in faith outside of" it, and the union in faith through the Spirit contains the union which takes place in the Supper: the latter is subsumed in the former.[153] That is, while the Supper occupies a prominent place within the union it is only a place within something larger.

The Personal Union

Nevertheless, the union is also a personal one, and it is this personal union I want to focus on now and carry into the conversations with Pentecostalism. Even if secondary to union in the church, the personal union is necessary to Calvin's conception and so important in its own right. The engrafting image is again very helpful here. A branch grafted into the church remains a branch—it is united to its source of sustenance, Christ, *via* the church, but the union is with *this* branch (among others, of course), and so remains a personal union with the one believer who is the branch. The believer engrafted into the church is truly part of the church and receives her sustenance *via* the church, but she remains unique in union with Christ: she enjoys a personal union with him. These personal and corporate attributes of the union are well captured by Tamburello when he says that "Christ's promises are made to individuals, but only insofar as they are members of the community." That is, while the Spirit does act towards each one by one, this is not towards any one person independent of the community.[154]

The union is of the fullness of God in Christ with the believer, through the Spirit who indwells the believer. The union, or bond, is within the believer, but is one between two distinct beings, between her and Christ, through the Spirit. Its function is to establish a communion between Christ and the believer through which the indwelling Spirit can transform her.[155] Its function is also to provide for the believer's God-centeredness to be effective,[156] and become more prominent in her as real communication with Christ and participation in him is possible through the Spirit in the union for the believer.

---

152. All this is energized and effected by the Spirit (IV.17.12).
153. McDonnell, *The Church, and the Eucharist*, 179.
154. Tamburello, *Union with Christ*, 97.
155. II.5.5.
156. II.5.14.

There is nothing passed to the believer that can be separated from Christ. If something was passed to the believer so that she received some ability that became intrinsic to her, for her use, then the Spirit would have separated something intrinsic to Christ from him and passed it to the believer. If this occurred, the believer would intrinsically be able to perform divine acts by herself, something beyond anyone, Calvin argues.[157] In addition, this would also destroy the intimacy of the union between the believer and Christ, as the Spirit remains distant while what was given is used.[158]

What of some rule which God might give which identifies how God will consistently act in particular circumstances?[159] Here the nature of the union means that this is tantamount to the believer as one distinct party determining how God as the other will act.[160] This would destroy the intimacy of the union, this time allowing the believer to remain distant while God acts. Such a gift would not constitute participation in God at all but allow the believer to reap benefits without participation.[161]

The union is used by Christ to provide a means by which believers can obtain the benefits he has for them. Its function, then, is to give effect to the call of the elect, to make effective the realization of election for each believer. This is a transformation of the believer which includes a growth in godliness, performing good works and imposing some restraint on evil.[162] It is the means by which Christ, through the Spirit, makes believers "good Christians" as they pursue piety throughout their lives.[163]

How this is done is all contained in the phrase "through the secret work of the Spirit," acting within the believer.[164] The Spirit works to sanctify the believer, to make her teachable and obedient, for example.[165] However, this is not a work done on an individual who need do nothing but allow the Spirit to work, who can essentially remain unresponsive and

---

157. II.1.5; Niesel, *The Theology of Calvin*, 80–81.

158. Canlis, "Calvin, Osiander and Participation in God," 172.

159. Real isolation is not possible, of course, because the union always exists. What is meant is that the believer can act in her old nature to apply the rule.

160. That is, if the believer produces the particular circumstance, God is bound to act as the rule requires.

161. It could be argued, of course, that participation in God would be a condition of any such law to be met by the believer. However, such a condition renders the law superfluous as any authentic participation in God is a real participation and can only produce what God desires.

162. II.5.14.

163. III.24.13.

164. III.11.5.

165. II.5.11; III.5.3; IV.16.31.

allow things to happen. In a discussion on prayer and the role of the Spirit (operating in the union, of course), Calvin suggests that it is the Spirit who shows the supplicant what to pray for and exerts control over his emotions. Everything associated with the believer's prayers: what he wants, any assurance of them being heard or generating a response, any direction on the subject for prayer or how anxieties for the future might be resolved; these all originate in the Spirit. But it is not the Spirit who prays: it is the believer who prays in the Spirit. The union is an entirely non-competitive relation where all happens as God intends but the believer must make real efforts. So, the believer is unable to wait and allow the Spirit to take control. Rather, that direction of the Spirit must be actively sought—the believer must be diligent and hardworking in persistently seeking the Spirit's direction and activity.[166] Because the Spirit's activity is secret, this diligent seeking must appear as if it is all the believer's effort—it is the believer who must have the discipline to apply himself to making opportunities for prayer and taking advantage of them, for thinking about what to pray for and actually speaking the prayers out. This is real effort, of course, but Calvin affirms that all this not only has its roots in the activity of the Spirit but is actually entirely, from beginning to end, the work of the Spirit.

What applies in prayer applies to all aspects of the believer's life in union with Christ. Calvin frequently refers to the need for believers to apply themselves to godly things.[167] While every godly thought or act of the believer is actually a work of Christ through the Spirit, because that action is secret each will appear to be the work of the believer. This will certainly be so for those observing the believer, but it will also be so for the believer herself. A single act of piety, for example attending a worship service, will appear to her to be the result of her decision to do so, given effect by the various actions required to get to the service and participate in it, each of which will be experienced by the believer as her own acts, although it's all the work of the Spirit. In fact, in all this, God is not apprehended directly by the believer, and she can consider that her activity arises from her faith. However, it is the very presence alone of this faith which is the indicator of the presence of the Spirit. There is not a minimum level of faith which must be reached, any amount of genuine faith is sufficient[168] as genuine faith is a work of the Spirit[169] and thus proof of the presence of the Spirit in his undivided fullness. If the decision to attend is something she feels she must do because of her

---

166. III.20.5.
167. III.6.3, 5; 11.1; 16.2; 20.5 for example.
168. III.2.20.
169. III.1.4.

faith, then what has actually occurred is that the indwelling Spirit has acted, producing the decision and accompanying actions.

The action of the Spirit has produced the decision, so the decision can properly be called a work of the Spirit, but it is certainly better to describe it as I have: the act of the Spirit has produced the decision rather than simply say the decision itself is an act of the Spirit. This is because the believer is certainly involved. It is her decision because she is in a real union with Christ through the Spirit; the activity of the Spirit in this union also belongs, derivatively speaking, to the other in the union, the believer. The believer can claim the decision as hers, but this is not a statement of ownership, rather a statement about her being: this decision is personal to her and her nature, transforming her being as it is in union with Christ through the action of the Spirit.

In summary, while there is no synergy or polarity in the union in that its formation and operation are solely works of the Spirit, the way the union is experienced by the believer is that effort is required on his behalf, to apply himself to the disciplines of piety and living the Christian life. While this does not comprise a contribution to the union on his part, there is no doubt that the union requires the involvement and response of the believer for the work of the Spirit in and through it to be actualized. Accordingly, what the believer does is due to the prevenient activity of the Spirit.

Moving on from this discussion, the importance of the union for Calvin can also be further demonstrated by considering his view of the character of salvation and the Christian life following. I will look at five issues: justification, faith, regeneration (or sanctification), self-denial, and cross-bearing.[170]

Justification

Humans require justification. This is because of sin in humans which, for Calvin, starts with Adam's sin which becomes for those following original sin. This he calls "a hereditary depravity of our nature" which makes humans liable for God's wrath and produces "works of the flesh (Gal 5:19)" which are sinful acts.[171] These acts are what Scripture does call sin or sins, and it is certainly the acts themselves which first come to mind when sin is considered. While a definition of sin could focus on the acts, Calvin correctly argues that such an approach is deficient as it draws attention to outward actions (works), missing the inner nature which is infected by sin.

---

170. See Ross, "New Life for Old," 23–42, from which the discussion hence draws.
171. II.1.8.

The acts result from this nature, they are not the nature itself. It is not as if human nature is neutral or good but subject to sinful acts at times; rather human nature is such that, apart from Christ, nothing but sin can result. It is a nature which is fertile ground for evil.[172]

This has come about because of the sin of Adam, who was disobedient or unfaithful to God in his eating of the fruit of the tree of the knowledge of good and evil, contrary to God's explicit instruction (Gen 3).[173] This breaking of trust was so abhorrent to God that for Adam, for whom spiritual life was to remain bound to God, it was "the death of the soul."[174] The impact was so profound that whereas at first human nature was good and pure, now it was totally depraved, wholly given over to sin.[175] That means that each subsequent human shares this depraved nature: it is not that humans are good or neutral, but inevitably sin because of their circumstances; rather they have this sinful nature from conception. Calvin demonstrates this by appealing to Ps 51:5.[176] However, this depravity does not extend to putting humans beyond restoration. They can be restored, and the start of this restoration is justification.[177]

Prior to justification, then, the human is sunk hopelessly in sin, estranged from God. From the post-justification standpoint, this is the old nature, the old person, the former self. In this state of depravity, the human can do no good, but is condemned to sin. He can only sin unless God does something.[178]

Justification is what God does first in human restoration.[179] Calvin gives at least four succinct definitions of justification: it is to be reckoned righteous in God's sight and be treated as such;[180] it is to "acquit of guilt" or, more strongly, to confirm innocence;[181] it is "the acceptance with which God receives us into his favor as righteous men . . . it consists in the remission

---

172. II.1.8, 9; II.2.8, 25, 27; II.3.5; Niesel, *The Theology of Calvin*, 82–83.

173. II.1.4.

174. II.1.5.

175. II.1.5.

176. II.1.5.

177. II.3.7.

178. Niesel, *The Theology of Calvin*, 80–81.

179. While the establishment of the union between the believer and Christ is logically prior to justification (see later), the union is the means by which the restoration is effected by God, rather than something which directly effects restoration.

180. III.11.2.

181. III.11.3.

of sins and the imputation of Christ's righteousness";[182] and it is being "engrafted into [Christ's] fellowship by the calling of his Father."[183]

Explicit to the first definition, and at least implicit in the other three, are two aspects of justification. One is that humans in Christ are reckoned by God to be righteous. This means that the estrangement due to sin has disappeared; justified humans are reconciled with God, to enjoy God's presence and God theirs. The other is that God now treats humans as righteous. God's dealings with us now, and for the future, are no longer conditioned by our sinful nature, but by the righteousness imputed to us. This has implications for human life in this world now, but also for humans in the eschatological judgement to come. The status of the justified human has changed— once depraved sinner, bound for judgment and eternal damnation, he is now made righteous and is destined for eternal life.[184] In respect of justification alone, the believer is who he always was, but there is something new which has changed: his status.[185]

This new status is not received until "Christ is made ours" in the "mystical union" where Christ comes to dwell in the heart of the believer, and the believer, in turn, is "engrafted into [Christ's] body."[186] In this union, Christ "makes us sharers with him in the gifts with which he has been endowed," that is, his righteousness is imputed to believers,[187] to the justified human is accounted the righteousness of Christ and it is that which matters for God. It is not that the union is a result of justification or is something which follows a decision by which God justifies: the establishment of the union is logically prior to justification and is necessary for justification to occur. While logically prior, the union is coincident,[188] so it is integral to what God is doing in justification; to the extent that justification must have occurred if the union exists, the union is justifying.

---

182. III.11.2.

183. III.14.6. Note that Calvin does not specifically say here that this defines justification, but it is clear from the context that this is what he means.

184. This change is real, but I have stated it above from the human perspective. From God's perspective, for Calvin, the justified human is one of the elect and was only ever destined for life.

185. Redding, *Prayer and the Priesthood of Christ*, 80–81, summarises justification as "the ungodly being clothed in Christ's righteousness," and observes that this takes place within the believer's humanity. That is, justification is a change in the human, not a declaration from afar.

186. III.11.10.

187. Ibid.

188. Tanner, *Jesus, Humanity and the Trinity*, 53–54. She cites Calvin, III.1.3, in support.

Until the engrafting of the union, humans are "the heirs of darkness and death and the enemies of God" and this only changes when the Spirit cleanses the engrafted believer.[189] The change comes with the union by which the benefits of Christ are brought to the believer: without this bringing, nothing changes; with it, all changes. Through the union the one person has a new altered status, an "objective alteration," because of the new presence in her of another person, Christ, and his activity, through the Spirit, within her. The union is the principal means by which justification occurs. Because of the presence of Christ, the believer is reckoned righteous by God as Christ is righteous; and God will treat the believer as righteous as Christ is treated. It is as if when God now engages with the believer, God sees Christ, not her, and treats her accordingly.

This new status, the making of the union, is, for Calvin, entirely a work of God. The experience of faith through which a sinner comes to salvation is the experience of encountering God by this work of God.[190] In a closely related way, it is also true to say that justification comes through faith alone[191] (note that he does not say that it is faith which justifies: it is Christ who justifies).Calvin is careful to point out at some length that this faith is itself not a human work, but a further gift from God. This, of course, inevitably follows from his view on election and double predestination, where God has predetermined, before the act of creation, which individuals will experience salvation and eternal life and which will not.[192] Salvation is then the calling of the elect, whereby each of the elect realizes their election, a realization which is actualized by God alone.[193] So the faith of the believer is something also determined by God through election. The role of faith in the union is important in understanding how it is that the union comes about and is discussed in detail below.

Note that the justified still sin. It is true that the sin is not counted against them as they are reckoned righteous, but Calvin notes that "traces of sin always remain" in the justified and that justification must be "different from reformation in newness of life," a reformation accomplished by God progressively throughout life.[194] This reformation Calvin calls regeneration,

---

189. III.14.6.

190. III.11.16, *encounter* is my term. As Zachman, *John Calvin as Teacher, Pastor and Theologian*, 18, points out, this encounter occurs in the church as it occurs through the preaching of the gospel of free grace and mercy of God in Jesus Christ through the power of the Holy Spirit.

191. III.11.19.

192. III.21.

193. III.24.1–5.

194. III.11.11.

which is the gradual emergence of an increasing obedience to God throughout the Christian life. Justification and regeneration are not to be separated, but they are distinct things;[195] justification is whole and complete in the believer at conversion, but regeneration is commenced but incomplete and ongoing from that time, and is itself a work of the Spirit.[196] In the justified believer, the old depraved, sinful nature "belongs" to one in union with Christ; but it has been supplanted by the righteousness of Christ imputed to the believer, the indwelling of Christ, and the work of the Holy Spirit. However, it still has influence. In other words, believers still sin because they are still in the flesh and the works of the flesh result.[197] In his discussion on this subject, Calvin does not explain how this is in terms of the operation of the union, which is entirely consistent with his thought.

Calvin's conception of the union means that to say believers are still in the flesh is to say that the believer retains his integrity as an "other" within the union; he is not swallowed up. There is a new creation comprising the believer now in union with Christ, changed as a result, but still ontologically the original person.[198] There is a spiritual bond by which the new creation is formed.[199] The existence of the union and the persistence of the believer means that the believer's behavior is dependent on the influence of either nature: Christ's or the believer's original, depraved nature. If driven by Christ, then behavior in obedience to him results; if driven by the believer alone, then works of the flesh, that is disobedience and sin, result. Just how this is so is a mystery, because in Calvin's account, the operation of the union is not one in which the believer is choosing one nature or the other from moment to moment. If it were left to the choice of the believer alone in any way, then the union would not exist in the first place, and even if it could, the believer would consistently choose disobedience according to his original nature. "Traces of our imperfection remain" in believers so that even they "do no good works of themselves," and even those who have progressed most in their Christian lives "have a great part of their heart and soul still occupied with fleshly desires."[200] Certainly, the sinful actions result from the believer's choice, but the godly actions are all the result of the action of the Spirit working through the union to produce them; they are truly acts of God, not the

---

195. III.11.11.

196. II.7.11.

197. III.11.11.

198. Edmondson, *Calvin's Christology*, 139, notes that it is a mark of Calvin's theology that he has an antipathy for any metaphysical union (i.e., any fusing of the persons) as it violates the integrity of persons and natures.

199. III.11.10.

200. III.14.9; 19.4.

acts of the believer. Nevertheless, it is the believer who applied real effort to carry them out and the believer who experiences the decision to do so as one he has made. This is the reality of life in union with Christ: the believer in his old nature sins, but by the work of the Spirit the benefits of Christ are present to him and godly works result. In fact, the Spirit's work means that the believer is seized by a new nature, one formed and effected by Christ through the Spirit. As life progresses, sin reduces as the believer's original nature holds less sway and his new nature as one in union with Christ gains ascendancy. In this new nature, God works through the Spirit so that godly works result more and more. This progression forms part of the work of regeneration, rooted in the concrete declaration that is justification.

Regeneration

Regeneration is something which occurs at conversion simultaneously with justification, but it is to be understood as something different.[201] However, like justification, it is a matter of faith. Only by faith does anyone know that regeneration is necessary; without a knowledge of God's righteousness and wrath, there can be no desire to escape the latter and partake in the former.[202]

Therefore, regeneration proceeds from an earnest fear of God.[203] It consists in a turning to God, the sense of both the Hebrew and Greek terms used in the Bible (*nacham* and *metanoeo* respectively) and usually translated "repent."[204] It is a "departing from ourselves, [in which] we turn to God, and having put off our former mind, we put on a new."[205] This action means that the human must put off the old nature and seek a transformation "in the soul itself."[206] As humans cannot change their natures, only God, regeneration is a free gift of God and so can only be found through faith.[207]

Here is what appears to be an act or decision made by the human, expressed as a turning to God. It is deciding to pursue something new—a new nature, a transformation, a new mind, a departure from oneself. Despite this phrasing, this is emphatically not a work by the human as it is a choice made by faith which is given to the human by Christ through the Spirit, a

---

201. Tamburello, *Union with Christ*, 59, citing III.16.1.
202. III.3.2.
203. III.3.7.
204. III.3.6.
205. III.3.5.
206. III.3.6.
207. III.3.21.

subject explored further below. It is a decision corresponding to the union with Christ, itself all a work of the Spirit, as discussed above.[208] However, it is useful to consider the issue in this way as it emphasizes that there is a point at which regeneration takes hold for the believer. This taking hold occurs simultaneously with justification and something new results. Where there were only human desires which are evil and charged to humans as sin there is now regeneration.[209]

Where justification is a change of status and treatment for the human, regeneration is a change of the human himself. Thus, while it is true to say that in considering justification alone the human is the same human, albeit with a new status,[210] it is not true to say it of regeneration. In regeneration, there is change in the human. An old nature is diminishing; it has faded and will fade more; a new and completely different nature with a new focus has come; through regenerating grace the image of God is partly and then progressively restored in the believer.[211] This transformation is wrought by God and so comes into being through God's operation in the human through the union established at conversion and, as we shall see below, in the Christian life.

Regeneration: Mortification and Vivification

To explain regeneration in greater depth, Calvin introduces the concepts of "mortification" and "vivification." These displace sinful human desires in the regenerate believer.

Mortification is the realization of the true nature of sin and judgement and an understanding of where human desire, the flesh, leads. It is the rejection of these which accompanies this recognition of the sorry state of the human.[212] By mortification, the old self, the flesh, is done away with.[213] This can be characterized as the negative dimension of regeneration, where the turning to God inevitably means a turning away from human desire.

---

208. The work of regeneration is accomplished by the Spirit through the church *via* preaching and the sacraments, the primary motif for Calvin. However, it has effect on the believer through the personal union. That is, while personal to the believer, it occurs *in* the church.

209. III.3.12.

210. That is, there has been ontological change for the human in the change of status and what it brings, but no such change in respect of the human nature in justification.

211. III.3.9.

212. III.3.3.

213. III.3.8.

Vivification could be termed the positive part of this turning, where the believer looks to God through Christ and finds there courage, hope, and a desire to live in a way devoted to God.[214] Vivification denotes a new self, wrought by the Holy Spirit acting in the mystical union: "the Spirit of God so imbues our souls, steeped in his holiness, with both new thoughts and feelings that they can be rightly considered new."[215]

Regeneration therefore consists of mortification and vivification, the old self passing away in mortification and the new coming by the Spirit.[216] These processes happen by "participation in Christ"[217] and their aim is to restore the image of God in the human, something which occurs "through the benefit of Christ",[218] a term which must mean the work of Christ both constitutively for the world and individually in the believer. Expressing this in terms of the union of the believer and Christ, the old nature becomes less and the new nature in union greater as the Spirit works so that the outcomes in the believer's life are less and less due to her choices and more and more due to the Spirit's work in her through her union with Christ

Regeneration continues for the believer throughout life[219] because "there remains in a regenerate man a smoldering cinder of evil."[220] Believers are still sinners and remain so throughout life in this world because sin is still a part of their makeup. Sin ceases to reign in them, but it still dwells in them.[221] There remains a life-long struggle with the corrupt human nature for believers, but the corruption of sin will diminish as the image of God is gradually restored.[222] The human being still exists in the union, with her old nature, however much the new nature is asserted. While the believer desires and seeks the ascendancy of Christ in her life by the work of the Spirit, the old nature still has an impact precisely because of the character of the union. This seems a dark prescription, but in reality it is not. Believers are to look upon this struggle positively, because if there were no struggle there would be no awareness of sin, so they would actually be non-believers. Calvin notes that believers dislike the evil they do within the struggle because of their familiarity with righteousness. One cannot hate

---

214. III.3.3.
215. III.3.8.
216. III.3.5.
217. III.3.9.
218. III.3.9.
219. III.3.9.
220. III.3.10.
221. III.3.11.
222. III.3.9.

sin unless she loves righteousness.[223] Put another way, those who are not in union with Christ know only sin, but do not know it as sin because they do not know righteousness. Through the union and the participation in Christ it effects, the believer is intimately familiar with righteousness and just as aware, if not more, of sin. Thus, the desire for mortification is evidence of the indwelling Christ and the work of the Spirit in union, together producing new life. New desire and new life are fruits of the hypostases active in the union and so attributable to them alone, not to the believer.[224] This fact of new life itself, of course, is positive and should remove any apparent darkness of the prescription by itself.

Calvin picks up this positive aspect to the struggle in a reference to Romans 7:24 and 8:38–39. If Paul looks to whatever righteousness he might call his own, he can only see how wretched he is, how hopeless that is (7:24). But the same Paul, looking to that righteousness granted him which is grounded in Christ, rejoices as nothing can separate him from the love of God (8:38–39).[225] Calvin therefore understands these passages as referring to the struggle each believer experiences as sin occurs, even as regeneration progresses. He does not see them as a comparison of the perfect life of a believer with that of the sinful life of a non-believer. Here, rather, is the Spirit at work through the union within each believer; Paul's old nature can assert itself in which case sin results, but the union means that the righteousness of Christ present in him leads to and effects new life in the Spirit, a life of the justified being regenerated.

Thus, regeneration is ongoing; Christ and the Spirit continue to work in the believer in the union he experiences with Christ. This ongoing process is still a work or gift of God[226] and it produces piety, good works, purity, and holiness in the believer.[227] But it is not "a process of development by which man attains the goal of perfection."[228] Rather, "through continual and sometimes even slow advances God wipes out in his elect the corruptions of the flesh."[229] Within the union the believer continually decides, as one being in union with another, to engage in acts of mortification and vivification, to choose the other more and more and so comprising a string of apparent

223. III.3.20.

224. This new life includes good works, which Tanner, *Jesus, Humanity and the Trinity*, 61, reminds us do not originate with the human as they issue "continually from the overflowing of Christ's virtues to us, as those virtues become ours by faith."

225. III.11.11.

226. III.3.20.

227. III.3.16.

228. Niesel, *The Theology of Calvin*, 128.

229. III.3.9

choices each day to participate in regeneration. These choices are only apparent, as in reality it is God working regeneration in the believer by the Spirit through the union, so that the regenerate human may glorify him more so as to repeatedly embrace this new thing God has done and is doing within the believer's person. Thus, more and more the new nature of the believer in union with Christ is seen and her original nature fades.

In a similar way to justification, regeneration is coincident with the union but is logically post. Regeneration is a function of the union and can be accomplished only because the union exists, but it is always only this; something which is facilitated by the union, something the union allows God to do in the believer's very being.

Faith

Several references have already been made to faith, with the suggestion that choices or decisions are made in faith by the believer. Faith itself comes to the believer and Calvin gives this careful treatment to show that it is not a human work and is truly given to the believer, although it functions in a way which can appear to be self-effort by the believer.

Calvin's definition of faith has already been considered and I will not repeat it here. It is sufficient to state that faith is a sure knowledge of forgiveness, founded on the promises revealed in Scripture. Faith is produced in the believer through the Spirit, the medium of the union of the believer with Christ. While faith is therefore entirely a work of the Spirit,[230] once this work is done, the believer has faith and can identify it as such, so much so that she can say "my faith." This is not a statement of ownership, but a statement about her being: she is now someone who has faith and it is personal to her and her new nature. This faith is truly a new thing created in the believer. It is not something she has developed or grown into; it is not a fruit of the old self or to be identified with it. She is a new creation in respect to faith because she now has, by the grace of God through union with her in Christ, something she did not have before.

However big or small this faith may seem to the believer, because it is a work of the Spirit it is sufficient. There is no question of whether someone has sufficient faith as there might be if it were a human work, when how much effort is required to "make contact," so to speak, might be discussed

---

230. Although saying this does not exclude Christ at all. As Shepherd, *The Nature and Function*, 1, points out, "Faith, then, results from the action of the exalted Christ upon men as he bestows himself upon them and binds them to himself in the power of his Spirit."

and decided upon. Even a little faith is real and ultimately it is enough for salvation.[231] However a believer might be tested and assailed, faith, however small, will allow him to win through to God;[232] doubt cannot smother it.[233] This must be so because of the union. If faith exists, then the union exists because the union is effected through faith. Therefore, any faith is clear evidence of the union, and if the union exists, the individual is justified.[234] But there is an expectation that faith will grow within the believer; become larger, more substantial.

However, "certain interruptions of faith occasionally occur."[235] The unfortunate fact that believers remain sinners demonstrates that faith is something to be nourished and increased.[236] Believers are subject to temptation and do fail because of this, something ultimately rooted, for Calvin, in the continued division of spirit and flesh in the world.[237] That is, the old nature of the believer in the union with Christ still exists despite her new nature in Christ. However, while faith may seem to wax and wane as believers struggle and are distracted by other thoughts, because it is ultimately dependent on the Holy Spirit through the union and not the believer, faith still remains (and will ultimately triumph).[238] It is not that believers in this struggle vacillate between being with Christ and being without him (or "with themselves" so to speak), which implies that the union comes and goes. No, the union, once established, always exists and, as elected, of course, there is no possibility of salvation being lost for believers. Actually, whatever the believer may feel in the midst of the struggle, even at its worst depths, Christ is nonetheless in him, cleaved by an "indivisible bond".[239] Whatever happens in the Christian life, believers continue to be with Christ, to have Christ dwell within; faith does not guarantee that the world will not fail the believer, but rather guarantees that God will not fail him.[240]

So, faith is not perfect, but it is new, and it is of God. It is perfect in itself because it is God's gift but has yet to be perfected in the believer because

231. III.2.20.
232. III.2.21.
233. III.2.37.
234. Pitkin, "Faith and Justification," 293–94, comments that "Mystical union with Christ is one of the principal effects of faith, and forms the ground of believers' assurance."
235. III.2.24.
236. IV.14.7.
237. III.2.18.
238. III.2.18.
239. III.2.18; III.2.24.
240. III.2.28.

of the remaining fleshly nature of the believer. Faith resides; but the new creation consists of one in union with another where the human participant has an original, or fleshly, nature brought into the union with Christ, so the original nature still has some influence.

Faith has a central role in Calvin's thought. Faith itself does not justify, but God justifies through faith.[241] It is what God does when faith is aroused through the Spirit—giving the new status of righteousness to the believer through union with Christ and treating her as such—which justifies. However, faith as the work of the Spirit in bringing the illumination of God's truth to the believer follows from the work of justifying.

Similarly, the work of regeneration can only proceed where faith exists. If there is no faith, there is no awareness of God and therefore there can be no regeneration. If a person does not know that Christ dwells within them, then they are reprobate.[242] This knowledge can only be acquired by faith. But regeneration and faith, while closely related, are different things which must be understood and considered as such. "They are held together by a permanent bond, [and] require to be joined rather than confused."[243]

The joining of regeneration and faith, and indeed the equally necessary joining of justification and faith, point to how important the mystical union is to Calvin's thought. Justification, regeneration, and faith are intrinsic to salvation, and the latter is the gift through which justification and regeneration come about: it is how God brings these other two into being in the believer. Through faith, the Spirit establishes a bond between Christ and the believer. By faith, *Christ* now dwells within the believer through the Spirit. It is in this communion and by this communion that Christ can give faith and so justify and also work in the believer thereby regenerating him. There must be this communion to ensure that what Christ does actually affects the believer; to share and impart his benefits, Christ must dwell within believers in this communion, this mystical union.[244] Without this union there is no way for Christ to have any impact in a life.[245]

This impact surely includes faith. Justification cannot occur without faith and, while it is true to say that the union is justifying, and that justification comes through the union, this does not exclude the role of the

241. III.1.7.
242. III.2.39.
243. III.3.5.
244. III.1.1.
245. Zachman, "*Communio cum Christo*," 370, sums this up well: "Faith not only unites us to Christ so that we may receive all of the benefits to be found in him, but it also leads the godly to cry out to Christ in prayer, so that they may obtain from him the blessings they know to be found in him alone."

union in faith. Faith also comes to the believer through or by the union—it is probably best to conceive of faith and justification being coincident at the point of conversion.[246] Similarly, to the extent that regeneration occurs at conversion, it is also coincident with the union. However, regeneration continues throughout the believer's life through, or as a function of, the union. Similarly, faith, once established through the union, continues to flourish and grow within the believer, coming as a gift to the believer from Christ through the union by means of the Spirit. Hence the key way in which conversion or salvation, understood here as faith, justification, and regeneration, comes to the believer (and conversion coming is the correct way to conceive of it for Calvin) is through the establishment and operation of the mystical union. This is the sharing of the benefits of Christ to which Calvin assigns the "highest degree of importance,"[247] it is the foundation for all descriptions of how the new creation has come for Calvin.

Self-Denial

Beyond these broad themes, the union is such that God is involved in all the details of the believer's life. Once justified and in union with Christ, God's work in the believer can extend to everything the believer does, both directly and indirectly, all of which arises from the work of the Spirit through the union. While this is God at work, the believer has a role in pursuing regeneration, which has as its object "to manifest in the life of believers a harmony and agreement between God's righteousness and their obedience, and thus to confirm the adoption that they have received as sons."[248] Part, at least, of this role is self-denial, an obedience to God in lieu of following one's own desires,[249] which must follow if the believer is to see the new nature in union with Christ manifested in her life and not the old nature, or self, acting in isolation.

---

246. While faith effects the union and so is logically prior to it although coincident with it, faith is not the one-time declaration that justification is, but continues and develops in the union.

247. III.11.2.

248. III.6.1. Boulton, *Life in God*, 79–82, represents this manifestation as living a life of piety where every good is ascribed to God and a program of learning about God's goodness and providence is pursued.

249. Niesel, *The Theology of Calvin*, 144, highlights that "The substance of Christian ethics" is not self-improvement, but that "The essential action which we are called upon to perform is rather the renunciation of all that is our own, that we may give scope to the action of God."

The motive for obedience lies with Christ through the union. In this union, and through the operation of the Spirit in it, believers perceive "the right understanding of Christ from the word of the gospel"[250] and thus a "love of righteousness"[251] promoting obedience is instilled by the Spirit within the very being of the believer as scriptural instruction in the gospel through the ministry of the church continues. However, this obedience is not instantaneously complete: believers remain imperfect. What is expected is that there will be small advances in obedience and towards righteousness every day throughout the Christian life.[252]

This occurs because believers recognize that they are no longer their own, they now belong to Christ.[253] Because of this, they pursue obedience to God, rather than obedience to self. They increasingly become God-centered, oriented to their new owner, and less self-centered, oriented to their old self. It is a gradual process of improvement in the Spirit as the old self is still present and has influence. This obedience, for Calvin, involves self-denial, a giving up of personal goals and an embracing those of God. No longer is the believer's life based on a philosophy centered around him; now there has been a transformation and his life and philosophy are becoming rooted in God's intentions for him. So, "The Christian philosophy bids reason give way to, submit and subject itself to, the Holy Spirit so that the man himself may no longer live but hear Christ living and reigning within him."[254] This transformation turns everything upside down as it promotes a way of life not related at all to the environment a believer lives in (which is separate from God even if under his providential care) but rather to God.[255] Thus the Christian life is not to be driven by personal desires; neither by standards the world views as appropriate; nor by how the world understands itself; nor by any rational deduction from any circumstances. It is to be completely divorced from this and instead be driven by Christ from within the intimate union he shares with the believer.

Calvin sees this re-orientation, this self-denial, as resulting in behavior which embraces "soberness," which includes good moral living, proper use of material possessions and acceptance of poverty; "righteousness," which is maintaining good relations with others; and "godliness" which is

---

250. III.6.4.
251. III.6.2.
252. III.7.5.
253. III.7.1.
254. III.7.2. Hence Niesel, *The Theology of Calvin*, 144: "It is not a question of resignation in itself, but of a resignation which relinquishes the control to Christ."
255. Zachman, *Reconsidering John Calvin*, 124.

maintaining good relations with God. "But, nothing is more difficult than this," he says.[256] Self-denial therefore has aspects directed to humans, but mostly its aspects are directed towards God.[257] This is because even those things which are overtly directed towards humans only arise because the Christian life is oriented towards God and correct Christian action results from proper attention to God through the union within, which alone makes that orientation possible.

Towards humans, self-denial means there must be a proper concern and helpfulness towards others.[258] Since believers cannot share their possessions with God, they can only share them with their neighbors, and this they must do.[259] Because this proper concern arises from believers' obedience to God, it is dependent only on God and the relation in union with Christ, through the Spirit. It has no dependence on anyone else, so what a believer might think of her neighbors has no bearing on what her attitude to them must be.[260]

Towards God, self-denial means devotion to his will,[261] and this devotion will prove to be to the believer's benefit because God will "bring a happy and favorable outcome for us."[262] This will be so even if what believers are led to do according to God's will makes no sense to them. In fact, this means that believers must not strive after anything other than God, and for all results (however fruitful) all credit must be given to God[263]—anything else is shamelessness. Self-denial is not a pious effort by the believer but originates in Christ.[264] This reminder of the basis of self-denial is a powerful antidote to how believers may rationalize the Christian life so that it can be lived

256. III.7.3.

257. III.7.4.

258. Zachman, "Deny Yourself and Take up Your Cross," 472, says "Far from domineering over our neighbours, we ought to be severe with ourselves and forbearing with our neighbours."

259. III.7.5.

260. III.7.6.

261. Zachman, "John Calvin on the Christian Life," 471, has it that Calvin claims believers need submit themselves to the "guidance of the Holy Spirit" so that Christ will govern their lives "from the inside out."

262. III.7.8. Boulton, *Life in God*, 119–20, when explicating "this liberating 'mortification of the flesh' notes that it involves effort and is gradual. "That is, the process of 'dying to sin' takes place over time, in and through the tangible, everyday, Spirit-led paideutic exercises of Christian life, and particularly in and through reformed versions of classic ascetic disciplines: 'self-denial', which Calvin calls 'the sum of the Christian life'; 'bearing the cross, and so on." He cites III.7 and 8 in support.

263. III.7.9.

264. Niesel, *The Theology of Calvin*, 145.

to their advantage. It means that nothing can be done in the name of God which is not securely bedded in the Word and promise of God. There can be no appeal to "godly principles" which promote the pursuit of something other than God, even if in his name. Believers cannot pursue possessions, position, health, or wealth, for example, under the assumption that God has some principles which set out that this is what he has commanded for believers. Calvin makes it quite clear that what God has for believers is God-self and life with God, and pursuit of this is the sole goal for believers. This means self-denial and a setting aside of the pursuit of anything for oneself. This will actually result in the best outcome for the believer. This does not mean that believers are barred from worldly success or comfort, but it does mean that if such things come to the believer, they do so as a result of pursuing God's will and there remains the responsibility of living with them in a continuing pursuit of God's will.

This focus will assist the believer to bear adversity.[265] When hard things come, the reliance on God will ensure the believer can persevere, as reliance on anything else is highly uncertain; such things tend to disappear or change and so provide no sure foundation.[266] It is interesting to consider the list of examples Calvin gives of adversity: disease, war, famine, frequent death, and a house burning down.[267] In Calvin's time, there was little or no control over such events. Even war, the result of human choice, was imposed on the populace in a way foreign to modern liberal western democracies. In the current environment, there is a greater level of control (although by no means complete and certainly not shared by much of the world) over all these kinds of events. Thus, the call to self-denial is more challenging for the modern western believer because it involves the apparent relinquishment of more control. Sixteenth century Genevans may well have willingly embraced self-denial as a deposit towards their future lives which promised relief from their " . . . nasty, brutish, and short"[268] lives on earth. Such denial is less attractive to the western believer who would not describe his life in such terms, either because it is not like that or he holds out hope that it will improve. The increased difficulty, however, does not diminish the strength of Calvin's appeal. Whatever the environment, wherever he is and however comfortable life appears, Calvin would remind

---

265. III.7.10.

266. Zachman, "John Calvin on the Christian Life," 474, picks this up by saying that if believers "look to God's blessing as the only source of value in [their] lives then they will not be prideful when prosperous but tranquil when in poverty."

267. III.7.10.

268. Hobbes, *Leviathan*, 57. Hobbes (1651) was a century later than Calvin, but his comment is undoubtedly applicable to sixteenth-century Geneva.

the believer that he owes his allegiance and obedience to God and that the prospect of the life to come is only delayed, not eliminated. Even in comfort, self-denial leads to the best for the believer.

The call to self-denial and its actualization is new in the believer at conversion. As the Christian life continues, the expectation is that self-denial increases so that obedience to God increases. Without Christ, the individual pursues sin which is a total rejection of the call to self-denial and a continued self-serving. With conversion, a transformation in behavior has taken place and continues. This transformation is wrought by Christ through the Holy Spirit, acting in the union the believer has with Christ. In the union the believer is led by the Spirit to be obedient, but it involves his apparent decision to be so. This is only an apparent decision because it cannot be a decision of an independent free will, as the decision is made by one in union with Christ, one in intimate relationship with Christ in that union. The will of the believer is more than just affected by that relationship; it is actually directed by the Spirit. Any act of self-denial in this context is a godly act and thus due to God's working. However, it is undoubtedly true that the decision appears to the believer to be his as the union is experienced by the believer as faith held by him, not as the directly perceived presence of the Spirit instructing him, so it is legitimate to consider it as an obedient act of the individual. This being the case, each decision to deny self is a symptom of the transformed life Christ is crafting through the union and, conversely, each such decision is a lessening of the influence of the flesh, a diminishing of the "old."

Bearing One's Cross

One particular part of self-denial Calvin sees is bearing the cross, or coping with adversity, something which is a function of regeneration.[269] However, it is self-denial indirectly because bearing one's cross is something which happens to the believer, rather than something which the believer chooses to do. It is the hard things, the persecution, the sufferings which happen to believers because of their Christian faith. Because it is what happens to believers, it is in this sense passive compared to the active sense in which self-denial is pursued. However, it is also self-denial, because crosses are to be borne, not avoided in the interests of comfort.

The cross, of course, speaks directly to the cross of Christ[270] and not only shows his obedience. In the union with him, his sufferings "help much

269. III.8.1.
270. As Zachman, "John Calvin and the Christian Life," 474, observes, inseparably so.

in promoting our salvation." That is, when believers share Christ's sufferings, they become much more aware of the power of the resurrection and ultimately they will share in it as they will share also in his death.[271]

No believer escapes cross-bearing. Each has to bear their own cross, endure their own hardships because of their faith, and as they do their fellowship with Christ is confirmed; in fact, the greater the suffering and so the heavier the cross, the more the fellowship with Christ is confirmed.[272] Each cross is personal, and God uses it to keep the believer in Christ, in union with Christ, to keep her from backsliding, and to train her in patience and obedience. In fact, it is God's chastisement directed at correction for her.[273] Thus, the Christian is to consider this suffering as a comfort as it identifies her with Christ and even if it results in her death, she will enter the blessed life with Christ hereafter.[274]

This means that God uses the individual crosses of believers in a positive way to train them. Bearing a cross is something believers are to embrace because God uses cross-bearing to prepare and train them.[275] Calvin certainly affirms this, but does he have an activist view of God's involvement in this area? That is, does God not only use crosses passively received but actively impose them on believers? Calvin makes a distinction between God's treatment of the elect for their sins, and the reprobate. The elect are chastised[276] for their sins, but God takes vengeance on the reprobate for theirs.[277] He uses "vengeance" here for the purpose of teaching—what he has in view is punishment. Thus, believers suffer punishment for their sins which is chastisement, but the reprobate suffer punishment which is purely penalty without the positive outcome chastisement promises; after all, there is no positive outcome for the reprobate. Note also that Calvin is talking of this life, as chastisement has no place in the life to come for the believer. Further, both punishments look the same (he uses flogging of a son and a

---

271. III.8.1.
272. Ibid.
273. III.8.4–6.
274. III.8.9.
275. Zachman, "John Calvin on the Christian Life," 475–76, notes the chief benefit for believers "has to do with the increase in self-knowledge" and that as cross-bearing brings them to closer conformity with Christ crucified, they should find "comfort and even joy" in their experiences.
276. By chastisement, Calvin means punishment meted out for the purposes of admonition and correction. That is, for the positive purpose of increasing godliness in the Christian, III.4.31.
277. III.4.31.

slave cited by Chrysostom as an example[278]), so whether something is chastisement or punishment is determined by the status of the recipient, not the character of the event. Care is needed here in analyzing Calvin's thought, however, as on the one hand he says believers are chastised for their sins, and on the other that they are chastised in bearing their cross.[279] Is chastisement common to both? This is a real question as cross-bearing can include suffering brought to the believer through no sin of his own, but through his complete obedience to God.

It seems clear that it is. Punishment for sin implies suffering, and suffering is something to be borne, however it has arisen. If punished for sin, the believer is to acknowledge that and bear it, resolving once again to deny self and remain obedient to God. Therefore, this suffering, for Calvin, is at least part of the cross that believer must bear, and it has been brought to him actively by God as chastisement, rather than being something which has been brought by others.

The chastisement of the cross is real: the suffering involves real pain and real hurt, even if it does build up the believer and add to the Christian life. Believers are not to expect to feel cheerful in suffering, there is no need to be stoic; it hurts.[280] Rather, as Jesus did, sorrow and hurt can be expressed, but like him, the believer is to remain obedient.[281] Even harsh, cruel things happen according to God's justice (again meted out in this world) and believers are to accept such things.[282]

Becoming a believer therefore changes the character of suffering for the individual—it is no longer vengeance, but is now chastisement.[283] In their new relationship through the union with Christ, believers can now recognize it as chastisement and adopt the new attitude their obedience requires.[284] This is

---

278. Ibid. The son is flogged for chastisement, the slave for punishment, but both are floggings.

279. III.8.6.

280. Niesel, *The Theology of Calvin*, 148. See also Zachman, "John Calvin and the Christian Life," 476.

281. III.8.8–9. But this is not an impossible situation. As Zachman, *John Calvin as Teacher Pastor and Theologian*, 253, points out "Christ gives us the power to endure the cross in this life so that we might inherit the kingdom of God, by sharing with us the Spirit he has abundantly received from his Father."

282. III.8.10.

283. Of course, for the elect, it was always so, but as it is only at conversion that the elect realize that they are elect, until then their suffering due to sin appeared as vengeance to them.

284. There is a difficulty for Calvin here, as he wants to say that God is involved in a very detailed way with the Christian and brings chastisement for correction in response to sins. However, he also wants to say that God no longer treats the justified as a sinner,

an important point, as it is not as if God can only act and direct the behavior of people through union with them. No, God actually directs everything which happens and a "lower working" of the Spirit is possible even among the reprobate.[285] The fact that chastisement and vengeance look exactly the same viewed externally is a good illustration of this. The distinction for the individual is only perceived by the believer because of the union he enjoys with Christ. It is not true to say that the union is what makes the difference, but the union is certainly evidence of the difference. It is most certainly true to say that Christ makes the difference and does so through the union. The distinction between the believer being chastised and the reprobate suffering vengeance is the presence in the former of Christ in union with her, and the lack of any union, and hence Christ, in the latter.

The union is therefore crucial in cross-bearing, as it is the only means by which the believer knows she is bearing a cross, the only means by which Christ can grow and teach the believer through the crosses she bears.[286] Without the union, this benefit of Christ cannot be embraced by the believer. The crosses need not be imposed through the union itself, although this cannot be ruled out; they need only be imposed through the general activity of God with the believer in company with the reprobate. But because of the union, Christ works with the believer and she can be aware of that and rejoice in his promises.

Cross bearing and self-denial must involve the full range of human life: there is no limit in the scope of what constitutes a godly act. Such acts can range from some small kindness for a neighbor to highly influential actions, and each act embraced and performed is also an act of self-denial. Equally, suffering ranges enormously in its scope, but each item is a cross which the believer must bear. Thus, just as the union is crucial in the broad themes of conversion and Christian life, it is also crucial in allowing God to direct and influence believers without limit in their daily lives. Not only is the union grand and sweeping, involving the limitless God as it does, but it is also close and intimate, allowing God to penetrate to all parts of the believer's existence, however small and trivial they may appear. The pervasiveness of the union cannot be understated.

---

so how can he chastise such a one? It would be better to say that cross-bearing is a passive activity in as much as God does not impose the suffering involved, but that in the same way as the believer may suffer the consequences of her being obedient to God, she also bears the consequences of her disobedience. However, this discussion is focused on Calvin's thought, not its critique.

285. II.4.1; III.2.13.

286. Zachman, *John Calvin as Teacher, Pastor and Theologian*, 253, notes that Christ gives the believer power to endure her cross.

Summary

In Calvin's theology the fullness of God in Christ through the Spirit is given to the believer. The union formed to do so brings simply this, not any "part" of Christ. Neither is there any fusing of Christ with the believer. Through that union the believer enjoys the benefits of justification and regeneration, experienced in faith brought through the union. In this union between Christ and the believer, every godly thought or act of the believer is an act of self-denial and a work of Christ through the Spirit, so allowing the Spirit to work in believers and, through them, in the world. All suffering also involves the Spirit as, whether imposed actively or passively by God, the Spirit uses suffering as crosses for the believer to bear through which he becomes more godly. In short, the union allows the participation in Christ which God desires for each believer, and this is a participation of the whole believer without deduction; nothing is too trivial as regards participation in Christ. All this, the believer knows and experiences by faith; there is no overt experience of the union in any other way. The union is established by the Spirit whose activity is interdependent with Word and Scripture and sealed by the sacraments. Therefore, believers in union with Christ through the Spirit must turn to the preached and written Word and its promises and the sacraments for illumination.

Such is Calvin's thought on pneumatology and union. Calvin conceives of a world where believers live as people with faith, whose perception of God's presence and activity in the world is revealed in faith, sought in the church through Scripture and its exposition in preaching and attested by the sacraments. It is only these three which believers can take hold of in any way which appears objective, or independent of God, although in reality each involves the intimate activity of God. Pentecostal theology claims such intimate activity, but its conception is one where there is an intense awareness of God as the Spirit. It is time now to examine how this is so in the way Pentecostals view pneumatology and union with Christ.

2

Pneumatology and Union
The Pentecostals

Turning from Calvin to Pentecostal doctrines, one faces a very different task in attempting to be definitive about what a Pentecostal theology of the Spirit and the union between the believer and Christ *is*. Pentecostals want to say that the Spirit has been poured out on many in a "latter rain," but once they turn to explaining what that means doctrinally, a broad diversity of views arises, something which has been noted by many.[1] This diversity is even present concerning such an identifiably "Pentecostal" doctrine as subsequence (see below) which is not universally accepted among Pentecostals and has been understood in different ways.[2]

Distilling a representative "Pentecostal theology" is therefore at present a forlorn task and perhaps may remain so. This is well illustrated by the existence of substantial streams within a broad Pentecostalism with differing emphases or theology. Steven Studebaker describes three "historical forms" of Pentecostalism, each of which can be called a separate stream, separated from the other two by time, locus and praxis:

1. Classical Pentecostalism, tracing its origins to the Azusa St revival or contemporary occurrences, emphasizing Spirit baptism and speaking in tongues;

2. the Charismatic Renewal, originating in the nineteen-fifties to the nineteen-seventies, occurring within 'mainstream' churches, affirming Spirit baptism but with less emphasis on tongues than Classical Pentecostalism; and

3. Neocharismatic, originating in the early nineteen-eighties with no connection to Classical Pentecostal or Charismatic Renewal churches,

---

1. Macchia, *Baptized in the Spirit*, 33–38, gives a brief survey.
2. Ibid., 35.

more interested in "charismatic manifestations" (or, "signs and wonders") than Spirit baptism and tongues.[3]

There is diversity within these streams—for example the Oneness Pentecostals, an offshoot of Classical Pentecostalism. Their origins can be traced to a Camp Meeting in 1913, where one R E McAlister asserted that the apostles baptized in the name of Jesus *only*,[4] and did not invoke the triune Name. The following night "John G Shaeppe . . . had a vision of Jesus and woke up the camp shouting that the name of Jesus needed to be glorified." Subsequently it was taught by a Frank J Ewart that those baptized using the trinitarian formula required rebaptism in the name of Jesus, with some being told that they would lose their salvation if they were not rebaptized.[5]

This focus on Jesus as one in lieu of the triadic formulation led to a modalist view of God. Jesus is the Name of one God in whom the fullness of God dwells, the "soteriologically efficacious name of the Godhead," and an historical human.[6] This doctrine of God as one Person fulfilling three offices was adopted by the Oneness Pentecostals who remain a substantial group. Yong suggests up to thirty percent of all black churches in North America affirm a Oneness understanding[7] and one leading denomination alone, the United Pentecostal Church International, claims more than two million followers.[8] This is a significant force with some influence, whose doctrine of the Spirit as one manifestation of the singular God cannot be reconciled with the classical trinitarian formulation held by most Pentecostals.

This "unity and diversity" in doctrine and practice means a consolidation of views is not possible, but nevertheless there are distinct currents which can be usefully examined and used in the engagement with Calvin. The first task here, then, is to identify those currents I will examine; but a word about terminology is required before proceeding.

In general, Pentecostal theologians use "revelation" in a much broader sense than Calvin. For Calvin, Jesus Christ is always the revelation—he is its content and visible representation and that is the extent of what he terms "revelation." Pentecostal writers would certainly affirm Jesus Christ as the revelation, but "revelation" is also used to mean divine knowledge imparted

---

3. Studebaker, "Introduction," 21. He also identifies the same three groups, calling them Pentecostals, Charismatic and "third wave."

4. The only formula used in Acts.

5. McRoberts, "The Holy Trinity," 171–72.

6. Yong, *The Spirit Poured Out on All Flesh*, 205–6.

7. Ibid., 185.

8. See http://www.upci.org/about-us/about-us.

to, or received by a believer,[9] something which is to be understood as much more an encounter than a simple reception of intellectual knowledge. In this discussion, I will restrict the use of the term to Calvin's meaning, which will mean occasional changes of terminology from the sources I use but hopefully eliminate confusion on the point in this work.

Pentecostalism can claim its genesis to have been at the Bible School of Charles Fox Parham when, in 1901, Agnes Ozman received the baptism of the Holy Spirit and spoke in tongues; however this is but one of many loci. Earlier and later initiations can be seen in "England, Germany, India, Russia, Wales, and North America."[10] It certainly sprang from earlier Wesleyan and Holiness roots, but came into being as an identifiable movement in the first two decades of the twentieth century before its development into its current status as one of four distinct forms of Christianity (the others being Roman Catholicism, Eastern Orthodoxy and Protestantism). It is therefore easily the youngest of the major forms of Christianity, and this shows in the breadth of its self-understanding and the way it has expressed its theology to date.

The movement's youth and birth in experience have had their impacts on Pentecostal writings. Andrew Gabriel, in a discussion focused on Pentecostal pneumatology and the access to it provided by trinitarian theology, describes the predominance of a drive among Pentecostals for a "biblical" theology, by which he means a theology tightly tied to Scripture; one which essentially uses only scriptural terms and relies heavily on the use of prooftexts as direct evidence. He carefully distinguishes this from the academic discipline of biblical theology (which is, of course, also scripturally founded) and notes that the practice is limiting as it effectively excludes exploration of important Christian doctrines like the Trinity.[11] This has broader implications than just the Trinity, of course, and has inhibited the development of specifically Pentecostal systematic theology.

Instead, Steven Land comments that "More comprehensive theological works by Pentecostals are essentially traditional outlines of evangelical fundamentals with a few extra chapters on Spirit baptism and gifts."[12] He

---

9. See Hocken, "Meaning and Purpose," 125–34, for one example.

10. Land, *Pentecostal Spirituality*, 16. See also Hollenweger, *The Pentecostals*, for a broad survey.

11. Gabriel, "This Spirit is God," 74–75.

12. Land, *Pentecostal Spirituality*, 24. Examples he gives are Pearlman, *Knowing the Doctrines of the Bible*; Duffield and Van Cleave, *Foundations of Pentecostal Theology*; and Sauls, *Pentecostal Doctrines: A Wesleyan Approach*. Other examples which use the "biblical" theology approach noted by Gabriel are Horton, *Systematic Theology*, Grudem, *Systematic Theology*; and Menzies and Horton, *Bible Doctrines*. Packer, *Evangelical*

goes on to suggest that this wholesale borrowing from one strand of Protestantism has occurred despite the fact that, in respect of its faith and practice which is true to its origins, Pentecostalism has continuities with each of the other three forms of Christianity. He illustrates this by observing that its emphasis on sanctification-transformation over forensic justification owes more to Catholicism than Protestantism; its high view of Scripture as authoritative over the church and tradition is the reverse; and its understanding of "spirituality as perfection and participation in the divine life" owes more to Eastern than Western traditions.[13]

The result of this borrowing and direct biblical linkages has been that much of what has been written has not extended itself to what might be called a "full" Pentecostal systematic theology, apart from the treatment of Spirit baptism and allied matters. It is only in the past three decades that serious work has begun on developing a global Pentecostal theology, and I will touch on some of this work. Before then, I will examine a number of currents with some broad acceptance within Pentecostalism which I think will create an admittedly particular picture of Pentecostalism that is nevertheless representative of much of its thought and so can be used in conversation with Calvin. There is overlap between currents, so there is not a neatly divided list, but I begin with an examination of evangelical pneumatology which has been adopted by Pentecostalism and then examine the high-profile role of the Spirit in the early church which is not reflected in that pneumatology. Pentecostals claim a recovery of that high profile, so I turn then to their account of Spirit baptism and its basis in Acts texts and Lukan theology before engaging directly with how the role of the Spirit is elevated by the full content of the experience of Spirit baptism. I briefly look at the implications this work has for the Pentecostal doctrine of subsequence before turning to the work of Amos Yong and Frank Macchia who propose similar christological and soteriological models which incorporate a much higher profile for the Spirit than typical Western Protestant theology allows. The basis for this inclusion of the Spirit is an appeal to a wider interpretation of Spirit baptism than an occurrence which gave only power for mission and witness, as will be seen. The discussion concludes with a consideration of

---

Influences, 276, 279, defines evangelical theology as one which asserts "the final authority of Holy Scripture in all matters of faith and life, and the centrality of justification by faith in the Lord Jesus Christ." He expands upon this by noting that justification is "apart from human works" and adding "acceptance through Christ *only*, without human merit and indeed in defiance of human demerit; and of salvation by grace *only*, not by human endeavor; and of glory to God *only* for salvation, without man having anything of which to boast; and of saving knowledge: by Scripture *only*, without human tradition or speculation coming in to supplement it" (emphasis his).

13. Land, *Pentecostal Spirituality*, 30.

the union between the believer and Christ as it appears within Pentecostal doctrine. These currents comprise a limited description which I contend is true to Pentecostalism and its origins and its present direction. Some of the currents examined are attempts to work towards a global theology, so striving for a "representative" position.

The Holy Spirit

I begin with what is not a distinctly Pentecostal theology: a brief rehearsal of the doctrine of the Spirit shared with the evangelical tradition. The majority of this I have taken from *Systematic Theology* (ed Stanley M Horton),[14] cited above, presented by the Assemblies of God, one of the largest, if not the largest, of the Pentecostal denominations. This will give a not untypical presentation of doctrine accepted by Pentecostals, without claiming to be representative of the stream's theology as a whole.

As a general statement, Pentecostals hold to the classical doctrine of the Trinity, where God is one in three hypostases, Father, Son, and Holy Spirit, as set out in the Nico-Constantinopolitan Creed of 381. The Oneness Pentecostals are an obvious exception to this rule. The Spirit is therefore understood to be fully divine and no lesser than the Father or the Son, and of one substance with them. It is likely that the Western, Augustinian, version of the Godhead is generally held rather than the Eastern view, but there is a close affinity with *theosis* in Pentecostal pneumatology, showing some sympathies with Eastern thought although not expressed in that manner.

The work of the hypostasis that is the Spirit can be rolled into a single statement: it is being "the active agent of the Trinity" in creation, without which "knowledge of God would be impossible."[15] This knowledge is granted by the direct work of the Spirit indwelling believers, proving the resurrection of Christ and teaching correct understanding of the Bible, and also being *the* sign to believers that they are included in the church. The indwelling of the Spirit occurs at salvation, but there is an ongoing transformation of the believer wrought by the Spirit as the Christian life is pursued.

This transformation is, of course, sanctification, but this term is understood in a very wide sense. *Sanctification* is used to mean the whole process by which God is cleansing the world from every taint of sin, bringing it towards its ultimate renewed destiny, which of course includes the transformation of the individual. Certainly, the means of this sanctification

---

14. Particularly McLean, "The Holy Spirit," 375–95; and Jenney, "The Holy Spirit and Sanctification," 397–421.

15. McLean, "The Holy Spirit," 375, 377.

is Jesus Christ and his saving work, but the Spirit is the agent, post-Easter and pre-*parousia*, sent to give effect to Christ's ministry. This broad understanding of sanctification as the work of the Spirit can be divided into four tasks:

1. to convict the world;
2. to cleanse the believer at the new birth (conversion) through the blood of Christ;
3. to make real God's righteousness in the believer's life (that is, the work of transformation, the conventional Protestant meaning of sanctification); and
4. to empower the believer to assist in the sanctification of others.

Note that an entire cleansing is not expected in this life—that is achieved at the end of time, with all that avoid the Spirit's work being cleansed by fire then.

While these tasks are for, and occur in, the world, they are accomplished one person at a time. Thus, convicting the world is accomplished by convicting individuals, one by one, and hence the Spirit's work is perceived to be within each believer and beyond them by operating through them on other individuals. This understanding has the effect of collapsing the four tasks into one (number three), but maintaining the distinctions is useful as it adds a considerable outward focus to the inward work of the Spirit in each individual.

Conviction includes revealing to individuals the reality of sin and the effect it has in making them guilty before God; showing them that the testimony about Christ is true; that righteousness is possible, available and desirable through the work of Christ and that those who do not avail themselves of it will face the judgement of God; and confirmation that the Word of God, Scripture, is true. The Spirit works in conviction on all people, and each is a non-believer when the work starts. Where conviction is efficacious, the grasping of the truth it contains is more than a simple intellectual acknowledgement that these things are true, although of course it includes that. Rather, it is a deep inner knowledge given by the Spirit to the individual to reveal to her the reality of her position and what she must do to deal with it. For Pentecostals, this inner knowledge is imparted, at least partially, by Scripture being confirmed by the Spirit to be true through "signs and wonders" following its preaching. The conviction is internal, but the means to its achievement is not exclusively internal. Appealing to "signs and wonders" is appealing to the miraculous as an agent of conviction, although this is certainly revealed by the Spirit, and the phenomena are works of the Spirit. There is a sense that sighting and recognizing the supernatural will assist the individual to be convicted and so respond to the Spirit's work of conviction. This is understood as an activity of the Spirit but, at a popular level, it tends to be expressed as the individual independently recognizing the supernatural as being of God. Whether this is the case or not, there is more than a simple, deep assent in conviction; there is also visual evidence that what is said and written is true.

Conviction does not necessarily result in conversion, as it can be resisted. The individual experiences conviction negatively as it is an uncomfortable experience to be confronted with God's reality and how it applies to her. But at that point she can deal with it by embracing the provision Christ has made and moving to conversion, or by avoiding it and putting it to one side. Doing the latter puts her outside the work of the Spirit for the present, although she may still experience conviction again and again. If she responds by seeking what Christ has done, then the Spirit works again in her by cleansing her and giving her new birth. Conviction leads her to be converted, to accept Christ. Her salvation has been accomplished by a combination of the Spirit's work and her faith which has led her to respond positively.

Should conviction lead to salvation or conversion, this is a single, instantaneous event initiated by the Spirit, who has a great deal to do with the response of the individual. What Christ has done to provide salvation is applied by the Spirit to the individual where not only conviction results, but faith in Christ is also produced.[16] This conviction includes pointing to the truth of Scripture (where the witness to Christ resides), so this arousal of faith is a convincing of the individual of the general truth in Scripture and its personal application to him. The object of the faith aroused is Jesus Christ as personal savior, as testified by Scripture. While faith is aroused by the Spirit, and thus the Spirit is crucial to its coming into existence, it is nevertheless the individual's faith, and it is him that responds. Thus, the Spirit's role in conversion is partial only, as conversion depends upon the individual using the faith aroused to respond to what the Spirit has shown.

This presents immediately as a semi-Pelagian construction, the "default theology of most American evangelical Christians" for Roger E. Olsen,[17] but this is not the case for Pentecostal theologians. It is probably not true to say that Pentecostals are Arminians, but it is true to say that most tend towards Arminianism, or are "More Arminian than Calvinist in [their] approach

---

16. "The Holy Spirit applies the work of Christ's salvation to the heart of the individual. He works in the human heart to convict of sin and to produce faith in Christ's atoning sacrifice" (Higgins, "God's Inspired Word," 110).

17. Olsen, *Arminian Theology*, 30.

to human agency and perseverance."[18] Certainly the above construction cannot be understood as Calvinist, but can fit well in an Arminian sense. Salvation as a gift is efficacious when received through faith, and as simple receipt of a gift is not work, there is only a work if the gift is refused, in which case salvation does not result.[19] So Pentecostal soteriology includes human agency in this sense—the work of the Spirit here can be resisted and rejected. As Arminianism can be interpreted to mean that the perseverance of the saints is not guaranteed, the possibility of eventual total rejection and the loss of a true salvation once gained is possible for Pentecostals, which can only be avoided by personal perseverance—never rejecting the gift. This being the case, Pentecostals do look to the Spirit for assistance in this perseverance and must rely on an economic pneumatology to do so, because it is *here* that the individual is, it is *here* that part, at least, of the decisions concerning his eternal salvation are being made, so it is *here* that the Spirit must be present and working.

What is established at conversion is a relationship with Christ by the Spirit's work, a union with Christ. The Spirit then dwells within the believer to maintain the relationship and continues working by making God's righteousness real in the life of the believer. This is the third task of the Spirit, the conventional Protestant understanding of sanctification, the process of effecting holiness in the believer. Very early in Pentecostalism, the idea that sanctification was instantaneous and complete at conversion, or even preceded conversion, enjoyed some support, but a doctrine of progressive sanctification which begins at conversion and continues through a believer's life is now generally accepted. The indwelling Spirit works to continually apply the sacrifice of Christ to the believer's life so that the believer is always holy before God, hence Christ's role is finished; the Spirit now applies what he has done.

The Spirit also increasingly delivers the believer from sin, something which includes direct guidance on behavior. In an analogous way to those who viewed the Law and its derivatives as guidance for day to day behavior, so the indwelling Spirit provides guidance by direct witness to the individual's heart and mind. However, this occurs through the believer's submission and increasing submission as his sanctification progresses. Thus, the Spirit's guidance is effective only as the believer steps aside, so to speak, and accepts the guidance given. In other words, the believer allows the

---

18. Land, *Pentecostal Spirituality*, 29–30.

19. See Olsen, *Arminian Theology*, for a presentation and defense of Arminianism, and Stanglin and McCall, *Jacob Arminius*, from where this and later comments are taken.

Spirit to work and commits herself to following what the Spirit reveals, thus contributing to her own sanctification.

The other way in which the Spirit works to make the righteousness of the believer real is by opening Scripture to the believer, giving insight or illuminating its truth as it is read or preached. The indwelling Spirit speaks authoritatively to the human heart to show that Scripture is the "Word of God" and to show its truth. However, the human mind is not bypassed in this process, so it is not a mystical content hidden behind the written words which is illuminated, but the truth of the actual words. Equally, the Spirit is not the universal remedy to the need for diligent study of Scripture, rather the Spirit works to give illumination to those who consistently apply themselves to Scripture. As the believer does this, she will find that her understanding grows and she gains in spiritual understanding; that is, that her intellectual understanding will grow and so will the strength of her belief, her faith.

The Pentecostal doctrine of the inspiration of Scripture means that this understanding of the illumination of Scripture is different from that of neo-orthodoxy (and Calvin, for that matter).[20] "Evangelicals [and Pentecostals] . . . view Scripture as the objective written Word of God inspired by the Spirit at the time of its writing."[21] Thus, the actual written words contain "true communication about God,"[22] are an objective expression of truth about him and so have an intrinsic authority. The reader can recognize this or fail to recognize it; can accept it or reject it. What the Holy Spirit does is cause the Word to be "heard by the heart as well as by the head"[23] so that the truth that is plainly there is recognized and accepted by the believer at a level of being beyond the intellectual. This contrasts with neo-orthodoxy's view that the truth is illuminated by an operation of the Spirit coincident with the reading or hearing which reveals the words as God's Word. This difference allows for the possibility that the truth revealed might be rejected more easily, at least, for the Pentecostal whereas it can be argued that the neo-orthodox position does not allow for any rejection of the Word of God so revealed. This repeats what has already been said in respect of conversion: the work of the Spirit can be resisted or accepted by the individual,

---

20. By "neo-orthodoxy" is meant a theology which claims that knowledge of God can only be obtained by revelation from God. Karl Barth was at the vanguard of this movement in the early part of the twentieth century, but it has many exponents and a wide variety of expression. Higgins, "God's Inspired Word," 112–13, uses the term in this sense without defining it.

21. Higgins, "God's Inspired Word," 113.

22. Ibid.

23. Ibid., 112.

who is involved in her salvation and continues to be involved with her sanctification, having a direct impact on its place in her life.

This brings us to the fourth point in the broad definition of sanctification: the empowerment of the believer to assist in the sanctification of others, which is the realm of Spirit baptism. Among the multiplicity of doctrinal views, perhaps the one thing which can be claimed with confidence is that Pentecostals uniformly assert that the Spirit has come in a way exactly as occurred at Pentecost and on later occasions recorded in Acts. This assertion is substantiated by what is experienced by the individual and evidence which (it is claimed) can be adduced by an external observer. Hence, "What unites the Pentecostal churches is not a doctrine but a religious experience, and this can be interpreted and substantiated in many different ways."[24] This experience is, of course, identified as baptism in the Holy Spirit or Spirit baptism. Although neither term is exactly replicated in the New Testament, Jesus does promise that the disciples will be baptized with the Holy Spirit (Acts 1:5), which clearly refers to the experience described by Luke as being "filled" with the Spirit (Acts 2:4). Similar occurrences are described as being "filled" also (Acts 9:17); or the Spirit falling on or coming on individuals (Acts 10:44, 19:6 respectively); or the Spirit being received (Acts 8:17).[25] So distinctive is this experience to Pentecostals that their pneumatological discussion has focused on the doctrine of Spirit baptism rather than on the Spirit *per se*, something seen in the relative space afforded to Spirit baptism and spiritual gifts compared to other doctrines of the Spirit in Pentecostal doctrinal works. Horton (ed.), *Systematic Theology*, devotes forty-four pages to discussion in chapters titled "The Holy Spirit" and "The Holy Spirit and Sanctification," and fifty-five pages to "The Baptism in the Holy Spirit" and "Spiritual Gifts," followed by a further thirty-four pages to the related "Divine Healing." Steven Studebaker makes the same point, citing four examples including Horton (ed.) with the most extreme being Higgins et al., *An Introduction to Theology*, which devotes "slightly more than one page to a section headlined 'the Role of the Holy Spirit in Salvation', whereas an entire chapter is devoted to the doctrine of the Baptism in the Holy Spirit."[26]

---

24. Hollenweger, "From Azusa Street to the Toronto Phenomenon," 7, cited in Macchia, *Baptized in the Spirit*, 34.

25. Generally I will refer to this experience as "Spirit release," using this appellation for how Pentecostals understand this experience in its fullness, after considering the nomenclature below.

26. Higgins, Dusing and Tallman, *An Introduction to Theology*, 108–9, 143–58, cited in Studebaker, "Pentecostal Soteriology and Pneumatology," 265. Of course, this present work repeats the pattern, but I am attempting to reflect Pentecostal expressions so the same result is inevitable.

The strong emphasis within the Western church on Christology is also cited as muting a wider interest,[27] a point which may seem curious, but the historical subordination of the Spirit to Christ within the western church was carried into Pentecostal theology, Spirit baptism excepted.

The Importance of the Holy Spirit in the Early Church

It is tempting to place this experience of Spirit baptism firmly in the background when discussing the Spirit theologically, on the ground that the inevitable subjectivity of any experience means that it can carry little weight. But, in fact, a good case can be made that such a direct experience of the Spirit was a central part of early Christian faith and, hence, that the experience must be somehow incorporated in any pneumatology. James Dunn summarizes such a case in his contribution to *The Work of the Spirit: Pneumatology and Pentecostalism*.[28]

He begins with the Old Testament concept of God's Spirit, captured in the Hebrew by *ruach*, an existential term as its root meaning of breath or wind implies it is something experienced, or observed by its effect: how it is experienced by some other being or object. Hence there is always an effect of the Spirit, there is always what he calls an existential aspect to the bestowal of the Spirit. There is no limit to this effect, something implicit in the use of *ruach* to denote "the cosmic and inescapable presence of God in Psalm 139:7."[29] The work of the Spirit, therefore, always involved a numinous experience for the person anointed in the Old Testament.

Certainly, God could bestow the Holy Spirit, but there was no expectation of a Spirit dispenser beyond this in Judaism, no expectation that the Messiah would give the Spirit. The idea that the coming one would do so seems to have originated with John the Baptist. It was entirely novel to him, something he expressed as the coming of one who would baptize with the Spirit. It is telling that all the Gospel traditions agree that the Baptist's preaching included this assertion, one of only two points common to all traditions,[30] as it indicates that understanding the Messiah as one who would impart the Spirit was a common idea among all early Christians. Despite this, Dunn thinks that the image of Spirit baptism coined by John

---

27. Bruner, *A Theology of the Holy Spirit*, 21; Burgess, "Implications of Eastern Christian Pneumatology," 24.

28. Dunn, "Towards the Spirit of Christ," 3–26. The summary following above is taken from this essay.

29. Ibid., 7.

30. Ibid., 8. The Spirit descending on Jesus in the form of a dove is the other.

was not much taken up by early Christianity (although it was not absent), and that it was only with Pentecostalism in the twentieth century that it came to the fore.

This does not mean that the somewhat different idea that the Messiah would be Spirit dispenser was not taken up. In fact, it is striking that the giving of the Spirit is associated with Jesus, the exalted Christ, who poured out the Spirit, a function of God in the Old Testament. This was a major development with critical implications for Christology. The one who had been empowered or inspired by the Spirit (recorded at his baptism by John) had become the dispenser of the Spirit—this was the early Christian distinctive, but a distinctive not without its awkward implications. Dunn thinks Paul, in Romans 8, is reluctant to say that the Spirit raised Jesus and so expresses this in a roundabout way because he knows the awkwardness of saying that the dispenser of the Spirit was resurrected by the Spirit (how could the dispenser be at the mercy of the dispensed?). It is easy to see here the sort of tension which eventually led to the formulation of trinitarian doctrine.

The early Christians understood that the Spirit was a vital factor in showing that the earthly Jesus was still important for theology, alongside the exalted Christ. The existence of the Synoptic Gospels by itself indicates this; but more directly, the Spirit was understood to be a Spirit of adoption who brought believers into "a participation in Christ's sonship" and transformed them into the image of Christ.[31] This image took concrete form in the earthly Jesus, so he and his mission are an indispensable part of Christian faith. Not only did the Spirit testify to Jesus and the Christ in this manner, but a further direct result of the Spirit's activity was to see Christianity develop out of and separate from Judaism, including the movement beyond Palestine. That is, what may have been understood as a messianic renewal which would be limited to Judaism with its attachment to Palestine became the separate religion of Christianity. That it was a compulsion of the Spirit which convicted the early church that the gospel was also for Gentiles, who would not be expected to become proselytes, is seen clearly in Acts, Dunn suggesting the clearest account being that of Cornelius and his household in Acts 10–11.[32] Here, the Spirit is poured out on the assembled Gentiles in a manner where Peter feels compelled to agree that God has accepted the Gentiles and that they should be baptized forthwith. Later, Peter reports to the Council at Jerusalem that God had indicated acceptance of the uncircumcised Gentiles by "giving them the Holy Spirit, just as he did to us" (Acts 15:8). It is the Spirit who informed and illuminated the early Christians on

31. Ibid., 16.
32. Ibid., 17.

Christology and the need for evangelization, both developments which were foreign to Judaism. The Spirit was intimately and identifiably involved in the establishment of Christianity.

In all this, the Spirit was still understood in existential terms. Dunn appeals to Galatians 3:2 as assuming that the *"receiving of the Spirit was something perceptible."*[33] That is, it was an event that could be recalled; an experience which marked conversion, the beginning of Christian life. This assumption receives support from Paul's question of the Ephesian converts at Acts 19:2: he wants to know if they had received the Holy Spirit. He clearly expects that this is something they will know, without any further prompting from him. It is at once a simple question, yet a complex one. Have they experienced something which, if they have, they will undoubtedly be able to identify as the Spirit? Yes or no? If the answer is yes, then they have been introduced to, and granted knowledge of, the complexities of the earthly Jesus becoming the exalted Christ for their salvation. A modern evangelist might want to quiz them on their belief,[34] but the definitive question for Paul is the experienced presence of the Spirit. Definitive it might be, but Dunn notes that we now know that no experience is unmoderated—the individual's involvement is conditioned by the lens of their history and understandings—so the experience is not a raw event which stands by itself but is inevitably an interpreted event. That is, what is experienced is given meaning for the individual by their interpretation of what it is or represents. The convert interprets what he or she encounters as being the Spirit, so the encounter is given the meaning of divine insight by the new believer. This might be thought to detract from the reality of the insight, but Jean-Jaques Suurmond makes it clear that this is not so. He observes that purely objective knowledge is an illusion: all knowledge involves the knower so that we "observe our interpretation of an object," which is an experience. Hence, "information which is not experienced cannot be personally meaningful to us . . . Apart from experience, redemption merely remains a word in a book."[35] In other words, the subjectivity of the experience is no bar to its validity, as all knowledge is subjective to a significant degree in any case. The highest profile example of the Spirit giving direct insight in action is Peter at Pentecost (Acts 2:14–41), where he interprets for the crowd what is happening—he passes on his insight that it is the Spirit who is producing the phenomena the crowd sees.

33. Ibid., 21 (emphasis his).

34. As Dunn suggests with a quote from Newbigin, *The Household of God*, 95, cited ibid., 21.

35. Suurmond, "The Meaning and Purpose of Spirit Baptism and the Charisms," 42.

So how could they be certain this was the Spirit? First, many of the initial experiences were "ecstatic"—of such a nature they demanded an unusual interpretation, and in fact the most disturbing interpretation of all—that God had been encountered. This means that such raw events were the features which facilitated the establishment of Christianity, the very sorts of events which the church has viewed with suspicion and usually dismissed in most of its history since. "*Christianity began as an enthusiastic sect!*" Dunn says.[36]

Second, there is the importance of "checking and evaluating claims to Spirit experiences."[37] The New Testament attests to the necessity and importance of doing so—its authors are aware that the enthusiast can be so confident that what she has experienced is the Spirit that no more consideration need be given to the question. But, in reality, the raw experience must fit within what is known to be the Christian framework. He suggests that Paul went beyond the "enthusiastic Luke"[38] to assert that the experience must produce grace to fit the framework—signs and wonders are great, but the test is whether the grace of God is working. This will be seen in a life which reflects that grace, and which particularly witnesses to Jesus Christ, one in whom God is displayed. In a longer version, it is by the power of the Spirit that believers are shown that what they see in Christ is identical with God's being, and it is by the same power that they are able to reproduce the grace that properly belongs to that being in their lives to some degree.

Dunn's view is echoed, with somewhat different emphases, by Pentecostal scholars. For Gordon Fee,[39] the context was that in the hoped-for new age the Messiah would be the "unique *bearer*" of the Spirit and that there would be an outpouring of the Spirit on all of God's people.[40] John the Baptist further extended this context with the claims that Jesus was the Messiah because on him the Spirit came; and that this same Jesus would baptize with the Spirit. It was this presence and activity of the Spirit which defined the new age, the coming of the Kingdom of God which Jesus proclaimed, "This is the key to everything in the New Testament."[41] At Pentecost, Peter can claim that the hoped-for new age has arrived *because* the Spirit has arrived. The early church understood that the primary factor in their new existence was their experience of the Spirit, a point he emphasizes by suggesting that

36. Dunn., "Towards the Spirit of Christ," 23 (emphasis his).
37. Ibid., 23.
38. Ibid., 24.
39. Fee, "Baptism in the Holy Spirit," 87–99.
40. Ibid., 92.
41. Ibid., 93.

they would not recognize modern distinctions. For them to say "This one is a Spirit-filled Christian, this one is a Christian who is not Spirit-filled"[42] is to say "This one is a Christian, this one is not." This is reflected in one of the selection of scriptural examples he uses to support his argument, 1 Cor 2:6–16, where Paul is contrasting Christians and non-Christians. Paul's criterion is the presence of the Spirit: the former has the Spirit, so is a Christian, the latter has not and so cannot be.[43]

This issue has also been taken up recently by Frank D. Macchia.[44] He starts by noting that God conceived as Father and breath are both present in the Old Testament, but there is no conception of God as Son. Luke identifies Jesus as the one who was conceived in Mary by the Spirit (Luke 1:35) and who was raised to send the Spirit ("clothed with power from on high," Luke 24:49).[45] He also reports John the Baptist proclaiming him as the one who will baptize with the Spirit (along with the other Gospel writers; see Matt 3:11, Mark 1:8 and John 1:33) and records Jesus promising that the disciples would be baptized with the Spirit after his departure (Acts 1:5, recalled by Peter at Acts 11:16).

It is this action in sending the Spirit which confirms the divinity of Jesus and reveals the trinitarian nature of God. "How then can he who gives the Spirit not be God?"[46] For the first disciples, who had no tradition of a Son within the identity of God, such an action in respect of the Spirit, whom they certainly could identify with God, revealed Jesus' identity as the Christ and, in turn, "Christ's ontological unity with the Father."[47] This is not in isolation from the resurrection, of course, but one of the goals, at least, of the resurrection is for Jesus to become the one who imparts the Spirit. Without this impartation actually occurring, the resurrection by itself is insufficient to support the testimony of the church to the divinity of Christ. Thus, the reception of the Spirit is crucial to the revelation of Christ as the divine Son.[48] Note how different this is from simply saying that the Spirit reveals that the resurrected Jesus

---

42. By which I mean this one is Pentecostal/Charismatic, this one is not; I am not suggesting the Spirit dwells in one but not the other.

43. Ibid., 94.

44. The discussion which follows is taken from Macchia, *Baptized in the Spirit*, 110–29 and 258 n. 25.

45. Macchia, *Baptized in the Spirit*, also cites John 1:14, 20:22; 1 Cor 12:13 and 15:14 in support of his proposition, but I have restricted the references here to those from Luke.

46. Well put by Augustine, *De Trinitatis* 15.46, cited by Macchia, *Baptized in the Spirit*, 111.

47. Macchia, *Baptized in the Spirit*, 110.

48. Ibid., 110–11.

is the Christ: while this remains true, there is a real experience of Jesus Christ imparting the Spirit to the believer as well.

The implication of this is that the presence of the Spirit must have been demonstrable for the early Christians. There is little point in his presence being the criterion of conversion if this was not so. Fee asserts that the Spirit was conceived of as a powerful presence which led to a powerful life: "The coming of the Spirit had phenomenological evidence; life was characterized by a dynamic quality, evidenced as often as not by extraordinary phenomena."[49]

If this was the case, the obvious question is, what became of this first-century norm? Dunn does not address this in his essay, but notes that, understood as Spirit baptism, it was not much taken up.[50] Fee does hazard an answer. He notes that throughout most of church history believers have understood the Spirit as a "quiet, unobtrusive presence,"[51] albeit a transforming one, a position which avoids the discomfort of having to confront raw, ecstatic experiences within the Christian life. However, this is at the expense of needing to grapple with the questions surrounding a Christian life without any great evidence of the Spirit working: is such a life a genuine Christian life? He then goes on to suggest two reasons for this anonymity of the Spirit. The first is that as the church matured it became dominated by believers who were second, third, fourth generation converts, and so on. For them, the conversion experience is not the dramatic experience of a first-generation conversion as they start from within a Christian environment where familiarity produces not contempt, but a lack in respect of the dynamism of the Spirit. His second (and, for him, more important) ground is the eventual link that was made between the coming of the Spirit and water baptism. Once this was accepted and infant baptism became the practice, the experiential dimension of the Spirit at conversion was lost.

There is plenty of support for Fee's view of the attitude of the Western church to the Spirit,[52] but his reasoning to support his view is questionable. This is particularly so if the Eastern tradition is considered, where a strong pneumatology has been developed and maintained incorporating a pneumatological view of salvation involving, as it does, the process of *theosis*. In the Eastern view, the Fall is not as "complete" as in Western eyes, giving ready material in the individual for the Spirit to work on in

---

49. Fee, "Baptism in the Holy Spirit," 95. He cites Acts 1:8, 2:33, 4:33, 8, 1 Cor 12–14 and 1 Thess 5:19–22 to support his assertion.

50. Dunn, "Towards the Spirit of Christ," 9.

51. Fee, "Baptism in the Holy Spirit," 95.

52. For example, Badcock, *Light of Truth*, and Williams, *Renewal Theology*.

transformation.⁵³ With the possible exception of glossolalia, there is no cessationism in Eastern Christianity although the tradition has an expectation of a wider range of gifts than Pentecostals and tends to emphasize "more subtle or intellectual . . . gifts."⁵⁴ Following the view Dunn ascribes to Paul, Eastern Christians give little or no attention to "evidences" along Fee's lines or those of early Pentecostalism, but rather see the "true indicator of the indwelling Holy Spirit is a life of genuine holiness," thus making a distinction between spiritual gifts and fruit (eg Gal 5:22–23).⁵⁵ For them it is the ongoing quality of life which clearly indicates the presence of the Spirit, not the phenomenology appealed to by Fee.

The Eastern tradition is a challenge to Fee, then. First, it has survived multiple generations since the first and adopted infant baptism. Second, while it has not abandoned the phenomenology to which Fee appeals, it does not give it the emphasis he does. Yet it *has* maintained a stronger pneumatology than the West, in its attempt to "stress each member of the Trinity equally in contrast to the western focus on Christology."⁵⁶ The common ground between eastern theology and the two scholars Fee and Dunn is that the Spirit is *experienced*. The process of *theosis* is an ongoing act of re-creation in which the human is made like God, is transformed into the image of God. Salvation is no forensic declaration for a completely lost human and resulting indwelling of the Spirit which must be attested to in faith; rather it is the coming of the Spirit to a human who is able to be transformed by the Spirit and for whom the transformation commences. Just as sanctification, which does not constitute salvation in the western tradition, can be observed externally and identified by the subject being sanctified as he is transformed over time, *theosis* can also be observed and self-identified. The fact that it is capable of self-identification means that it is experienced by the individual, just as sanctification must inevitably be able to be experienced.

What this discussion shows is that it is legitimate to claim that the presence of the Spirit was the crucial factor in identifying Christians in the early church and that this presence was demonstrated experientially. It is true that this depends upon the New Testament, and Acts in particular, being historically accurate, rather than being a theological justification for a position taken by the early church. One such manifestation of the latter idea

---

53. Burgess, "Implications," 25–28.

54. Ibid., 24, 31. Burgess specifies knowledge, wisdom, teaching, administration and aids as the "more subtle or intellectual of the gifts."

55. Ibid., 28–29.

56. Ibid., 24.

is that the coming of the Spirit was the Lukan solution to the delay of the *parousia*, and so was a late development after the early expectation that the imminent return of Jesus was not fulfilled. In discussing this point, Howard Marshall takes issue with it, tellingly noting that "the experience of the Holy Spirit as the decisive evidence of the reality of the new age goes back as far as we can trace."[57] That is, there is no identifiable point before which there is evidence that no appeal to the Spirit experienced was necessary as the marker of faith, but after which this marker appeared. This is strong evidence that the marker existed from the very earliest beginnings and thus that the Scriptures which attest to it are historically reliable. While this marker has been largely lost through most of the history of the Western church, it has continued strongly within the Eastern tradition, although without much of the distinct phenomenology of the first century. It is fair, then, to say that an experience of the Spirit is not an unmoderated action which must at least be doubted, if not rejected outright, but is rather a legitimate core of Christian faith. Pentecostals' claim to an experience is consonant with the first century witness, and resonates strongly with Eastern pneumatology which traces a continuity with the first century experience.

In saying this, it must be conceded that, broadly, the Pentecostal claim to an experience is limited to a Spirit baptism where equipping for mission and witness is central, whereas the above discussion is much wider than that. This wider experience is the life-changing experience of conversion, of the insight that Jesus Christ is *the* savior of humanity and that in a deep and personally meaningful way, this now means salvation for the one who possesses the insight.[58] In fact, the insight is given by the Spirit and it is this gift which is understood as real and experienced as such. This is much more than empowerment for mission, although it undoubtedly includes that. The relationship between the narrower Pentecostal claim and this wider consideration needs examination to determine whether they are best understood as being separate (although inevitably linked in some way), or as integrated. Whatever the outcome of that investigation, the ubiquity of experience among Pentecostals means that their claims are a serious basis for the consideration of sound Christian doctrine and deserve evaluation to draw out the full richness they may offer to global theology.

---

57. Marshall, *New Testament Theology*, 174.

58. I am not equating the insight with salvation here—it is who is apprehended in the insight, Jesus Christ, who effects salvation. To possess the insight means to see that this is true.

The Acts Testimony

The examination must begin with the Pentecostal account of Spirit baptism which in turn can only be founded in Acts, using the five references noted above. The Pentecostal experience came to people who were already Christian. However they understood their personal conversion, there is no doubt that prior to Spirit baptism they were believers. Their experience was of such a quality that they were immediately convinced that what had occurred was a genuine encounter with God and that whatever change it had wrought in them was a change accomplished by God in the person of the Holy Spirit. This being so, there must be a Biblical warrant for their experience, and it was found in Acts. What had happened to them in the twentieth century is equated with these historical occurrences, so the claim can then be made that this experience was intended to be normative for all Christians. As it was in the first century, now it is in the twentieth and twenty-first, as perhaps it should have been all along, so what do the five Acts' references tell us?

In Acts 2:1–4, the 120 were filled with the Holy Spirit in an occurrence where there was a sound of a violent wind, what seemed to be tongues of fire resting on each person and those present began to speak in tongues. There seems no question that they were believers: Luke refers to them as "brothers" (Acts 1:15,16); they organized a replacement for Judas to restore the twelve leaders (Acts 1:21–26); and the disciples had already received the Holy Spirit in some fashion (John 20:22). The resultant clamor drew a crowd who were impressed with what was occurring, some puzzled as to what it meant and others sure they were witnessing drunkenness (Acts 2:6, 12–13). Peter seized the opportunity to explain to the crowd what had occurred: this was what the prophet Joel had predicted, that the Spirit would be poured out on all people and the key to participating was to recognize that the Messiah had come, Jesus the Christ. To participate they had to repent, be baptized in the name of Jesus Christ for the forgiveness of sins, and they would receive the gift of the Holy Spirit (Acts 2:38–39). This establishes the sequence for Pentecostals: repentance, then baptism, followed by receipt of the Spirit; non-Pentecostals stop at baptism.[59]

Acts 8:4–25 describes the preaching of the gospel in Samaria. An unspecified number of people, men and women, believe the gospel and are baptized in the name of Jesus (Acts 8:12–13), and when the apostles in Jerusalem hear of it they send Peter and John to the Samaritans where they

---

59. According to Bruner, *A Theology of the Holy Spirit*, 64; here understanding receipt to be Spirit baptism, not the indwelling of the Spirit coming at conversion/baptism, which is, of course, affirmed by Pentecostals and non-Pentecostals alike.

find they had not received the Holy Spirit. Following prayer and the laying on of hands, the new believers receive the Spirit, although no particular phenomena are reported as associated with the receipt.

Paul's so-called conversion[60] in Acts 9 incorporates an encounter with Jesus whom Paul first identifies as "Lord" before being told his identity (4, 5). Three days later he is filled with the Holy Spirit as Ananias places his hands on him, after which he is baptized (9, 17–18). Evidently, the filling is accompanied by some phenomenon as "immediately something like scales fell from his eyes, and his sight was restored." (18).

The extension of the gospel to Gentiles is inaugurated at the ministry of Peter to the household of Cornelius, "an upright and God-fearing man" (22) in Acts 10:22–48. There is a large gathering who are there to hear from Peter, who gives a brief account of the gospel, in the midst of which the Holy Spirit comes on all the hearers, something evident to Peter and his companions as they spoke in tongues and praised God (44–46). Peter accordingly instructed that they be baptized in the name of Jesus (48). As in Acts 2, the coming of the Spirit is specifically associated with unusual phenomena, the speaking in tongues and praising God strongly suggesting an ecstatic experience.

The fifth Acts text is 19:1–7, where Paul comes across a group described as "disciples" (1) in Ephesus who had not even heard of the Holy Spirit and had only received John's baptism. Paul identifies that as a baptism of repentance and tells them of Jesus whereupon they were baptized in his name and the Holy Spirit "came upon them" when Paul afterwards lays his hands on them. This is followed by the phenomena of the disciples speaking in tongues and prophesying.

Pentecostals looked for, and found, two parallels with their own experience in these texts. One is the occurrence of unusual phenomena, particularly glossolalia which is specifically said to have occurred in three of the five events. Paul's experience is not said to have included glossolalia, although it certainly did later, at least, on his own evidence (1 Cor 14:18), but was accompanied by his loss and recovery of sight. The Samaritan event is the only one where no unusual phenomena are recorded, although Pentecostals tend to infer that as the Spirit was bestowed, so phenomena must have followed, particularly glossolalia, on the basis that something must have occurred to convince Peter and John that the Spirit had been given.[61]

---

60. He himself calls it a "revelation," Gal 1:15–16.

61. So Wyckoff, "The Baptism in the Holy Spirit," 443, who cites several others who share his opinion.

The second parallel is the order observed in the events narrated in Acts. In three of the texts, but most notably the Pentecost experience, there is repentance, baptism, then receipt of the Spirit. Pentecostals looked to their own experience of receiving the Spirit some time after conversion and baptism and saw it mirrored in this sequence in Acts. Spirit baptism was subsequent to their conversion, and subsequent to water baptism in Acts, so was a subsequent occurrence in Christian experience. Of course, there are some difficulties faced by this parallel which do not afflict the first. One is that both Paul and Cornelius' household were baptized *after* receiving the Spirit, a fact dealt with by noting that Paul had certainly been converted before receiving the Spirit—his baptism merely confirmed what had already happened. This is not so straightforward for Cornelius' household, where the claim is that, as Cornelius was a "God-fearing man" before Peter arrived, he could have been a believer already.[62] This is possible but is not obvious from the text. Another is that the Ephesian group, although described as disciples, may not have been Christians. Many Pentecostals certainly view them as such,[63] although Fee demurs, thinking they were "obviously not Christian."[64] Others do not consider them Christians, more likely being disciples of John,[65] or believers in a Messiah to come preached by John. The reader knows that this is of course Jesus, but they have no knowledge of him.[66]

Whether these difficulties can be resolved or not, there are three instances in Acts where it is arguable that the early Pentecostal experience of Spirit baptism following conversion is paralleled, and perhaps as many as five.[67] The resulting Pentecostal contention is that there is good scriptural support for the experience of Spirit baptism being intended for all Christians and hence normative for Christian life, as an event separate from conversion and subsequent to it. The maintenance of this position requires that Luke must be viewed not only as a historian, but also a theologian. That is, that he is not merely recording historical curiosities, but that his narrative has the legitimate theological purpose (in these texts at least) of establishing the place of Spirit baptism. This is exactly what Pentecostal theology asserts, which raises two pertinent questions.

---

62. Bruner, *A Theology of the Holy Spirit*, 66–67, suggests this, although notes it is a minority view.

63. See for example, Duffield and Van Cleave, *Foundations of Pentecostal Theology*, 310; and Menzies and Horton, *Bible Doctrines*, 126 n. 4.

64. Fee, "Baptism in the Holy Spirit," 94.

65. A case put by Trebilco, *The Early Christians in Ephesus*, 128–33.

66. So Bruner, *A Theology of the Holy Spirit*, 207–12.

67. Although Fee reduces it to one, "Baptism in the Holy Spirit," 90–91.

The first is how narrative texts like Luke-Acts should be viewed compared to didactic texts like the Epistles. Pentecostals would say that to assign a priority to didactic texts on the ground that they set out to teach doctrine or practice while giving a lesser place to narrative texts is arbitrary and ignores Paul's own injunction that all Scripture is useful for teaching (2 Tim 3:16).[68] Some go so far as to assign a priority to narrative texts.[69] Taking the contrary view means that Luke-Acts is read through the didactic lens instead of giving it standing in its own right by recognizing that its author had a theological intent. In fact, there is significant recent scholarship arguing the legitimacy of recognizing that Luke was a theologian, so Roger Stronstad can claim that *Witness to the Gospel: The Theology of Acts*, ed. Marshall and Peterson "illustrated that something like a scholarly consensus about the theological significance of Luke's narratives had arrived."[70] He also makes the points that Luke's two books need to be read together and that at the start of his Gospel, he specifically claims a theological intent in his writing (Luke 1:4), so this should be taken seriously when reading Acts.[71] However, it is not necessary for the question here to evaluate Luke as a theologian in depth. Acts has been subject to a plethora of readings,[72] but it is difficult to depart far from C. Kavin Rowe's contention that it is best read as intended for Christians and to do so "is to think Christianly in the late first century Graeco-Roman world" and see it as a "lively political theology."[73] To put it another way, the book is recognized as Scripture and read as such by Christians; while it is a narrative, inevitably the views and opinions of its author can be deduced from the narrative (with greater and lesser certainty), thus a theology can be distilled from the story. With such a theology at hand, this is as far as it is necessary to go to construct a Pentecostal pneumatology from a Lukan base. While this may result in doctrine which views the New Testament through a Lukan lens, so treating the narrative on a footing equal to that of the didactic, the very fact that it is a scriptural narrative with a theology gives any doctrine distilled from it legitimacy. No more need be claimed.

This does lead to the second query, however, which arises from the task of deriving a pneumatology from Luke-Acts. Even accepting the resultant pneumatology is legitimate, it does differ from pneumatologies

---

68. Wyckoff, "Baptism in the Holy Spirit," 433–36.

69. Williams, *Renewal Theology*, 2:181 n. 6, for example.

70. Stronstad "The Charismatic Theology of St Luke," 104. See also the discussion on this point in Yong, *The Spirit Poured Out*, 83–86.

71. Stronstad, "The Charismatic Theology of St Luke," 102–4.

72. See Penner, "Madness in the Method?," 223–93.

73. Rowe, *World Upside Down*, 7, 10–11.

found elsewhere in the New Testament, so how are these to be related or reconciled? More specifically, the question revolves around the relationship between Lukan and Pauline pneumatologies. For Paul, the Spirit is the one who incorporates the individual into the body of Christ, or into Christ himself, the divine one who indwells the believer. His interest is primarily soteriological, so the work of the Spirit is one of regeneration as the believer is first incorporated, then more deeply rooted in Christ. Spirit baptism is what initiates the individual into faith in Christ and enables the ongoing growth of that faith. In short, Pauline pneumatology is interested in the indwelling Spirit imparting new spiritual life, the life of Christ.[74]

Luke's pneumatology is about the individual *functioning* in Christ by the Spirit,[75] where the individual (and, together with other believers, the community which is the church) is empowered for mission. The Spirit fills each believer, imparting a power for service, a power of the Spirit that proceeds from faith, so Luke is focused on the work of the Spirit *through* each individual believer to others—so much so that Chan can suggest that he shows little interest in the renewal of the individual.[76] Spirit baptism therefore initiates *service* by the believer empowered by the presence of the Spirit—the one who shares new life through the indwelling Spirit also does the work of Christ by the infilling Spirit.

Pentecostal pneumatology does not ignore or discard Pauline pneumatology in favor of the Lukan version. It is, after all, impossible to suggest that Paul is unaware of the Spirit's activity depicted in Acts. Chan even suggests that Paul's pneumatology contains all of Luke's.[77] Rather, Pentecostal pneumatology has historically given regard to the Pauline account, but has placed its real interest firmly in Luke's camp by focusing its efforts on Spirit baptism. There is an order involved, for Pentecostals. At conversion, the Spirit comes to *dwell* within the believer. Later, at Spirit baptism, the Spirit *fills* the believer in an event different in character from the pre-existing indwelling. It is as if the already-present Spirit is somehow activated at Spirit baptism. Pentecostals want to assert that, while personal salvation and sanctification through the indwelling Spirit are crucial, in fact necessary conditions, clearly God, by

---

74. See Macchia, *Baptized in the Spirit*, 14, 15, 29, 87; Chan, *Pentecostal Theology*, 47–49: Williams, *Renewal Theology*, 2:268–70; and Duffield and Van Cleave, *Foundations of Pentecostal Theology*, 281 for this brief description and that of Lukan pneumatology which follows.

75. Macchia, *Baptized in the Spirit*, 14 (emphasis his).

76. Chan, *Pentecostal Theology*, 47, although Yong, *Spirit Poured Out*, 89–91 can also suggest the gift of the Spirit for Luke enables salvation in all its aspects.

77. Chan, *Pentecostal Theology*, 49.

the Spirit, does something else powerful through Spirit baptism and this is where attention ought to be focused.

To maintain this position, Pentecostals must at least separate Luke's account of Spirit baptism from Pauline pneumatology by this focused attention. If Pauline pneumatology is given precedence, then being filled with the Spirit cannot avoid collapsing into indwelling, so Lukan pneumatology must somehow be subsumed within the Pauline and the Pentecostal distinctive risks being lost. To avoid this and so give life and weight to the Pentecostal conviction concerning the Spirit's activity, Lukan pneumatology must be given its own place and adopted as the ground on which Pentecostal pneumatology is founded. It is not necessary to claim a primacy for Lukan over Pauline; it is merely necessary to allow the one to have some distinction from the other and treat them as complementary.

Thus, the same position concerning the relative pneumatologies is reached as was attained in considering Luke as a theologian. It is legitimate to give a place to Lukan doctrines, so the Pentecostal position is tenable and a full Spirit baptism theology is possible. This, of course, is only a partial resolution of the second query as the possession of legitimacy for Lukan views and the associated need to see them as complementary to other New Testament voices still leaves the task of working out how the complementarity is to be understood.

The Re-emergence of the Spirit

The beginning of this task is to examine what may eventually prove to be Pentecostalism's greatest contribution to Christian theology: its participation in the rehabilitation of the Spirit. I noted above Dunn and Fee's comments about the place of the Spirit in the history of the Western church which have been echoed by others. Badcock notes that the historical "practical subordination of the work of the Spirit to the Word" has diminished the "ontic" role of the Spirit and, he suggests, impoverished the church and spiritual life.[78] Although he goes on to suggest that Pentecostals represent excess in the reverse, there is no question that Pentecostal theology champions the activity of the Spirit in empowerment for service at least, and he ignores the determinedly christological focus of Pentecostal theology (the latter perhaps well represented, not without irony, in Oneness Pentecostalism). Williams makes a similar comment contrasting the proclamation by the church of "the *ontological* equality of the Spirit and the Son" on the one hand with a "*functional* subordination" of the Spirit to the Son on the

78. Badcock, *Light of Truth*, 233.

other. That is, the tendency has been to acknowledge an equal place for the Spirit with the Father and the Son, but subordinate the role of the Spirit, understanding it as conveying the benefits of Christ and revealing him with little or no emphasis on any reciprocal activity by Christ.[79] Ontologically, the Spirit is co-equal with the Father and the Son and recognized as such; economically, the Father and the Son are revealed, but the Spirit is neither experienced nor perceived. The Spirit performs crucial tasks in God's salvation economy, but is not directly experienced as they are done. In sum, the Spirit has been assigned a high degree of anonymity in Christian thought.[80] In itself, this is not intrinsically negative, but it does invite the formation of an incomplete view of the work of the triune God.

This anonymity is not the sole preserve of the Western church, something illustrated in Eastern theologian Vladimir Lossky's description of the place of the Spirit in the activity *ad extra* of the triune God where he says: "Every energy, every manifestation, comes from the Father, is expressed in the Son, and goes forth in the Holy Spirit."[81] This leaves quite some ambiguity between "expressed" and "goes forth" which serves to blur the role of the Spirit and hence imbue some anonymity as the Spirit's activity cannot be separated from that of the Son. The same ambiguity is even present in a Pentecostal account where works are said to originate with the Father, are done by the Son and are "brought to fruition" by the Spirit.[82] Pentecostal theology certainly wants to affirm the involvement of each of the hypostases in God's economic activity, but generally its experiential base in Spirit baptism claims that the anonymity of the Spirit has been stripped away, so the ambiguity must be resolved.

At one level, it does this by simply saying that the Spirit is "the active agent of the Trinity,"[83] by which is meant that it is the Spirit who is active in the world in the entire breadth of God's work including salvifically and in empowerment for mission, and without that activity God would not be known. This gives a distinct place to the Spirit, but does nothing necessarily concerning his anonymity and, in any case, is hardly the sole preserve of Pentecostals. The declaration of early Pentecostals at least was that, in Spirit baptism, the Spirit is most certainly not anonymous and is inaugurating a renewal of the Spirit's obvious presence and activity, reclaiming the

79. Williams, *Renewal Theology*, 2:207 (emphasis his).

80. Hence, Vladimir Lossky can write, "Roman Catholic and Orthodox theologians agree in recognizing that a certain anonymity characterizes the Third Person of the Holy Trinity" (Lossky, "The Procession of the Spirit," 74).

81. Ibid., 91.

82. So Duffield and Van Cleave, *Foundations of Pentecostal Theology*, 271.

83. McLean, "The Holy Spirit," 375.

place occupied in the early church. Despite this, Spirit baptism itself was "reduced to empowerment for life and service" in doctrinal statements,[84] which limits the Spirit to being no more than the active agent of God in the above sense, and also risks isolating the Spirit from the Father and the Son. I will take up this latter point later, but perceiving the Spirit as "active agent," whether anonymous or not, is capable of a range of ontological interpretations. At one end of the spectrum, he can remain co-equal with the Father and the Son, but be the hypostasis who "gets his hands dirty," so to speak, in the world. Somewhat less classically, he can be understood as this, but be isolated from the other hypostases as I suggested, where the Father and the Son are acknowledged, but it is to the Spirit that believers look when wanting to see God revealed by their experience of him. The modal interpretation of Oneness Pentecostals moves outside the classical presentation, and furthest away is what I term a unitarian interpretation, where the Spirit is the power or influence of a distant singular God by which that God operates in the world. This last interpretation can be discerned among Pentecostals in practice, if not in doctrinal statements.[85] This reduction to empowerment and alignment with "active agent" views carries not insignificant risks and in fact is a formulation which falls far short of the richness of the experience of early Pentecostals according to Peter Hocken, who showed that "Spirit-baptism was a powerful 'revelation' by the Spirit who brings the believer into a new relationship with the triune God."[86] This richness carries within it the mitigation of such risks.

Before pursuing this richness further, the implications of a highly visible Holy Spirit for conceptions of the Trinity should be touched on, noting that this will also bear on later discussions concerning soteriology. The implications can be summarized in a simple question, which can be stated two ways. If Pentecostals adopt what is understood as the dominant western view of the Trinity which emphasizes the unity of the Godhead before moving to considering the hypostases within, how can the Spirit be understood to have such a visible presence? Even more simply, how can the *Filioque* hold for such a visible Spirit?

This is an issue which Pentecostal thinking has not yet addressed in any substantive way,[87] but it is an important point. A highly visible Spirit having an essentially reciprocal role with the Son, coupled with the fact that

---

84. Chan, *Pentecostal Theology*, 21.

85. This is touched on further below.

86. Hocken, "Meaning and Purpose," 125–34, cited in Chan, *Pentecostal Theology*, 21, from whom the quote is taken.

87. Yong, *Spirit Poured Out*, 225.

Pentecostals place little emphasis on the Father or creation,[88] fits very well with the Eastern conception of the Trinity. The monarchial Father remains transcendent, acting in the world "through the Son and Spirit as the 'left and right hands of God.'"[89] who can easily maintain an equal status and visibility. It does not fit so well with the Western view on first consideration, as understanding the Spirit as the bond of love between the Father and Son, proceeding equally from each, invites anonymity for the Spirit. However, as Yong notes, "the Spirit both sends Jesus and is sent by Jesus" (Luke 3:16b, John 20:22),[90] which does not risk anonymity to the same extent. A sending and sent Spirit can surely be accommodated in the western view and emphasizes the one thing which must be maintained: there is no subordination of the Spirit implied by the *Filioque*. If there is no subordination, then increased visibility cannot be denied to the Spirit as doing so implies some subordination. In any event, as Yong suggests, there is a broader context available for trinitarian discussion than the East-West *Filioque* debate.[91]

Returning to Hocken's observations, there was evidently much more to the activity of the Spirit in Spirit baptism in early Pentecostalism than what is reflected in doctrinal statements; so what early Pentecostals understood as the content of Spirit baptism is important in this discussion. In one sense, the content is the Holy Spirit and this constitutes its totality, but I am taking *content* here, and later, to mean the activity of the Spirit in Spirit baptism. This certainly included an endowment of power, but was also repeatedly asserted as giving new (meaning deeper) insight or knowledge in respect of Christ.[92] Hocken identifies the former as its purpose, aimed at mission and ministry, and the latter as its "meaning or spiritual content,"[93] which is summarized as lying in "the believer's changed relationship to the persons of the Trinity, and in particular to the Lord Jesus Christ, in whom the Spirit is manifest and through whom we have access to the Father."[94] In itself, this illuminating activity of the Spirit is not new to Christian history (and may not be new to the recipient) but the way it is perceived is new.[95] It is perceived through a direct experience and recognition of the Holy Spirit,

---

88. Macchia, *Baptized in the Spirit*, 113.
89. Ibid., 119.
90. Yong, *Spirit Poured Out*, 226.
91. Ibid., 226–27.
92. Hocken, "Meaning and Purpose," 125. He uses "Revelation" which I have expressed as insight or knowledge of Christ to maintain consistency with Calvin's usage.
93. Hocken, "Jesus Christ," 3.
94. Hocken, "Meaning and Purpose," 125.
95. Ibid., 129–30.

who is anything but anonymous in the process. No longer is the Spirit self-effacing, pointing only away, now the believer is confronted by the Spirit. In classic Pentecostal pneumatology, Spirit baptism is for believers,[96] in whom the Spirit dwells and has been working, albeit secretly. Now, in Spirit baptism, they are confronted by a powerful presence, who is recognized as the Holy Spirit, in a completely novel way, even for those whose conversion was years before. The shattering of the Spirit's previous anonymity means that this is inevitably at least a greater and deeper identification of the Spirit and possibly a first "sighting" for the believer. This richer insight must, in turn, mean a greater and deeper recognition of Jesus Christ and the Father because of the role of the Spirit as revealer, but also through the intra-trinitarian relations the Spirit shares with the other hypostases. The act of one is the act of all, so the action of the Spirit in Spirit baptism is also the action of the Father and the Son and so inevitably gives greater knowledge and recognition of them.

This is exactly the new and overwhelming insight testified to by many early Pentecostals which has been shorn off in the formulation of Pentecostal doctrine, but which is now being recovered. Through Spirit baptism, the Spirit brings a greater and deeper knowledge and appreciation of Christ, and similarly the Father, to the believer. For the believer, the announcement of the Spirit by the Spirit makes the appearance of Christ and his role as Spirit baptizer clearer and more distinct. Along with this must follow a similar deeper awareness of the Trinity by the same means—it is no longer a "theoretical construct with little apparent relevance, but is the truth about God as he reveals his inner being."[97] Of course, it must be conceded that Oneness Pentecostals would not accept this as an appropriate ontological insight, but the revelation of Christ is certainly a key theological point for them.

Based as it is on the personal encounter with the Spirit, this is certainly a pneumatological perspective which is developed "from below": it is an economic pneumatology. Pushed too far, the economic focus can give rise to a theology where God seems to be at the disposal of the creature. This is the potential and unfortunate outcome from the focus of Pentecostal doctrine on Spirit baptism as empowerment for service: the temptation I noted above to isolate the Spirit from the Trinity and see the work of the Spirit through empowered believers as divine, but done by the Spirit alone. In one sense, this presents no difficulty as the ontological place of the Spirit is recognized, but it brings with it the risk that the Spirit and Spiritual direct activity is all that is sought, with little attention being paid to the other two hypostases or

---

96. Even if it is "coincident" with conversion.

97. Ibid., 130.

Scripture. More damagingly, it is then a relatively short step to take the isolation further and suggest that the work of the Spirit produces some supernatural abilities which are placed at the disposal of individual believers. This is particularly so if the unitarian interpretation I suggested is taken up. It is this latter interpretation which I suggest has a presence in Grudem's definition of spiritual gifts as *"any ability that is empowered by the Holy Spirit and used in any ministry of the church,"* following which he goes on to assert that "They are given for the work of ministry and are *simply tools* to be used for that end."[98] While he certainly does not adhere to a unitarian viewpoint, this definition places spiritual gifts at the disposal of the believer, something suited to a unitarian practice but which can place God at the disposal of the creature. My own experience suggests that this praxis, if not intellectual assent, is not uncommon within Pentecostal circles. Ensuring the content of Spirit baptism includes both empowerment *and* insight not only accurately reflects the experience and teaching of early Pentecostals, but serves as a corrective to this tendency. The insightful content must clearly identify the empowerment as linked just as much to Christ and the Father as it is to the Spirit. The recovery of this aspect of the Spirit's work in Spirit baptism also aids substantially the development of a Pentecostal theology which better integrates the activity of the Spirit with that of Christ in particular.

Subsequence and Spirit "Release"

This recovery, and the integration which results, have implications for the Pentecostal doctrine of subsequence. This doctrine can be viewed in some quarters as the classic Pentecostal position on Spirit baptism, although it is probably fairer to describe it as the majority North American view. Its shape is evident from my description of the Pentecostal approach to Acts and the evaluation of their own experiences; now a statement of the doctrine can be made. Subsequence arises from the early Pentecostal experience of Spirit baptism which occurred for individuals who already had a Christian faith: for them, conversion had occurred and Spirit baptism was a later enhancement of their position in that faith. Spirit baptism was therefore viewed as a work of grace by God in the Spirit which was additional to the grace experienced at conversion and which occurred after that event. They found support for this sequence of events in the accounts of the Spirit's coming in Acts; so developing the doctrine of subsequence where Spirit baptism is treated as a further work of the Spirit, separate from that at conversion, occurring *subsequently* to conversion. It is recognized

---

98. Grudem, *Systematic Theology*, 1016 and 1031 (emphasis his).

that conversion and Spirit baptism, so separated, may occur at the same time, but a form of subsequence is maintained by describing Spirit baptism as separable and distinct from conversion, even if occurring immediately upon conversion.[99] This separation is emphasized by the suggestion that there are conditions to be satisfied before Spirit baptism can occur—Williams says, in reference to Spirit baptism, "*There is a certain moment in faith, whether at the outset or somewhere along the way, when the Holy Spirit may be received.*"[100] He makes it clear that a faith sufficient for salvation may be reached before a faith sufficient for Spirit baptism exists, a position necessary for subsequence to hold and which indicates there must be conditions to meet before Spirit baptism can occur. He prefers to call the conditions he identifies "contexts" which allows him to broaden the concept of *conditions* somewhat. He identifies five.[101]

1. God's sovereignty: an overall context as any individual context cannot be interpreted as requiring God to respond.

2. Prayer: particularly essential as it is "in a special way the context or atmosphere in which the Holy Spirit is given."

3. Obedience on the part of the believer: a "willing obedience to *whatever* Christ commands."

4. Yielding: an atmosphere of surrender to Christ, a "total availability" of the believer.

5. Expectancy: the gift comes to those who expect, little comes to those who do not.

Bruner also extensively describes a doctrine of conditions for Spirit baptism,[102] identifying that appealing to conditions is necessary to explain why Spirit baptism must occur after conversion, with tongues as evidence following, and why it is that Spirit baptism and tongues are not universal among Christians. His conditions are similar to those of Williams and he summarizes them as a pre-condition of conversion followed by obedience and faith.

---

99. Wyckoff, "Baptism in the Holy Spirit," 431–32.
100. Williams, *Renewal Theology*, 2:272–73 (emphasis his).
101. Ibid., 2:293–304.
102. Bruner, *A Theology of the Holy Spirit*, 87–129.

Subsequence is widely held and taught within Pentecostalism,[103] but has been challenged from both outside Pentecostal circles and within.[104] The very existence of conditions which must be fulfilled for Spirit baptism to occur must give pause to affirming subsequence, particularly as Pentecostals affirm salvation is through faith, not works. Aside from that, Gordon Fee thinks that, in arguing for the biblical basis for their experience, Pentecostals have given equal weight to the character of their experience *and* its timing. He notes that this has had the unfortunate effect of making those who oppose the Pentecostal view think that debunking the timing also debunks the experience.[105] He certainly wants to affirm the character of the experience, but in his exegesis of the three Acts texts above where Spirit baptism is specifically identified as coming after salvation (Acts 2 and 10 being excluded. Although he considers the former in his discussion, he omits any reference to the latter), he concludes that only one (the Samaritan believers in Acts 8) gives a biblical precedent for subsequence (and, incidentally, for tongues as evidence). This one occurrence is too thin a ground for him—is it precedent or unique occurrence?[106] He therefore affirms the character of the experience, but abandons subsequence.

Theologically, subsequence can only be maintained by differentiating between the "indwelling" of the Spirit and "being filled" with the Spirit. Both are understood as the coming of the Spirit to the believer, but the former occurs at conversion where the Spirit illuminates Christ but remains anonymous while the latter is a distinctly different event occurring as Spirit baptism after conversion. Williams has a particularly full description of Spirit baptism, calling it a *"taking possession"* by the Spirit where the believer is "enveloped in the reality of the Holy Spirit" in a way involving the whole person analogous to water baptism; where a fullness of the Spirit comes from beyond the believer to inwardly pervade "every aspect of individual and communal life,"[107] all of which occurs in a way that the believer directly experiences. This is in contrast to the indwelling, where it is still the fullness

---

103. In addition to Wyckoff, "Baptism in the Holy Spirit," see Duffield and van Cleave, *Foundations of Pentecostal Theology*, 312; Williams, *Renewal Theology*, 2:187, 205; Menzies and Horton, *Bible Doctrines*, 123–30; Stronstad, "The Charismatic Theology of St Luke," 112–21, etc.

104. For example, non-Pentecostals in Bruner, *A Theology of the Holy Spirit*, 155–218; and Dunn, *The Baptism in the Holy Spirit*; Pentecostals in Fee, "Baptism in the Holy Spirit"; Yong, *Spirit Poured Out*; and Macchia, *Baptized in the Spirit*.

105. Fee, "Baptism in the Holy Spirit," 87 (emphasis his).

106. Ibid., 91.

107. Williams, *Renewal Theology*, 2:197–202 (emphasis his).

of the Spirit who comes, but experience of him is indirect, revealed only by the convictions concerning Christ.

This differentiation is reflected in Pentecostal soteriologies which have generally picked up the soteriology of what Steven Studebaker calls Protestant scholasticism[108] and hence treated justification and sanctification separately from Spirit baptism and assigned differing roles to the Spirit in each. Ironically this means that Pentecostal theology, expressed in this way, asserts a subordination of the Spirit soteriologically but a primacy of the Spirit in empowerment for service through Spirit baptism. The tendency to isolate the work of the Spirit noted above makes it easier to maintain this position and hence hold to subsequence. This is not to say that the Spirit is isolated entirely from the other hypostases in this tendency, but it is to say that while his divinity and relations within the Trinity are acknowledged the latter play little or no part in his work in believers. Thus isolated, the Spirit can easily be said to come separately in an obvious manner after earlier coming so quietly as to be hardly noticed, if at all.

Integrating the work of the Spirit and Christ as illuminated in the wider content of Spirit baptism I have already discussed makes subsequence very much more difficult to hold. Simply put, in this case subsequence means saying the integrated work of Christ and the Spirit in conversion is so different from the same integration in Spirit baptism as to be able to be separated from it. While Spirit baptism is said to contain a *deeper* knowledge or illumination of Christ, it is still a recognition of Christ of an essential character identical with that which occurs at conversion. To maintain subsequence means having to either abandon this aspect of the full content, or separate out the work of empowerment while still holding to Spirit baptism as a single event. That is, subsequence can be maintained if Spirit baptism is only empowerment as that can be separated from other parts of the Spirit's work; or empowerment is said to be qualitatively different from the Spirit's other work so as to enable its separate operation. The first of these alternatives abandons the richness of the original experience as it denies a real part of it. The second introduces an inherent clumsiness as it demands some boundary be established between empowerment by the Spirit and other work. For example, how can such a boundary be easily established between empowerment for mission and transformation of the individual by the sanctifying work of the Spirit, thus making her more suited for mission?

This clumsiness only serves to confirm disquiet over subsequence. Nevertheless, the experience of Spirit baptism remains, so how is it to be construed? Macchia notes that there is a current tendency to move from subsequence to

---

108. Studebaker, "Pentecostal Soteriology and Pneumatology," 248–70.

view Spirit baptism as a "release" of the already indwelling Spirit.[109] While this move is a result of many other influences (not the least of them attempts to develop a theology which sits comfortably with the entire New Testament witness), it is true to the increased recognition of Christ in Spirit baptism. The concept of release moves away from any idea that the Spirit is internalized for the believer in a new and different way from the initial indwelling upon conversion. Rather, the already indwelling Spirit is "released" within the believer with his cooperation so that something new and phenomenal occurs within and for the believer. It can be conceived of as the Spirit manifesting in a new way in the believer. It must be admitted that "release of the Spirit" is terminology even more distant from New Testament terms than "Spirit baptism," but it carries several advantages as a concept.

First among these relevant to this discussion is that it does away with any separation between "indwelling" and "filling". Rather than being separate, they become linked—filling is the release, or even "expansion" of the already indwelling Spirit so as to be more pervasive and effective in the believer. Along with this, it allows an easier integration of the activity of the Spirit in salvation and sanctification with that in Spirit baptism and therefore offers associated promise in working out a comfortable relation between Lukan and Pauline pneumatologies. While the concern over conditions still remains, one might expect to see greater obedience, increased activity and acuity in prayer and a greater expectancy concerning God's activity in the world as a Christian life deepens and matures, all building a context in which greater activity of the Spirit in the believer, an extension of the depth and character of the indwelling, in short, a release of the Spirit, might be expected. Spirit baptism, understood as release in this manner, is entirely consonant with the Pentecostal experience and, further, offers ground for repeated dramatic experiences of the Spirit. Spirit baptism as described by Pentecostals is a one-time experience—having come in this manner, the Spirit stays.[110] This leaves the problem of explaining how it is that Stephen is filled twice according to Acts (6:5 and 7:55). However, if "release" is understood as a greater manifestation of the Spirit, then there is no bar to future manifestations which have the same character.

I will return to this topic in the concluding chapter, where I will explore in more detail whether the use of "Spirit release" as a suitable metaphor to describe the occurrences in Acts is appropriate for Pentecostal theology. At the risk of telegraphing the result of that consideration, I will henceforth use the term to describe the Pentecostal experience which they

---

109. Macchia, *Baptized in the Spirit*, 77–78.
110. Williams, *Renewal Theology*, 2:197.

claim to be a resurgence of the Acts occurrences in current times. Where I wish to refer to the totality of the coming of the Spirit represented by the indwelling at Christian initiation and a subsequent release, I will continue to use "Spirit baptism."

New Understanding

Returning to Spirit release itself, recognizing its dual content is leading, it appears, to new understandings of Christology and soteriology within Pentecostal theology, as is hinted by the preceding discussions. Pentecostalism has a substantial christological focus, but the tendency to isolate the Spirit does place this at risk. Recovering the deeper insight experienced in the full content of Spirit release reverses this and makes it truly christological as well as pneumatological. This allows a reassertion of the Spirit Christology eclipsed within the church since the time of the Fathers.[111] By "Spirit Christology" here is meant a Christology focused on Jesus as the Spirit-anointed man by which he is revealed as Christ and can function as Christ. This is, of course, a Lukan Christology, with its emphasis on the Spirit coming to one in the world and transforming him in a manner which reveals his true home and empowers him for his mission. The man, Jesus, is now Jesus, the Christ. The classic locus for this is his baptism, where the Spirit descends on Jesus, the Father declares him to be his Son, and his ministry commences with him being led into the wilderness by the Spirit (Luke 3:21–23; 4:1–2). This contrasts with a Logos Christology, meaning here a Christology focused on the divine Son incarnated in the man Jesus, which looks on God coming. It is not the man already here to whom the Spirit comes, it is God coming and doing so as a man. The classic statement of this is John 1:1–18, where the divine Word becomes flesh and gives to those who receive him "the right to become children of God." While there is no less potential intimacy in becoming a child of God compared to the Spirit descending, the latter speaks of God coming and involving himself in the believer, the former of a familial relationship, something which can be conceived of as allowing distance between the believer and God, surely encouraged if the Spirit is understood as self-effacing.

Yong suggests such a form of Spirit Christology: "Jesus is the revelation of God precisely as the man anointed by the Spirit of God to herald and usher in the reign of God."[112] In this Jesus is one who is so thoroughly anointed

---

111. Macchia, *Baptized in the Spirit*, 107–13; Yong, *Spirit Poured Out*, 109–12. This does not mean that Calvin ignored a Spirit Christology, see II.12–15.

112. Yong, *Spirit Poured Out*, 86. The immediately following discussion owes a debt to him, 86–88 and 109–12.

that he is always completely identified with God's will and so able to be perfectly obedient and hence, sinless. While his whole life was so anointed, at his baptism the Spirit "descended upon him in bodily form" (Luke 3:22) in a development which enabled or empowered his public ministry. Such a Christology cannot supplant Logos Christology as that would become adoptionism, but each has substantial scriptural warrant, so must be considered as complementary. Because Spirit Christology has not had a profile to speak of since the early church, simply recognizing its complementarity brings it to the fore, announcing it as a worthy subject for study.

Such a Christology speaks powerfully to the believer, who, after all, is human as Jesus is and can look for the same human-to-God contact enjoyed by Jesus: she can claim a parallel experience.[113] She will not have been conceived by the Spirit, but can point to being born of the Spirit (John 3:5) inasmuch as the Spirit came to indwell her at conversion. She can see her equivalent to the descent of the Spirit on Jesus at his baptism in her own Spirit release, with its deep recognition of Christ and empowering. Her claim to a direct encounter with the Spirit who she perceives in a way which makes his identity obvious and beyond question, reflects the Spirit descending on Jesus "in bodily form like a dove" (Luke 3:22; see also Matt 3:16, Mark 1:10, John 1:32). At Jesus' baptism, the Spirit had form, seen and recognized by the Baptist as the Holy Spirit in John, although in the Synoptics it is implied that the crowd so perceived the Spirit. So in Christ is revealed the pattern of her experience which is validated by the Spirit who reveals it. The conviction that it is *Christ* she is given sight of indicates that he reciprocates by showing her that the equivalence of their respective experiences means it is the same Spirit at work. In this way, the divinity and place of the Spirit she has encountered is established. It is this interaction which informs Badcock's insight that the reciprocity between Christ and the Spirit in a Spirit Christology facilitates a relationship with the believer in which there is a correspondence between the Spirit and human spirituality.[114] The close association engendered is part, at least, of the participation with God, of being taken up into God, which constitutes the place of the believer in the kingdom of God. Another way of putting this is that a close identification with the human who is anointed by the Spirit comes more easily than any identification with God who is incarnated in Jesus Christ, even assisted by the anonymous Spirit. Certainly, the outcome sought in a soteriology proceeding from such a Logos Christology is the same taking

---

113. Not an identical experience. As Yong, *Spirit Poured Out*, 87, notes, Jesus was fully anointed by the Spirit: his "life from beginning to end was of the Spirit," something which is qualitatively different from any other human.

114. Badcock, *Light of Truth*, 271.

up, but a complementary Spirit Christology offers a pneumatology which provides a ready mechanism for the taking up.

This suggests a synergistic activity on the part of the Spirit and Christ towards the believer in his Christian journey and hence the opportunity of conceiving a pneumatological soteriology. If Spirit release were simply empowerment then it would offer little to the renewal of the believer, something Bruner, who ignores its deeply insightful content, observes.[115] However, on the above reading, the Pentecostal experience is charismatic *and* soteriological.[116] As empowerment, a contribution of the Spirit to a believer working out his salvation (Phil 2:12), or to the process of "being saved" can be argued, but this requires no synergism. Neither is any synergism required in Protestant scholasticism, whose soteriology has Christ objectively justifying the believer and the Spirit subjectively sanctifying him, alongside the Spirit revealing Christ for who he is without also being revealed.[117] As insight and conviction as well as empowerment, Spirit release can be described as "the experience of the resurrection life of Christ," where the believer is seized by the Spirit in a way which allows her to "experience the exalted Christ" in the Spirit.[118] That is, she apprehends the risen Christ in a manner which penetrates her very being and involves her participation in him and his life. This is an encounter which occurs by the directly perceived activity of the Spirit: she knows who it is who is showing her these things, and is deeply affected by that knowledge and felt power of the Spirit. Here, she is "liberated for the authentic life of Christ" and so participates with him in his place and his work.[119] Here also, the direct activity of the Spirit in justification is implied, a view shared by Macchia who asserts "We are justified by the Spirit of God through our participation in Christ by faith" (although he does not mean this is a complete account of justification) and that the saved "self lives on, fulfilled through participation in Jesus' filial relationship to God in the power of the Spirit."[120] Paul's favorite description of the justified believer is one who is "in Christ,"[121] exactly an experiencing of Christ or the participation Mac-

---

115. Bruner, *A Theology of the Holy Spirit*, 73–75.

116. Yong, *Spirit Poured Out*, 81 (emphasis mine).

117. Ibid., 82.

118. Suurmond, "Meaning and Purpose," 35.

119. Ibid., 43. The quote is cited from Hermann, *Kyrios und Pneuma. Studien zur Christologie der paulinischen Hauptbriefe*.

120. Macchia, *Baptized in the Spirit*, 172, 175.

121. A text search for "in Christ" in the New International Version translation returns 84 instances in the Pauline letters. Witherington, "Christ," 98–99, notes Paul's use of the phrase *en Christo* 164 times in the chief Pauline letters and a further 6 times as *en Christo Iesou* in the Pastoral letters. He also notes that Paul does speak of Christ being in the believer (Gal 2:20; Rom 8:10) but that this "is not nearly so characteristic."

chia is referring to. In this Spirit-Christ reciprocity, it is the Spirit who takes the believer into Christ. Without diminishing the salvific work of Christ on the cross or in his ministry, the work of shifting the one who is brought into Christ is done by the Spirit. The reciprocal activity of Christ and the Spirit is also reflected in Yong's proposal for a pneumatological soteriology where salvation is a work of both Christ and the Spirit in *all* its aspects.[122] Not only are both involved in justification, but the synergism must also extend to sanctification if there is to be synergism at all. The justified believer is to live life "in Christ"; it is there that her growth in holiness will occur: it can hardly occur if she is apart from Christ. If this can be expressed as her place, the character of her place must have a bearing on her sanctification, hence Christ is involved in her sanctification in a corollary of the Spirit's role in her justification. This conception stands apart from the soteriology adopted by Pentecostal theology from its Protestant roots; the distinction made there between the work of the divine hypostases, Christ justifying and the Spirit sanctifying,[123] is dissolved by the strong synergistic link in the involvement of both in justification and sanctification.

Redemptive Justification and Pneumatological Soteriology

Macchia described something similar when he introduced a redemptive model of justification in his presidential address to the 2000 annual meeting of the Society for Pentecostal Studies[124] which "allows Christ and the Holy Spirit to assume essential roles in the entire redemptive process."[125] His model relies on the interaction of Rom 4:25 and 8:11:

> [Righteousness] will be reckoned to us who believe in him who raised Jesus our Lord from the dead, who was handed over to death for our trespasses and was raised for our justification. (4:24b–25)

> If the Spirit of him who raised Jesus from the dead dwells in you, he who raised Christ from the dead will give life to your mortal bodies also through his Spirit that dwells in you. (8:11)

---

122. Yong, *Spirit Poured Out*, 82 (emphasis mine).

123. Studebaker, "Pentecostal Soteriology and Pneumatology," 254.

124. Published in *Pneuma*: see Macchia, "Justification and the Spirit," 3–21, and discussed at length in Studebaker, "Pentecostal Soteriology and Pneumatology," 266–70. The above discussion is taken from both. Macchia used the term *redemptive justice*, but Studebaker uses *redemptive justification* which I also use above.

125. Studebaker, "Pentecostal Soteriology and Pneumatology," 266.

Christ was raised for our justification (note the distinction made between that and his death being for our trespasses), and it was the Spirit who raised him, although somewhat clumsily expressed as Dunn notes (see above). This is not reflected in the tendency in Protestant theology "to confine justification to the cross," where God's justice is satisfied, and base sanctification in the resurrection which brings new life.[126] Thus formulated, the Spirit is not directly involved in justification, a contradiction of 4:25 which commentators have had to work their way around.[127] But the text makes it clear, on the face of it, that the purpose and effect of the Spirit in raising Christ was and is justification of the creature. It is the God who resurrected Christ who will give life to the creature's mortal body through the same indwelling Spirit who raised him, to be ultimately fulfilled when the Spirit also raises the creature, the ultimate adoption as children of God for which believers wait (Rom 8:23). Macchia claims this adoption implies "that our justification is ultimately fulfilled only when the Spirit fully duplicates in us what the Spirit has done in Jesus."[128] Therefore, the Spirit has a direct role in justification, defined in the model as "the creation of new life in the person through the gift of the Spirit."[129] The model achieves the close correspondence between the Spirit and human spirituality mentioned by Badcock,[130] in that the work of the Spirit in relation to the "death, resurrection, and ascension of Christ" is replicated and paralleled in the human in his death to his old life, his new life and "restoration to fellowship with the triune God."[131] Redemptive justification is inherently pneumatological and so offers to Pentecostal theology a soteriology which gives a full role to the Spirit in contrast to that of Protestant scholasticism. It also offers a link between Lukan and Pauline pneumatologies with its basis in a Pauline text, so challenging any rigid differentiation between how each conceives of the work of the Spirit.[132]

Studebaker gives a brief outline of how this works.[133] The Spirit's role is subordinated in the historic soteriology, so that the death and resurrection

---

126. Macchia, "Justification and the Spirit," 9.
127. Ibid.
128. Ibid., 10.
129. Studebaker, "Pentecostal Soteriology and Pneumatology," 266.
130. Badcock, *Light of Truth*, 271.
131. Studebaker, "Pentecostal Soteriology and Pneumatology," 266.

132. An example of which is Dunn, *The Baptism in the Holy Spirit*, cited in Macchia, *Baptized in the Spirit*, 29.

133. Studebaker, "Pentecostal Soteriology and Pneumatology," 267–69. The above is a considerably abbreviated version of his discussion where I have conflated some of his terms, but is, I think, accurate to his intent.

of Christ are seen as primarily his works and, while the Spirit is his agent in justification and sanctification, the redemption he offers is entirely his. However, in redemptive justification, it is in or by the power and involvement of the Spirit that Christ lives and dies and is raised. Justification and sanctification are both works of the Spirit also, received in Spirit baptism, understood as constituting or taking place at conversion. The Spirit is fully introduced at all points making salvation both christological and pneumatological. It is not that Christ is excluded, but that the Spirit is included in a way which recovers the Spirit's status and asserts the integrated work of both Christ and the Spirit in human salvation. Note, too, that this elevates a Spirit Christology, something Macchia makes clear:

> Jesus was the justified Son of God precisely as the Person of the Spirit, a justification that was fulfilled in the resurrection, and that we are justified in him as bearers of the Spirit, an experience that will culminate in our resurrection.[134]

Yong makes a similar proposal,[135] envisaging salvation as an all-embracing transformation of the individual, dealing with sin, deliverance, healing, liberation and the placement in a new community. In his proposal, he adopts a definition of Spirit baptism after first reviewing the three views of Spirit baptism held within the broader Pentecostal community:[136]

a. Spirit baptism as a single work of grace which is initial conversion or salvation, and the later experience is a release of the Spirit (see above);

b. Spirit baptism as a second work of grace, separate from and following initial conversion; and

c. Spirit baptism as a third work of grace, following conversion and sanctification. The last is conceived as being complete at conversion, but being increasingly appropriated throughout the believer's life.

On the grounds that the patristic understanding was that salvation was an event which incorporated conversion, receipt of the Spirit and charisms following, in which they accurately reflect the New Testament witness, Yong prefers Spirit baptism as initial conversion. Thus it is a single work of grace, a single event, which "denotes Christian salvation, broadly considered, as nothing less than the gift of Jesus Christ himself to us in the totality of his

---

134. Macchia, "Justification and the Spirit," 10.

135. Yong, *Spirit Poured Out*, 79–120 sets out his position, of which the following discussion is a summary.

136. Ibid., 98–100.

Spirit-anointed life, death, and resurrection."[137] The activity of Christ and the Spirit is therefore linked in the totality of salvation through Spirit baptism in the following ways:[138]

1. Spirit baptism is anticipated by Jesus' offer of the Spirit.
2. Spirit baptism is the culmination of Christian initiation.
3. Spirit baptism connects Jesus being raised "for our justification" (Rom 4:25) with his being raised by the Spirit (Rom 8:11), so our justification is pneumatological as well as christological.
4. Justification is therefore linked with sanctification—"God *declares* sinners righteous through Jesus Christ and *makes* sinners righteous through the purifying fire of the Spirit."
5. Spirit baptism unites believers with the resurrected Christ, hence equipping them for ministry.
6. Spirit baptism is the "down payment" for God's "eschatological redemption."

This is a pneumatological soteriology which links well with the dynamic nature of salvation testified to by the New Testament. Christians have had an initial experience of repentance, justification, and receipt of the Spirit, so *have been* saved. They continue to have "ongoing experiences of being filled with the Spirit" which are material influences in their movement from sin to holiness and so are equivalent to the traditional understanding of sanctification, so *are being* saved; and will experience a fullness of Spirit baptism without any taint of sin at the *parousia* and so *will be* saved. Such salvation is the "reorientation of the totality [of the individual] to the revelation of God in Jesus Christ," accomplished by the Spirit's "assimilation [of the individual] with Jesus" and their gifting for service.[139] This is different from some other theories of the atonement which Yong considers (he calls them "ransom, satisfaction, penal-substitutionary and moral-influence"),[140] which allow a static declaration of righteousness for the individual, but is complementary to them rather than in conflict. For example, if Christ saves through paying the ransom for a believer, then that creates the conditions necessary for the Spirit to come to indwell and transform the believer: it is the foundation on which the Spirit can work.

---

137. Ibid., 101.
138. Ibid., 102.
139. Gelpi, *The Conversion*, cited in Yong *Spirit Poured Out*, 107.
140. Yong, *Spirit Poured Out*, 112.

The ransom is the atonement, the Spirit baptism it allows is how it is given effect for the individual. The same can be said for any other model of the atonement. Hence, Yong suggests that his pneumatological soteriology relates well to these models of salvation as it allows each of them to have its contribution without championing any.[141]

This understanding of salvation injects a dynamic element into the event, which stretches it to include all the believer's life. Salvation is not simply a static forensic declaration, entered into through faith, but is now also a living of a life reoriented to Christ, a life which is to be true to the resurrected Christ. By the Spirit, the believer is taken up to participate with Christ in an analogous way to the resurrected Christ's being taken up in his ascension. If this is the case, then a Christian life envisaged as a life of faith in a distant (ontologically and historically) Christ mediated by Scripture and the church with its attendant temptation to treat this in practice as separate from everyday life is not possible. Neither is a life construed as empowered by the Spirit who refills us periodically, in much the same way vehicles are refueled—where there must inevitably be times when the believer has "run out" of the Spirit. Rather, life is to be lived continually in Christ; life is to be lived in the ever-present, ever-indwelling Spirit; in fact salvation is intimately linked with living life. The believer, in a sense, comes to Christ in Spirit baptism as if she is boarding a new life, one in which Christ and the Spirit act reciprocally to take her into their fold and so share their journey with her. Such a view, of course, seems to involve her in her salvation to an extent beyond it being a work of God's grace received in faith; to talk of her boarding points to work on her behalf. Yong recognizes this, so concludes by saying:

> the dichotomy between salvation being of God and salvation as demanding human response is a false one. We do better to see salvation as human participation in the saving work of God through Christ by the Holy Spirit. In this way, salvation is not some abstract or speculative deal but the concrete experiences of embodied, social, political, economic and spiritual beings as the Holy Spirit is poured out on them.[142]

Summary on the Spirit

The line of enquiry followed by Macchia and Yong has arisen a century after the arrival of Pentecostalism itself. Born out of an experience as it was,

141. Ibid., 112–20.
142. Ibid., 120.

Pentecostalism has held to a mistrust of theology, so its development of a characteristic theology has been slow and is very much in its infancy. One result of this has been that Pentecostalism has borrowed much of its pneumatology from its Protestant roots and concentrated its efforts on explicating its experience of Spirit release. This has resulted in a theology of the Spirit which asserts an anonymous activity on his part in revealing Christ as savior to the believer and then working on his sanctification, while discarding his anonymity in confronting and empowering the believer for mission in Spirit release. To maintain this high-profile place for Spirit release, Pentecostalism relies on Acts to give it a theological basis, an entirely legitimate stance provided the resultant pneumatology is understood as complementary to other pneumatologies found in the New Testament.

This high profile given to the Spirit in Spirit release by Pentecostals is reflected in the experience and attitude of the early church. For them, it was the identifiable presence and activity of the Spirit which showed genuine Christian conversion, just as the activity of the Spirit in raising Jesus showed him definitively to be the long-awaited Messiah. Recent work has shown that the Spirit release experience of early Pentecostals included not only empowerment by the Spirit, but also a deeper insight into the person of Jesus Christ, revealing him in a new way as savior and one of the hypostases within the triune God. This fuller content of Spirit release than commonly understood accords the Spirit a similar role for Pentecostals as for the early church. This brings the Spirit's work to the fore, while not diminishing the work of Christ, thus asserting a reciprocity between them in the justification and sanctification of the believer. This reciprocity is fatal to the Pentecostal doctrine of subsequence, as the work of the Spirit is no longer separated from the work of Christ, so the separation implied by subsequence can no longer hold. This does not diminish the experience of Spirit release, which is better understood as a release of the already indwelling Spirit or a greater manifestation of his presence in the already Spirit-indwelt believer, neither does it lessen its content or impact on the believer. The reciprocity also allows the development of a Spirit Christology, on an equal and complementary footing to a Logos Christology, of the sort proposed by Macchia and Yong. Both then develop a pneumatological soteriology which introduces the Spirit to a greater role in the fullness of salvation, in particular claiming a role for the Spirit in justification previously left to Christ, without diminishing the place of Christ or his work on the cross.

What Macchia and Yong offer to Pentecostalism is the beginnings of an integration of the meaning and content of Spirit release with the pneumatologies previously borrowed from Protestantism. Ultimately the hoped-for outcome is a characteristic Pentecostal account of pneumatology which is consistent in its expression across all its aspects, while continuing to champion its experience. The work of Macchia and Yong suggests that this could be a theology in which the Spirit is intimately involved in a Christian salvation which is dynamic and directly experienced by believers as they live their lives.[143]

This accords well with the suggestion of Alistair McGrath that the defining characteristic of Pentecostals is the belief that God is involved with them and their lives on a day by day basis, in contrast to the mediation of the church practiced in other Protestant traditions and Roman Catholicism.[144] There are competing opinions concerning what the defining characteristic of Pentecostals is,[145] but that does not make McGrath's observation of the pervasiveness of the belief invalid. The soteriological models presented by Macchia and Yong are true to this belief, including, as they do, a dynamic and ongoing interaction between the believer and Christ through the Spirit in the creation of a salvation journey for each convert. This ongoing interaction occurs through what Pentecostals most often refer to as a relationship with Jesus Christ, but which can also be termed the union between the believer and Christ.

Union Between the Believer and Christ

In evangelical theology this union is not obvious from direct experience for the believer although the reality of its existence through the anonymous work of the Spirit needs to be asserted to cross Lessing's ditch.[146] In contrast, the Pentecostal experience of Spirit release makes it obvious to the believer that something has come in such a manner that he recognizes that he has been "filled" with something of God (or, better, someone), so, in a sense, he has been thrust into a relationship with God that he cannot ignore. The filling itself is so pervasive that it is obvious to the believer that this will now have an impact in his life beyond anything else. This is the experience behind Land's comments that Pentecostal soteriology "emphasizes salvation as participation in the divine life more than the removal of guilt"[147] and

---

143. Note that this does not mean that salvation is completed in their worldly lives, an eschatological reserve remains.

144. McGrath, *Christianity's Dangerous New Idea*, 424, 431–32.

145. See Macchia, *Baptized in the Spirit*, 24–28, for a brief survey of other possibilities suggested.

146. Lessing, *Lessing*, 85–87. This is how Lessing characterized his view that historical truth could not be used to prove eternal metaphysical truths.

147. Land, *Pentecostal Spirituality*, 23. This and the subsequent comment both have obvious affinities with the pneumatological soteriology discussed earlier, as well as being relevant here.

that "the Christian life is a matter of the experienced power and presence of the Holy Spirit today."[148] Thus, "Pentecostals . . . place great emphasis upon the reality of a relationship with God that affects every aspect of the human being."[149] It is through this relationship that God by the Spirit can give the everyday guidance and growth in holiness that McGrath refers to, but the existence of the relationship is often assumed rather than being given specific attention in their doctrinal writings.[150] There is a number of possible reasons why this might be the case. First, it is as if there is no need to address the subject as the existence and operation of the union is so obvious that no explanation is required. The lack of attention may also reflect the suspicion of theology within early Pentecostalism[151] and, in a related way, be an outcome of the tendency Chan identifies for Pentecostals to be better at telling their story than explaining it to their children.[152] What might be called the conventional Pentecostal soteriology adopted to date, borrowed from Protestant scholasticism but infused with Arminian tendencies where salvation is understood to involve some synergistic activity between God and the human, also serves to mask the union. If salvation is all God's work, then the human is taken up into a union as grace is irresistible. However, if there is some human contribution, then the human is conceived of as availing herself of an opportunity provided by God. In this construction, it is not obvious that a union is established in salvation, however much it might be inferred from how the process is understood.

This lack is not universal, however, with Williams giving the issue an extended treatment, and other commentators visiting the matter on occasions. He begins by making a similar observation to Calvin, that Christ's saving work requires our participation for it to be salvific for us.[153] For him, salvation can only occur if there is a response to the gospel preached—the Word "going forth in the power of the Spirit,"[154] provoking a response which arises from faith but is also faith itself. This faith has three elements: it gives a knowledge of what God has done in Christ; it is an "assent to God's offer

---

148. Newbigin, *The Household of God*, cited in Land, *Pentecostal Spirituality*, 33.

149. Railey and Aker, "Theological Foundations," 44. See also Williams, *Renewal Theology*, 2:237, and Duffield and Van Cleave, *Foundations of Pentecostal Theology*, 282.

150. See, for example, Horton, *Systematic Theology*.

151. Chan, *Pentecostal Theology*, 24.

152. Ibid., 20–21.

153. Williams, *Renewal Theology*, 2:13.

154. Ibid., 23, 28. It is not the response which is salvific: while it is required, it is always Christ who saves. Note also that he does not restrict this preaching to the church—all Christians can do it anywhere, at any time, individually or collectively. This preaching is incorporated within the activity of "witnessing."

of salvation in Jesus Christ"; and it is a complete reliance or trust on the promises God gives in the gospel.[155] The faith which is provoked could be said to be the response itself, but there is also a receipt of what God has done which contains a human element also related to faith. It is not that the human reaches out to God, but that she receives what God has provided for her. Her faith is built as she moves through the three elements and as, in complete trust, she receives what God has done for her in Christ, it becomes saving faith for her. This "climax of faith is union with Christ," exactly the kind of intimate relationship implied by that description, where she is in Christ and Christ is in her, inseparably. Therefore, "most profoundly [faith is] the reality of being united with Him. The climax of believing in Christ is being in Him." This union is not one in which the believer loses his identity, rather it is a union best understood as "a unity of relationship," where his life and existence finds its center in Christ without any loss of personhood, with the believer "constantly being invigorated and renewed by the life of Christ."[156] Within this, there remains a human component to faith. Duffield and Van Cleave have a similar construction without considering the issue in the depth of Williams. For them, there is a relationship established at salvation which believers understand through the influence of the Spirit, a relationship which has its basis in faith in God and the Word.[157] They also describe this relationship as a union which is "identification with Christ," so that his life is present in the believer's flesh.[158]

The role of the Spirit in faith, and hence the establishment of the union, is muted in Williams' account. He certainly views the union as spiritual, so being established at the deepest personal level in the believer, and notes that the reality of Christ in the believer is not a bodily indwelling, but a spiritual one, where the "indwelling of Christ . . . is identical with the indwelling

---

155. Ibid., 29–31.

156. Ibid., 31–32. He cites III.14.6 as emphasizing the importance of this union.

157. Duffield and Van Cleave, *Foundations of Pentecostal Theology*, 253, 305.

158. Ibid., 408. There is no attempt in the sources I have consulted to enquire concerning the two natures of Christ in contemplating the union. Whilst there is certainly affirmation that the one person, Jesus Christ, possesses both fully human and fully divine natures and that this is necessary to his saving work (see Williams, *Renewal Theology*, 1:306, for example), the union is always with the one Christ. There is no consideration whether it is accomplished in his human nature, no consideration as to the point of contact, so to speak. It is sufficient for Pentecostals to acknowledge the union with the one Christ. This is consistent with their testimony to Spirit release, where God himself is encountered directly not only in the Spirit but also in his triune fullness, so a direct relation with the deity presents no problems in Pentecostal theology. There is no necessity for believers to obtain access to the deity of God by means of the human nature of Christ in hypostatic union with his divine nature.

of the Spirit." Christ is in the believer as a spiritual presence through the agency and actual presence of the Holy Spirit.[159] However, viewing the union as the climax of the sort of faith he describes inevitably mutes the role of the Spirit. This is because faith here, even understood as identified with the union, is, to some extent at least, the proper possession of the individual in the specific sense that he has contributed to its formation. It is a great deal more than intellectual assent, it is a decision to commit the whole of oneself, to the deepest possible level, to what the believer now understands to be true about God and God's offer of salvation. God, through the Spirit, plays a real part in the establishment of this faith in the believer, as the Spirit shows the gospel to be true to the individual and identifies that God *is* making an offer of salvation, but faith is not the creation of the Spirit alone in the individual. So, while the Spirit does God's part in the creation of the union, that part does not constitute the whole creative act; the believer is also creative, albeit assisted by the Spirit.

This conception has its difficulties when confronted by the Protestant and Pentecostal affirmation that humans cannot save themselves and must rely entirely on God. To say that the faith through which someone is saved is to some extent the creation and possession of the believer appeals immediately as semi-Pelagian. Pentecostals, however, from their generally Arminian view of the process, would say that salvation is the result of faith, properly possessed by the individual (albeit formed under the direct influence of the Spirit), allowing the receipt of the gift of salvation, the passive receipt not constituting a work. If this is accepted, then salvation is a gift, but the faith through which it is effected is the possession of the saved. This, in turn, has its effect on the union between the believer and Christ, the mutual indwelling of salvation. This union has the character more of a real mutual interest, a unity in which two parties continue to each have influence on the union, rather than that of a unity where one party (the human, of course) is in complete submission to the other. Nevertheless, complete submission is properly the goal of the human, and the union allows this goal to be established and a real progression towards it to occur. This establishment and progression are based in the union between the believer and Christ and are considered under several headings.

---

159. Williams. *Renewal Theology*, 2:32.

Regeneration

The first of these is regeneration,[160] understood as "the decisive and instantaneous action of the Holy Spirit in which he re-creates the inner nature" of the human which occurs instantly at conversion.[161] The new nature is one re-oriented to Christ, characteristically a nature of "holiness and righteousness" and so very much more than a new inclination, rather it is a radical redirection of the human.[162] It is a spiritual new birth of the individual which results in a *new being*, something which *must* occur, as outside regeneration humans are dead in sin.[163] Regeneration is being born again, "literally the impartation of the divine nature (sic) to the heart and life of the sinner, which makes him a new creation. It is brought to pass through a personal union with Jesus Christ," something possible through the power of the Holy Spirit who comes "into the heart of the believer [bringing] the life of God, thus enabling [the believer] to be a partaker of the divine union."[164] Williams is somewhat more definitive than this about the creator of regeneration. For him, it is primarily the work of the Spirit who is the "resident factor in the believer's life" who enables the believer to be radically re-oriented.[165] Higgins is most definitive, the Spirit working in the human heart to apply what Christ has done for the individual to her through her union with Christ.[166]

Understanding conversion as the moment when the union with Christ is formed, an instant regeneration of the human occurs then. This can only happen because the union exists—the Spirit has come to indwell and creates the link with Christ whereby Christ also indwells the believer and he, in turn, dwells in Christ through the Spirit. This link therefore gives access to Christ for the believer, an access the Spirit can use to impart the

---

160. I have used "regeneration" in my discussion of Calvin to cover both an instant work in the believer at conversion and an ongoing work of growing holiness after conversion. Here, my Pentecostal sources mostly separate "regeneration" from "sanctification," the former an instant work at conversion, and the latter an ongoing process of growing holiness after conversion, although with a start at that point. I follow that practice in this discussion.

161. Pecota, "The Saving Work of Christ," 365.

162. Willimas, *Renewal Theology*, 2:55.

163. Ibid., 2:35–36 (emphasis his).

164. Duffield and Van Cleave, *Foundations of Pentecostal Theology*, 235, 236–38. The use of "divine nature" in the first quote is unfortunate. It is not a reference to the ontology of the Son, but means a change within the being of the believer to produce the desire and ability to be obedient to God.

165. Williams, *Renewal Theology*, 2:49–50. He goes on to conclude that the one true mark of the Christian is the presence of the Spirit.

166. Higgins, "God's Inspired Word," 110.

effect of what Christ has done salvifically to the believer and actualize it in the believer so his conversion is accomplished. While Higgins seems to think that this is all the work of the Spirit, both Williams and Duffield and Van Cleave leave an opening in their expressions which allows something of the believer to contribute. Thus, for them, it is at least possible that the union allows the believer to access Christ on her own merits, even if this is only possible with the assistance of, or even initiation by, the Spirit. Whatever the relative contributions of the Spirit and the believer, the link allows the regeneration of the individual to occur, sourced in Christ and conveyed by the Spirit.

The result of regeneration is a new creation, in which the believer has a new orientation to God in lieu of his previous orientation to self. What must be appreciated here (although little commented on in the sources consulted), is that it is the pervasiveness of the union in the individual that makes possible a regeneration that is similarly pervasive.[167] Of equal importance, the union is now part of the being of the individual and cannot be excluded when describing the person after conversion. That is, the new creation is still the individual, but this individual is now one in union with Christ, who is intimately linked with her. For the believer, there is a concrete path for the reorientation to use: she need only look to her union, to the link it provides, to *be* reoriented. Further, the existence of the union, and the indwelling Spirit, mean that, as long as the union exists, this reorientation is inevitable; it will also exist. Hence the coming into being of the union must mean regeneration for the believer. What this does not mean, however, is that regeneration is a complete, once for all reorientation which always operates in the believer and so produces complete holiness and righteousness. The Pentecostal view of the contribution of the believer to her faith with its consequent understanding of the union as two in relationship means that the believer can look elsewhere as well as to Christ in her life. Her reorientation is not perfect and, in fact, requires perfecting: she still requires sanctification.

Justification[168]

Before this can begin, one more change occurs at conversion: the believer is justified. Justification is needed for all humans, each of whom falls short of

---

167. Williams, *Renewal Theology*, 2:40, specifically notes regeneration is of the whole person.

168. The discussion here follows the broadly accepted evangelical view of justification imported into Pentecostalism, not the proposals put forward by Macchia and Yong as they have yet to gain broad acceptance.

God's standard of righteousness and is unable to change this by themselves. It is to be declared righteous by God, the ground for which "is God's act of redemption in Jesus Christ," a *costly* act which allows God to declare "a profound alteration for the human situation."[169] The declaration of righteousness includes a non-imputation of sin to the human; and an imputation of the righteousness of Christ to the human. There is thus a negative and a positive aspect: the individual's sins are forgiven, made as if they never occurred; and the perfect righteousness of Christ is applied to the human— it is not a lack of unrighteousness, but the positive status of Christ which becomes the individual's own.[170] Thus, in justification there is a distinct shift for the human, whose status before God is completely changed in an entirely undeserved way.

It is this change before God which distinguishes justification from regeneration. While both occur simultaneously and instantaneously at conversion, the latter is a change within the human, the imparting of a new nature, in contrast to the imparting of a new status in justification. In consequence, there can be some confusion between the two, and comment made concerning one aspect may be equally applicable to the other.

This change before God has its impacts in the human. It is not that the past is covered up, it is that the human becomes "*constituted* as righteous" in Christ, she actually *becomes* righteous.[171] The decisive moment that allows justification is the moment of repentance, which Williams defines as the moment where one turns from the "old to the new, from darkness to light," "a movement of the whole self away from sin to God,"[172] that is, the moment when the decision to accept what God has done in Christ is made. That acceptance is made by the human by faith, so the justification which results has occurred through faith, which acts as a channel through which God's saving action can flow. It is not that faith justifies, it is that faith is the instrument by which God can justify, and that God justifies those who have faith.[173] Duffield and Van Cleave make essentially the same point when they say that God saves those who repent.[174] For Williams, the "primary result of justification is . . . [that] we become [children] of God,"[175] also

---

169. Williams, *Renewal Theology*, 2:68–70 (emphasis his).

170. Ibid., 2:63–68.

171. Ibid., 2:70–71 (emphasis his).

172. Ibid., 2:44–45. Williams makes this comment in relation to regeneration, but he applies the concept equally to justification.

173. Ibid., 2:72, 75.

174. Duffield and Van Cleave, *Foundations of Pentecostal Theology*, 215.

175. Williams, *Renewal Theology*, 2:78.

echoed by Duffield and Van Cleave who talk of the new birth making a "believer a child of God."[176] They make this comment in the context of a discussion on regeneration (for which they use "new birth" synonymously) but it more properly refers to justification as it is a change of status for the believer. This adoption as children speaks of a new relationship being established, a reference, of course, to the union between the believer and Christ, so the change of status before God incorporates the establishment of the union. While God, of course, could sovereignly declare believers to be righteous in any manner he chooses, and treat them as such, it is better to consider the union as the link which God uses to impute righteousness to the believer because to do anything other is to place God at a distance while making his declaration. This, of course, would be Lessing's ditch, which is eliminated by the union. In turn, as justification comes through faith, Williams is right to say that faith is the "means of our being *united* with Christ,"[177] which must be understood as the medium through which God communicates the benefits of justification to the believer, not as the cause of the union or its energizing factor.

There is very little mention of the Spirit, if any, in the sources I have used, until Yong and Macchia's works. For example, Duffield and Van Cleave's nine pages of discussion on the specific doctrine contain only one mention of the Holy Spirit, and that only in reference to the inspiration of Scripture. If the Spirit is involved at all in justification, for these sources, the involvement is substantially anonymous. However, when the place of the union is considered, the work of the Spirit in its formation and continuance means that there is at least a supporting role for the Spirit in justification.

Sanctification

Sanctification, here understood in Jenney's limited sense as it affects the individual (see above), follows regeneration and justification. It is defined by Williams as having to do with holiness of life; it is to *make holy* or to *be made holy*. Consequently, it is both an action and a state.[178] Thus, a believer is sanctified by nature of his salvation, but is also being sanctified, also by nature of his salvation. Duffield and Van Cleave express it as primarily being set apart for God and secondarily being cleansed progressively,[179] both

---

176. Duffield and Van Cleave, *Foundations of Pentecostal Theology*, 239.
177. Williams, *Renewal Theology*, 2:73.
178. Ibid., 2:83.
179. Duffield and Van Cleave, *Foundations of Pentecostal Theology*, 242–43.

speaking of holiness, although it is doubtful whether assigning primacy to one aspect over the other is helpful.

The Wesleyan/Holiness tradition, in which Pentecostalism has its roots, maintained sanctification was a separate work of grace preceding Spirit release and spoke of entire sanctification prior to Spirit release. This has the advantage of firmly rooting Spirit release in the wider Christian experience, according to Chan, and was characteristic of Pentecostalism in its initial decade. However, in 1910 William H. Durham repudiated this and adopted the Reformed view that "righteousness was imputed followed by progressive sanctification." This was a beginning of fragmentation within Pentecostalism, and his view carried with it the possibility that one might receive Spirit release with little, if any evidence of sanctification. This tends to weaken the place of Spirit release within Christian experience (an obvious challenge to Pentecostalism) and can result in power being divorced from holiness with the attendant travesties and failings among purveyors of signs and wonders.[180] Despite this risk, progressive sanctification is the dominant view within Pentecostalism today.

Sanctification as progressive does not mean that there is a time when the believer is not sanctified, most obviously at conversion when his Christian life begins. No, sanctification is a state and holiness is a setting apart, both aspects also inherent in justification and regeneration. As these occur at conversion, then the believer must also be sanctified, although in an incomplete fashion, at conversion. Hence, Williams can say "Sanctification relates to the beginning, the continuation and the goal of the Christian life."[181] Of these three, the continuation is the primary focus here as sanctification at the beginning has already occurred, and sanctification as the goal is perfect sanctification, an ever-present goal in this life, but not attained completely until the complete realization of the kingdom of God.[182] Nevertheless, all three are contained in the continuing process of sanctification as, like any process, it has a beginning and an end. Williams sums up sanctification as a *continuing process*, which is a *progressive transformation* that is a growth *in* sanctification, not a moving *toward* it. This growth is properly understood as applying to the whole person, and to comprise "renewal in the likeness of God, or *conformity to Jesus Christ.*"[183] This points to something which is crucial to a proper understanding of sanctification, and which can only occur because of the existence of a real

---

180. Chan, *Pentecostal Theology*, 67–68.
181. Williams, *Renewal Theology*, 2:86.
182. Ibid, 2:90–92.
183. Ibid., 82:88–89, 93, 100 (emphasis his).

union between the believer and Christ. Sanctification is not the process of a believer learning to imitate Christ, rather it is allowing Christ, through the union, to actualize himself more and more in the believer with the corollary that the believer, through the union, moves ever deeper "in Christ"—a process of *identification*[184] with Christ. It is this actualization and movement which constitute the transformation of the believer that is sanctification; if it were only the effort of the believer to imitate Christ, then no transformation need occur. It is God in Christ through the Spirit who effects the transformation by actualizing himself in the believer, and it is God through the Spirit who draws the believer to Christ, both through the union. Thus, Williams can say that "sanctification is primarily the work of God: its source is Him," and that Christ is the *agent* of sanctification and the Spirit its *energizer*.[185] Duffield and Van Cleave assign the work to the Spirit who, indwelling, imparts new life and is the "greatest agency" in sanctification, transforming "the believer into the image of Christ." This gives a focus on the indwelling Spirit located within the believer, rather than the union, reinforced by their noting that the Spirit filling the human heart gives "little relish for that which is displeasing to the Lord."[186]

To talk of a*llowing* Christ to actualize himself and talking of the believer *moving* into Christ, while giving primacy to God in the process of sanctification, does leave open the opportunity for a human contribution, and this is exactly what my sources assert. Williams says that sanctification is also the task of the human, but not in a fashion where a clear distinction can be made between the tasks of God and the creature—he blurs the issue by saying it is "God all the way through [the human] all the way."[187] For Jenney, "Christians choose to be sanctified by the Spirit, a process that requires each individual's continuing cooperation," a construction which makes the human task passive.[188] This passivity is present to a lesser degree in Duffield and Van Cleave, for whom "The definite surrender of the life to God constitutes the supreme condition to practical sanctification," in pursuit of which "there is much that we can do." However, what humans do cannot be done by themselves, but can be accomplished only by using the means God has given, which they

---

184. Duffield and Van Cleave, *Foundations of Pentecostal Theology*, 246 (emphasis theirs).

185. Williams, *Renewal Theology*, 2:101 (emphasis his).

186. Duffield and Van Cleave, *Foundations of Pentecostal Theology*, 280–82, 249. By "image" they do not mean one who looks like Christ, which would mean only imitation is in view, but one who is identified with Christ.

187. Williams, *Renewal Theology*, 2:102. He uses "man" where I have inserted "the human."

188. Jenney, "The Holy Spirit and Sanctification," 412.

list as faith, obedience to Scripture, yielding to the Spirit and personal commitment.[189] Whatever the character of the contribution, in each case there is a distinct human role. Common to all three is the acknowledgement that sanctification is a joint exercise, which cannot be accomplished by either party involved without the cooperation, at least, of the other party. Such an arrangement points once again to the necessity of the existence of the union of Christ and believer in order to allow sanctification.

As might be expected from his more active construction, Williams gives more specific detail about the human task than the other sources, dividing it under two headings. One is dying to sins, reflecting the turning away from sin in repentance. For him, "the flesh is wholly evil and must be totally renounced," so dying to sin is a positive renouncing of sin, a disowning of sin and sins. He uses Calvin's term for this activity, calling it a *mortification*, although of sins rather than the flesh, which is a real putting to death that the believer can only accomplish by the power of the Spirit. This is a serious business to which believers must attend, as each must do it, using the power provided by the Spirit. In his extended discussion, he gives attention to sins, rather than sin, so is focused on sinful acts and the work of reducing those in the believer's life. Doing so is necessary because they are inimical to the new nature in Christ, so are now foreign to the believer. Each sinful act is treated individually, so that mortification proceeds by a series of mortifying acts directed to particular sins, in which there is a *putting away* of the sin—a forceful removal so that it is no longer present. Because the attention is to discrete acts, the putting away may be complete for one act, but the potential exists for further acts to occur, so he concludes that believers can put away sins, but that the putting away is continual through life.[190] Duffield and Van Cleave give passing reference to mortification, but direct it to the flesh rather than sins, although they clearly understand the flesh as capable only of sin.[191] Hence, they make the important point that "the great conflict within us is . . . between the indwelling Holy Spirit and the flesh."[192]

The counterpart to dying to sins is living for righteousness, the turning to God that repentance incorporates. It is characterized by "an intense desire for and commitment to righteousness"[193] which is both nurtured by

---

189. Duffield and Van Cleave, *Foundations of Pentecostal Theology*, 249–51.

190. Williams, *Renewal Theology*, 2:103–8 (emphases his).

191. "The flesh always opposes the Spirit" (Duffield and Van Cleave, *Foundations of Pentecostal Theology*, 246).

192. Ibid., 283, 454.

193. Williams, *Renewal Theology*, 2:109.

and produces three activities—"*Obeying God's Word*," "*Looking to Christ*," and "*Walking by the Spirit.*"[194] Living by all three is living for righteousness.

Obeying God's Word is a matter of "living according to Scripture," which is regarded as a relatively simple matter of studying it to become familiar with it, although guidance can also come through preaching, and then obeying what is learnt. Looking to Christ is actively following Jesus, looking to serve him and others. This includes applying what one knows about Jesus and his teachings, but also incorporates a taking on of his attitudes and appropriation of what he has provided for believers. Williams summarizes all this as "*abiding in Him*," which he views as quite active, a movement by the individual towards Christ, something done by individual actions rather than a simple choice, although the choice is, of course, necessary.

Walking by the Spirit is the most ill-defined of the three activities. The Spirit enables believers to live righteously, but this is done in a liberating fashion where they are unencumbered by a written code but guided by the indwelling Spirit. The Spirit therefore gives inner direction to enable righteous living in a recognition that such living is only possible with the aid of the Spirit. What results (although imperfectly) is a walking "*in love*," which he regards as a summary of the preceding two activities.[195]

So, the third activity summarizes the first two, but it is not clear just how "walking by the Spirit" can be manifested in the believer. There is no obvious activity analogous to reading Scripture which is something objective to which the believer can apply himself in order to be equipped to obey God's Word. At one level, Pentecostals can join with the Protestant tradition and accept the anonymous working of the Spirit by faith, trusting that as they apply themselves to living out what they can discern from Scripture and Christ, whom they discover there, they will be walking in the Spirit. However, this gives a role to walking by the Spirit which is subordinate to the other two, not the reverse which Williams implies. Pentecostals therefore take up their own tradition of Spirit release in which the Spirit is encountered directly, recognizably divine and giving empowerment for mission. As such, there is no real scope to be definitive—to encounter God is to encounter also what God wishes to reveal or accomplish in divine freedom and sovereignty, not to encounter some mediated construction of the creature. It is assumed that the quality of this encounter will be such that recognition of the Spirit is established, and that through the Spirit's infilling future recognition will be innate. Hence, to say that believers need to walk in the Spirit, and that this

---

194. Ibid., 2:109–14 (emphasis his). The following discussion under these three headings is taken from here, all emphases his.

195. Ibid., 2:116.

summarizes the other two activities, is to say all that needs to be said for the one who is intimate with the indwelling, recognized Spirit. This understanding carries the tendency to isolate the work of God to the Spirit alone as the hypostasis encountered, and the potential for unmoderated understanding and action, with the attendant risks that travesties will result, both aspects already discussed. Nevertheless, while recognizing these potential undesirable outcomes, the response to the direct experience of the Spirit is still a faith response—the individual believes this is the Spirit, believes that this is what the Spirit is saying, and so acts on that belief. Pentecostals want to say that there is no difficulty with this, provided the outcome is consistent with what is learnt from Scripture and the Jesus found there.

Perseverance of the Saints

Before concluding this part of the discussion, it is illuminating to look briefly at the perseverance of the saints as presented by Williams, which he calls "*persistence in salvation.*"[196] After assigning differing roles in perseverance to the Father, Son, and Spirit, he concludes that the "Triune God provides . . . the solid basis for persistence in salvation," so perseverance "is primarily a work of God," but then goes on to assert that there are conditions to be met before God will act. These conditions he summarizes as keeping one's *faith* after listing five individual conditions: believers must continue to abide in Christ; remain steadfast; endure in Christ no matter what; be firm in faith; and remain faithful to the end. The necessary cooperative operation of human action with God's action he explains by saying that God operates through the believer's faith. So, if that faith fails, God's action is not effective.[197]

What is presented starkly here is the task of the human. Remaining in salvation until life's end is totally dependent on human action, even if it is primarily God's work. Without the human action, perseverance, which is, of course, endurance of the union between the believer and Christ, is not possible. This necessity of human action is present throughout the Pentecostal accounts of regeneration, justification, and sanctification.

The union with Christ is necessary to make available his work to the believer in all aspects of salvation. Sanctification can only occur if Christ, through the Spirit, is able to directly work with the believer, and this can only occur through some union. However, this union remains a distinct "I and thou" union, where Christ and the human remain separate parties with

196. Ibid., 2:120 (emphasis his).
197. Ibid., 2:120–30 (emphasis his).

equal abilities to end the union. Christ has this ability because he is divine and his action is free, but the believer can be confident that he will always be available for the union as he is entirely faithful to his promises. The believer also has the ability to end the union, which can occur if she does not apply herself to her tasks faithfully. Williams specifically states this as possible,[198] but it follows inevitably if the human has tasks to perform within the union to secure their salvation—non-performance must place the union at risk. While the union is inter-penetrating to the extent that it allows the indwelling of Christ and the Spirit within the believer, and the believer in Christ, it is not so inter-penetrating as to be unbreakable. The difference is perhaps one of degree, where God allows grace to be resistible so that God does not exert his ability to so inter-penetrate as to make the "escape" of the believer impossible, rather God limits the inter-penetration so as to allow the possibility of "escape." There are still two poles to the union, both of which retain an independence which can be asserted. The implication for the believer is that she can be confident that her salvation remains as she applies herself to meeting the conditions set, although doubt is possible should she slip. Her Christian life consists then of her walking with Christ by her choice and action, which she perceives correctly as under her influence. While Christ saves and gives the means for her salvation to persist, her salvation is a co-operative effort as she lives in union with him by faith in the power of the Spirit.

Union and a Pneumatological Soteriology

This borrowed view of the union is challenged and extended by the pneumatological soteriologies proposed by Macchia and Yong which give it a more distinctly Pentecostal flavor while also expanding its focus somewhat. Their suggestions not only elevate the role of the Spirit compared to the traditional Protestant model to a place alongside Christ, but also inject a significant trinitarian aspect to the union. So, salvation is a "participation in the saving work of God through Christ by the Holy Spirit"[199] for Yong, implying an intimate union with a trinitarian locus. Macchia views Spirit baptism as being Christian initiation, encompassing "repentance and new life, cleansing and infilling" for people who become temples in whom the Spirit dwells.[200] This gift of life comes from the triune God to humans by the outpouring of the Spirit, so confronting the human with the "trinitarian fellowship of the Father and the Son" and the Spirit, a communion the human is invited to join by participating in it. This gives Spirit baptism a "trinitarian structure of a

---

198. Ibid., 2:131.
199. Yong, *Spirit Poured Out*, 120.
200. Macchia, *Baptized in the Spirit*, 100.

"two-way movement from the Father through the Son in the Spirit, and then from the Spirit through the Son toward the Father."[201] The self, saved in Spirit baptism, "lives on, fulfilled through participation in Jesus' filial relationship to God in the power of the Spirit."[202] In this conception, the union is with Christ, yes, but is actually more a union with the triune God *in toto* through participation in the loving communion which is the Godhead. In one sense, this changes nothing, as the believer is still in union with God who acts externally in unity—the believer still has his tasks to attend to as a partner in the union. In another, it changes a great deal, as the other party in the relationship is no longer a single hypostasis accessed through the agency of another, but is the three hypostases of the Trinity in all their dynamic and loving inter-relations. This dynamism must affect the believer through the union, contributing to defining his new nature. Hence, the believer can expect his experience of salvation to be dynamic and not only life-changing because of his regeneration and justification, etc., but also because his divine partner is unchanging, but not static; dynamic but not mercurial. There is potentially great richness in the future exploration of this concept.

Union and the Church

Some comment needs to be made concerning the church, for Pentecostals "the divinely constituted body through which the gospel is preached and believers are nurtured."[203] There is certainly an aspect of union as the church is the body of Christ, but the body is not as important in the Pentecostal view of the union as in some others. For Pentecostals, the church is the group of people who are genuinely saved: it is constituted by this group, which includes those Christians who have died.[204] Thus, the church comprises all those who have entered into union with Christ individually and is being built as more enter into that union, less any who exit it. As either conversion with Spirit release following or Spirit baptism as Christian initiation comprise the direct work of Christ through or with the Spirit in the individual, the church plays only a supporting role in the actual establishment of the union. It may well be the environment within which the union is established, or which proclaims the gospel collectively outside itself to incite the union, but the union is individual and requires only God and the eventual believer.

---

201. Ibid., 116–17.

202. Ibid., 175.

203. Duffield and Van Cleave, *Foundations of Pentecostal Theology*, 425.

204. See the definitions in Duffield and Van Cleave, *Foundations of Pentecostal Theology*, 426; Grudem, *Systematic Theology*, 853; and Menzies and Horton, *Bible Doctrines*, 158; for example.

Maintenance and growth of the union is enhanced by participation in the church as it pursues its roles of evangelisation, worship, edification (understood as teaching, building each other up and sharing in the life of God) and social responsibility,[205] roles in which all members are expected to participate.[206] But, as the church has been created by the initiation of unions, one by one, it doesn't bear directly on the initiation of each one. Salvation may be found only in the church, but this is because that is where the believer finds herself after entering the union with Christ.

Summary

While the union between the believer and Christ is not a focus to any great extent in Pentecostal doctrine, its existence is certain and often simply assumed. This is because the Pentecostal distinctive of Spirit release involves a confrontation and experience of God coming into the believer of such an intensity that the resulting existence of some relationship or union with God is a trite question. When the union is considered, Pentecostals have borrowed traditional Protestant doctrine, where regeneration, justification, and sanctification, together comprising the core of salvation, are accomplished through a real union between Christ and the believer. However, the believer remains a distinct partner in the union, with actual tasks to perform: while the work of salvation primarily belongs to God, there is human work required also. Without changing this human contribution (although hinting at a more passive role), recent work on pneumatological soteriology has pointed to a distinct trinitarian focus within the union which holds much promise for a distinctly Pentecostal treatment in the future.

This review of Pentecostal pneumatology and its treatment of the union between the believer and Christ is by no means complete. However, it comprises, I suggest, an accurate representation of doctrines which are Pentecostal and widely held within the tradition, together with an indication of some fruitful directions to explore as Pentecostalism searches for a global theology. As such, it comprises a good base for the conversation with Calvin which can now commence.

---

205. Dusing, "The New Testament Church," 543–45; Klaus, "The Mission of the Church," 588.

206. Williams, *Renewal Theology*, 2:25, comments: "All are urged to proclaim the word, to bear witness, to share the good news. It may not, and will not, always be sermons from a pulpit or even on a street corner, but often the simple, unostentatious conversation about Jesus and the new life in him."

3

The Assurance of Faith

Before engaging Calvin and Pentecostal views in conversation, the arena of discussion needs to be defined. This is because much Pentecostal theology has been borrowed from Protestant evangelical theology, which in turn has a debt to Calvin if not a direct affinity. If a broad arena was adopted, then much of the discussion would be trite as evangelical theological roots would be examined, rather than anything peculiar to Pentecostalism. To avoid this, the discussion in this and subsequent chapters will focus on issues in relation to Spirit release as Pentecostals understand it. This will achieve an outcome where Calvin is asked to interact with the experience all Pentecostals testify to in one way or another.

The assurance of faith is a relevant subject to discuss concerning pneumatology and union between the believer and Christ as faith is a crucial work of the Spirit in its entirety for Calvin and at least substantially so for Pentecostals. Equally, the union is understood in very similar ways by Calvin and Pentecostals respectively as an intimate union accomplished within the believer by the indwelling Spirit, although it is, of course, entirely a work of Christ through the Spirit for Calvin and a synergistic work of Christ and the Spirit[1] in the account of the previous chapter for Pentecostals. While a work of God, it is established through faith; this faith is a necessary condition for the establishment of the union, but is in no way a cause of the union. Further, the knowledge of the existence of the union is a matter of faith for the individual believer, as is the operation of the Spirit in the union, and through it in the life of the believer. Put another way, for Calvin, how can the believer know that he is in union with Christ? Through faith. How can the believer know that the Spirit is active in him? Through faith. For Pentecostals, how can the believer know that he is in union with Christ? Through faith. How can the believer know that the Spirit is active in him? Because there are direct encounters, occasions where there is an

---

1. The synergy being between the believer and the Spirit.

unmediated apprehension of the Holy Spirit, which begin with Spirit release and are expected to recur. But how can these encounters occur? Only by entering union with Christ through faith. How does the believer know it is the Holy Spirit he encounters? Through faith. Faith is a common factor which operates to convince the believer of the reality of what he believes and how God is active in and with him, and thus underpins the accounts of pneumatology and union for both Calvin and Pentecostals. Without faith, pneumatology and union reduce to speculation for each.

Calvin on Faith

For Calvin, faith is the sure and certain knowledge that the revelation of God, Jesus Christ, is reliable and true and hence to be trusted. This knowledge is tightly tied to Scripture, for it is there that the revelation is properly apprehended, and in fact, only there that it can be apprehended, and it is the Spirit which illuminates Scripture to the believer so that faith is aroused. It is not that some external standard has been demonstrated to be true in any objective sense such that Scripture can now be viewed as properly true, or that what is taught by the Church can be accepted as truth. For the individual, faith is both more concrete than that, but also less assured. This seems a curious dichotomy, but it is nevertheless true. Faith is more concrete because there is an internal operation of the Spirit within the individual through her union with Christ which acts to utterly convince her at every level of her being that Jesus Christ is God's revelation, to be trusted and his Word to be believed and obeyed. As the union has become part of her being in the new creation she is, the Spirit transforms her being so that her faith becomes incorporated within it, thus her faith is as solid and real as concrete because it is now part of who she is—if it were to disappear, she would be diminished. This is the real character of faith, although this does not exclude doubt. While there is a new creation, the believer's old self remains, and sin continues so the believer attempts to deny the existence of her faith and so doubts.

However, faith is also less assured in a way for the individual. This is because she cannot appeal to any external human or natural agency to demonstrate the truth of what she believes in faith. Her own human judgement of her piety or works cannot suffice; neither can others' judgments of the same. However, this is not a hopeless situation where the argument is internal to her and, in a way, circular. The Church, where her engrafting occurred, acts through its proclamation of the Word and celebration of the sacraments to function as an external agency for her.

Its ministries do provide her some assurance which is external to her. Of course, this is no human or natural agency, but the church, nourished and sustained by Christ through the Spirit.

For Calvin, this activity of the Spirit is secret. The believer knows that the Spirit is present in him through his faith; in the same way, the believer knows that the Spirit is present in the preaching of the Word and the Supper. So, he can trust the Word he hears and truly participate in Christ in the Supper. Of course, he is also engrafted into Christ in the Church, so is surrounded by others who are exercising their faith by their presence in the Church. This must also serve to encourage his faith. In any event, however small and wavering his faith might be, it is sufficient because his salvation depends on the work of Christ through the Spirit, not on any faith he has generated himself. So, perhaps, even the fact that he has "just sufficient" faith to ensure he engages in the Church can function to assure him that he is united to Christ.

All of this is no doubt encouraging for the believer, but Calvin does admit that even the reprobate can experience faith where they "are sometimes affected by almost the same feeling as the elect."[2] The difference is, of course, the absence of the Spirit in the reprobate. Thus, the assurance of faith for the elect still rests on the Spirit, albeit aided by the Church and its Spirit-effected ministry. The outcome, then, is that faith is a real, concrete, inner conviction for the individual believer which rests on what the Spirit does within her in relation to Christ. But this work is secret—she does not encounter the Spirit directly, but is only aware of his work because of the resultant existence of faith within her. She cannot appeal to any human agency to demonstrate the truth of her faith, so the only external agency she can appeal to is God, who has acted, and continues to act, secretly within her by the Spirit to confirm the truth. So, any assurance of her inner conviction is internal to her, albeit provided by the Spirit.

Thus, her faith is objectively based because it relies on God's activity in her but it is subjectively experienced. Certainly, there is external human agency (such as affirmations from fellow believers) and her worldly activity which can provide evidence of her faith, and in fact Calvin insists that internal faith must produce external evidence: "For we have been adopted as sons by the Lord with this one condition: that our life express Christ."[3] But neither of these factors can ever be more than pointers to what may be real. She alone can judge whether her faith is real, seeking assurance through her union with Christ.[4]

2. III.2.11.
3. III.6.3.
4. Zachman, *Reconsidering John Calvin*, 152–53, notes that, in this conception, the

Pentecostals on Faith

For Pentecostals faith is a deep trust in the promises given in the gospel of Christ, something reached after apprehending what God has done in Christ and giving assent to the salvation God offers in Godself. While the formation of this faith is assisted by the Spirit, in a real way it is the faith of the individual, in part a creation of the individual and truly his possession. This faith operates to allow the individual to accept the free gift of salvation, so a result of that faith is the formation of that "unity of relationship" where the believer centers his life on Christ and, while remaining who he is, allows Christ to breathe life into his life.[5] This is similar to Calvin's union, but the creature is writ much larger in the Pentecostal conception.

The believer here faces the same dichotomy touched on above. His faith is a concrete conviction, because he feels it as a "whole of being" commitment to Christ, but the fact that he has a considerable stake in his faith weakens the concrete somewhat as the sinful creature itself has an impact on his own faith. Thus, doubts arise, not simply because the sinful creature remains, but also because there is surely a risk that his faith might wax and wane, part creaturely as it is. On the other hand, some legitimate appeal can be made to external human agency to bolster faith. If it is creaturely in part, at least, then not only can it be affected by the creature himself, but it can be affected by other creaturely influences. Thus, the creature can assign to Scripture and its proclamation some intrinsic truth and similarly allow that the Church has some authority in matters of faith. While this may appear helpful to the individual, it occurs within a clear understanding that faith is individual and hence that the unity an individual enjoys with Christ is unmediated by the Church. This fact ushers in the "freedom" for the individual to reject the authority of the Church and offer his own interpretation of Scripture. This all carries with it a variety of possible outcomes for an individual and their faith, but provided he maintains a secure grip on his faith, it remains that certain knowledge at a deep level that he belongs to Christ.

Nevertheless, assurance of faith remains problematic. While the believer may feel helped by human agency, understanding his faith as rooted in his individual relationship with Christ does confine it to his person. In fact, if human agency does not accord with his understanding, that agency may actually damage his faith. It is exactly at this point that Pentecostals can turn to the experience of Spirit release as an aid to assurance. In Spirit release, they can say, the Spirit is encountered directly and in its full content

---

believer is most sure of his own election and less sure of others, while he thinks Christianity works best the other way around.

5. Williams, *Renewal Theology*, 2:31–32.

there is also a new and greater appreciation of Christ and, through him, the whole Trinity. Faith is required for Spirit release as it occurs in believers, and a function of Spirit release is to bolster that faith, and hence increase assurance as to its truth, as one who is very God is directly encountered in a raw, unmediated way. Pentecostalism feels it can legitimately claim that its adherents know God because they have met God, not face to face, but in a way where he was ecstatically present with them.

It is easy to see that Pentecostals could claim assurance through Spirit release, and the ongoing unmediated encounters with the Spirit which could follow, and hence suggest that they are not subject to the dichotomy in Calvin's view. However, the very fact that Spirit release is unmediated carries with it the seeds of its own questioning. Even admitting the ecstatic nature of the experience, as it is unmediated, how does the believer know that it is God she is encountering? Further, the same question can be asked of any subsequent encounters. Far from being the definitive assurance, Spirit release still leaves the enigma of assurance being almost entirely internal to the believer, so how can faith be assured?

An Anchor for Faith: Calvin

In respect of faith, which underpins the union between the believer and God, and is heavily dependent on an active pneumatology, both Calvin and the Pentecostals agree as to its concrete nature, but also to its lacking an anchor external to the believer which can offer assurance other than God, its very object. This is a similarity to be explored in some detail which I will start by considering Calvin's position more closely in two specific respects, being led by the work of Victor Shepherd and Randall Zachman[6] on the subject.

Victor Shepherd on Faith and Predestination

Shepherd addresses the core of this issue in his discussion on faith and predestination.[7] Salvation is only available to humankind through the mercy of God, an attribute which Calvin substantially identifies with Jesus Christ. For example, the gospel is "the clear manifestation of the mystery of Christ"

---

6. Shepherd, *The Nature and Function of Faith in the Theology of John Calvin*, Zachman, *The Assurance of Faith: Conscience in the Theology of Martin Luther and John Calvin*. I have chosen these two works because they directly address the subject I am pursuing here, albeit in different ways.

7. Shepherd, *Nature and Function of Faith*, 39–96.

which includes the mercy of God which had been shown to the patriarchs and is also the "proclamation of the grace manifested in Christ." Christ coming has expressed exactly what God expressed to the patriarchs in a "new and unusual sort of embassy" such that "the truth of [God's] promises would be realized in the person of the Son."[8] That is, the mercy of God is realized in the person of Jesus Christ and so is properly identified with Christ. Hence, Shepherd can confidently start his work by stating that Jesus Christ "*is* the Father's act of mercy."[9] Such a conclusion also follows from Calvin's identification of Christ as the revelation of God, or being the content of God's revelation of Godself to humans. This being so, what humans can apprehend of God must be identified in Christ in whom our salvation is found, made available by grace on account of God's mercy towards humankind. Therefore, God's mercy is found in Jesus Christ.

Humans, seeking salvation, find it in Christ as they come to faith in him. Salvation is available through mercy, but the faith which comes is a gift of Christ through the Spirit. While faith is the work of the Spirit, nevertheless the one Christ who is the mercy of God is also the originator and bestower of faith upon saved humans. The existence of such faith is evidence of the presence of the Spirit and hence one's salvation, the latter a gift which can be trusted because of the faithfulness of Christ, testified to by Scripture. However, humans do not avail themselves of salvation: they are dead in sin and the dead cannot avail themselves of anything.[10] Rather, salvation is entirely a gift of God through Christ, but it is given, for Calvin, only to the elect. There are those who are not of the elect to whom the gift is not given, in fact to whom the gift is not available, and it is in the interaction between this fact and Christ as the mercy of God that problems arise for Calvin.

Calvin's doctrine of predestination he calls an "eternal decree" by which God has determined, within Godself, what is "to become of each man. . . . eternal life is fore-ordained for some, eternal damnation for others." That is, "God adopts some to hope of life, and sentences others to eternal death."[11] Humankind is divided by God in God's "eternal and unchangeable plan" into "those whom he long before determined once for all to receive into salvation, and those whom, on the other hand, he would devote to destruction." Those chosen for life, the elect, have been chosen by "his freely given mercy, without regard to human worth", but the reprobate are doomed to destruction "by his just and irreprehensible

---

8. II.9.2.
9. Shepherd, *Nature and Function of Faith*, 1 (emphasis his).
10. Ibid., 42, 64.
11. III.21.5.

but incomprehensible judgement."[12] This judgement is not to be subject to human questioning or enquiry; it is simply to be accepted. Humans cannot comprehend it and are foolish to attempt to do so: it is God's right to make the decree and there the matter must rest.[13]

It may seem curious, then, that Calvin has no difficulty affirming that God calls all humans to Godself, yet has elected only a proportion of them, something he does on a number of occasions in *Institutes*.[14] This creates the situation where God calls all, including the elect and the reprobate, but only brings the elect to salvation by a free gift which confirms each believer's prior election. The remainder who are called are not brought to salvation: although some may be brought to a temporary illumination of sorts,[15] they will always be ultimately reprobate. This raises the obvious question concerning the merciful God who came as humankind's redeemer in Jesus Christ: is this the same God who can also call persons to salvation he has already rejected? If so, what assurance can anyone have as to their salvation if it is dependent upon an incomprehensible and completely unavailable decision made before creation, let alone the coming of God's mercy in Christ?[16] It is this question which Shepherd considers in some little detail.[17]

As contradictory as this is—the merciful God calling all having already refused salvation to some—Shepherd notes that Calvin is even stronger in the contradiction than this. Calvin declares that it is God's will that all be saved, but also that "Whomsoever God wills to snatch from death, he quickens by the Spirit of regeneration."[18] This willing, of course, is contained within the hidden decree of election, so while there is a revealed will of God which is mercy in Jesus Christ, there is also a "secret" will of God by which he determines who is to be saved.[19] Shepherd claims that Calvin's representative view of Scripture texts which indicate God's promise to humankind is that he invites all to salvation, is "they do not simply and positively declare what God has decreed in his secret counsel, but what he is prepared to do for all who are brought to faith and repentance." He then

---

12. III.21.7.
13. III.23.5.
14. III.3.21; 22.10, 11; 24.
15. III.24.8, cited in Shepherd, *Nature and Function of Faith*, 86.
16. Shepherd, *Nature and Function of Faith*, 88, makes this point also.
17. Ibid., 83–90. The following discussion is sourced from there, although my reasoning differs at some points.
18. III.3.21, cited in Shepherd, *Nature and Function of Faith*, 85.
19. Shepherd, *Nature and Function of Faith*, 84, makes the same point with slightly different reasoning. He also cites Warfield making the same point in "Calvin's Doctrine of the Knowledge of God," in *Calvin and the Reformation*, 178, 84 n. 226.

goes on to correctly note that the content of the promise and God's secret counsel are not the same, as all who are brought to faith is a subset of all who are subject to the double decrees.[20] Mercy is not offered to all, despite Calvin's assertions to the contrary.

The suspicion of a capriciousness of God by which the eternal destination of each human is determined might remain just that if God were a simple unity. But he is not, God is triune and the contradiction has serious problems for the Trinity. For those who are brought to faith, their faith is a gift, created in them by the Spirit. It is this same Spirit who must be applying the decrees of election as they were made within Godself, hence who must be condemning the reprobate to death. This challenges the unity of the Trinity as it suggests one or the other activity of the Spirit is not shared by the other persons within the deity. Equally, Christ who brings and is the mercy of God, and who consistently displays such a face to humankind, must have participated in the decrees in contradiction to him as God's revelation of Godself. Can it be that one or other of the hypostases is acting in ways contrary to the will of those with whom he shares communion within the Godhead, or contends in some way with the other within the deity? On this point, Shepherd refers to Calvin's commentary on John 17:6, noting that there he says that "the Son wanted to call all men to God, but only among the elect was his call efficacious" and later that "'faith flows from the outward predestination of God; it is not given indiscriminately to all, because not all belong to Christ.' This is a most clear statement that faith flows *not* from mercy [i.e., Christ] . . . but from the decree of the Father which the Son happens to implement."[21] He goes on to point out that if this is the case, then Christ ceases to be the full revelation of God as there are unknown areas within God which are not illuminated by the Incarnation; in fact, Christ becomes only the means by which God accomplishes one decree, to whatever degree he may reveal God.[22] If this is the case, then it raises questions over the Son's ontological status within the deity as it implies some subordination of the Son to the Father or, if not, a "difference of opinion" between the Father and the Son in the matter of election.

I do not intend to pursue this point further, but this short discussion suffices to point out the difficulties with Calvin's position on faith and predestination, of which Calvin was evidently aware. However, Shepherd thinks that he does not satisfactorily resolve his embracing of Scriptures

---

20. *De Aet. Dei Praed.* 106, cited in Shepherd, *Nature and Function of Faith*, 85.

21. Shepherd, *Nature and Function of Faith*, 86. (emphasis his). He cites Calvin's *The Gospel According to St John 11–21 and the First Epistle of John*, 17:6.

22. Ibid., 87.

which state that God's will is that all be saved alongside his doctrine of election, his attempts being weak at best.[23] His conclusion that, in the double decrees, "The origin of faith is not mercy, but the Father's determination to give some men to his Son"[24] encapsulates the ambiguity surrounding the relationship between the Incarnation and election for Calvin. If faith is based on the unknowable eternal decree of election, then, despite the revelation of the Incarnation, how can anyone be assured of their election and hence that their faith is genuine or well-placed? I will return to discuss this question after considering Zachman's work.

Randall Zachman on Conscience

Zachman begins by setting the question within Calvin's doctrine of God who "is our Father in his Son through the Holy Spirit."[25] As such, justification and sanctification occur when the human comes to a knowledge of God as her Father who has redeemed her to ensure her adoption as a daughter of God. This is exactly paralleled by Calvin's understanding the result of justification and sanctification as being drawn into a participation in God—such a participation is shared with the Father, Son and Spirit in close and intimate relation. However, the human need also know God as Lord, a knowledge which identifies the complete lack of merit of the human which drives him to the Father to seek "every good thing" he lacks.[26] These two aspects of the knowledge of God held by the believer are not to be understood as separate, rather God as Lord must be seen in the context of God as Father. They work together in the believer as knowing God as Father is to know he is the source of all good, and knowing him as Lord is to drive him to the Father as the only source of the good he needs.[27] Calvin also makes a distinction, giving it a further two-fold aspect: God, known to the believer as Father and Lord, is God the Creator and God the Redeemer.[28] "First, as much in fashioning the universe as in the general teaching of Scripture the Lord shows himself to be simply the Creator. Then in the face of Christ [cf 2 Cor 4:6] he shows himself the Redeemer."[29]

---

23. Ibid., 84–86. The texts he uses to illustrate his point are 1 Tim 2:4 and 4:10.
24. Ibid., 90.
25. Zachman, *The Assurance of Faith*, 91.
26. I.1.1, cited in Zachman, *The Assurance of Faith*, 92.
27. Zachman, *The Assurance of Faith*, 92.
28. Ibid., 93.
29. I.2.1, cited in Zachman, *The Assurance of Faith*, 93–94.

Zachman summarizes three concepts behind this distinction of the two-fold knowledge of God as Creator and Redeemer. The first two are that humans have no excuse for their ignorance of God as Father; and that the true God needs to be set before humans so they may know how God is to be worshipped. Together, these show human sin as the sole reason for the Father sending Jesus Christ. The third concept is that once the human knows God as her Father in Jesus Christ she receives assurance that this God, who rules the universe, has special regard for "the community of believers." All three "directly involve the testimony of the conscience." The believer's conscience makes her aware of sin and judgement, of a divinity to worship, and provides her with certainty that she has the good things the Father wants to bestow on her.[30] It is not that Zachman is applying a particular reading to Calvin's theology here so as to involve the conscience, it is that this is a genuine key within Calvin's understanding of the human reconciliation with God.[31] It is the conscience of the individual which tells him he is a sinner and so subject to judgment; it is his conscience which makes him aware that there is a divinity who is worthy of worship; and finally it is his conscience which assures him *he* has the good things the Father wants to bestow on *him* by its quietened, "good" state. Of course, this is not to be understood as being the result of any intrinsic human ability to detect his sinful state, etc., rather it is *God through the Spirit* who gives the knowledge in all three facets to the elect believer.

Calvin is specific in his definition of conscience,[32] confining it to the "spiritual" jurisdiction in contrast to the "temporal" jurisdiction, the former being government in humans in respect to God, the latter being a political government for good order among humans. "The former resides in the inner mind, while the latter regulates only outward behavior." He admits that Paul complicates matters by commanding obedience to civil authorities for conscience' sake (Rom 13:1, 5), but he maintains that conscience is concerned with the "inner forum," not the "outer." With this distinction made, he defines conscience as "a sense of divine judgement, as a witness joined to them, which does not allow them to hide their sins from being accused before the Judge's tribunal." This he describes as "a certain mean between God and man," a creation within the human which does not allow her to suppress what she knows from herself, to hide it or contain it completely within herself, but wherein God convicts her of what she understands in her

---

30. Zachman, *The Assurance of Faith*, 97.

31. Zachman, *John Calvin as Teacher Pastor and Theologian*, 175, reaffirms this point.

32. Zachman calls it a "very precise definition" (Zachman, *Reconsidering John Calvin*, 127).

conscience of spiritual things. The conscience holds not a "simple knowledge" which has no impact within her, but a knowledge through which God can work inwardly to actually transform her.[33] Zachman describes this as a sense or awareness which leads to the judgement seat of God, so in contrast to general knowledge where the knowing subject is the human, for conscience, the "knowing subject . . . is God the judge."[34]

Because it is God working at this "mean" within the believer, when her conscience convicts her of sin, it is actually "the judgement of God accusing [her] of sin," so "The condemning testimony of the conscience should therefore be considered to be the condemning judgement of God."[35] This testimony does not give any "certain and stable knowledge of God," but only confirms that there is a god whom humans need to acknowledge.[36] Here it seems that the conscience is established as an unmediated point of contact between humans and God, separate from the work of Christ. This is not to say that Christ is not involved in the contact, as the Spirit certainly is. This must be so to be consistent with Calvin's acknowledgment that the Spirit works within the reprobate as well as the elect, but there he is careful to make clear that it is in a different way from his work of illumination and regeneration within the elect, being of a different, lower order.[37] Here, he is making a similar distinction. Conscience allows humans to apprehend the nature of God and our appropriate response in God's self-revelation to the world, but does not give any ability to obey that revelation.[38] Certainly, humans think they are able "to do what we ought to do and thereby merit the favor of God" and so seek to "placate God's judgement" by "self-invented" rituals, but instead of having any real impact, these merely allow guilt-free sin.[39] For Calvin, Zachman says, "the . . . awareness of conscience leads the sinner to offer false expiations to God in order to sin with impunity."[40] The genesis of this reality lies in Adam's sin: if he had not fallen, then this knowledge of God to the conscience would have led to true religion. But, he did fall, so humans have no ability to respond to this apprehension of

---

33. III.19.15, cited in part in Zachman, *The Assurance of Faith*, 99.
34. Zachman, *The Assurance of Faith*, 99–100.
35. Ibid., 100–101.
36. III.19.15, cited in Zachman, *Assurance of Faith*, 104.
37. III.2.13.
38. Zachman, *The Assurance of Faith*, 106.
39. Ibid., 122.
40. Ibid., 123. He also notes elsewhere that humans try to hide, Zachman, *Reconsidering John Calvin*, 128.

God in any way efficacious in their redemption or salvation.[41] Nevertheless, this apprehension of God as judge and hence of human sinfulness is crucial: "The awareness of divinity in the conscience is . . . the irreducible foundation of both true and false religion."[42]

This is so because of the different responses of the reprobate and the elect to the Word of God in the light of this knowledge of God held by the conscience. In the reprobate, the conscience, confronted by the Word of God, flees from God because his only awareness is that of his judgement by the Lord.[43] In this confrontation, to a general knowledge of God and sin is added a knowledge of the law, which serves only to intensify the dread of judgement and desire to flee as the conscience becomes fully aware of the implications of sin and its result, so developing an appropriate 'dread of death'.[44] The elect individual is affected differently, once he is awakened to his election, because in that awakening God through the Spirit has revealed true knowledge of Godself as Creator and Redeemer to the elect conscience, and also true knowledge of the elect as a child of God. The Spirit illuminates the Word of God to the elect so he is convicted that "God's testimony in the Word of Scripture," as one who is seeking to adopt the elect and give him all good things, is true.[45] The elect human therefore turns to cleave himself to God in Christ through the Spirit rather than fleeing in the manner of the reprobate. However, this turning commences with the same "dread of death" in which the elect conscience becomes aware of sin and the need to turn to God—this is the beginning of repentance, given in its entirety by the Spirit, which sees a longing for God's grace in contrast to a hatred of God generated in the reprobate by the terror he feels.[46] The ultimate result of this repentance in the elect is faith, in which he is adopted by God and participates in Godself, with all this entails.

Calvin's scheme concerning the role of the conscience in his theology revolves around his understanding of the conscience as that faculty within the human where an awareness of God resides. This is a real, connected sense, not a sense at a distance, as it is in this faculty that common ground between God and the human exists, where there is a point of contact between the human and God. It must not be thought that this attribute of the conscience is inherently human, that is, entirely creaturely. No, the

---

41. Zachman, *The Assurance of Faith*, 106.
42. Ibid., 113.
43. Ibid., 125.
44. Ibid., 148–49. The quote is from III.8.3.
45. Ibid., 126.
46. Ibid., 153–55.

conscience is only like this through the grace and activity of God. In fact, if this common ground, existing by the grace of God, is not present, the implication of Calvin's position is that there would be no awareness of even the possibility of God at all in the human. Each human experiences and is informed by her conscience concerning God as God uses the conscience to give knowledge of Godself to her. At one level, this is knowledge of God as righteous Lord and judge, so the conscience identifies for the human her sin and fate of condemnation because of it, something only intensified as she gains an awareness of the law through the Word of God. By itself, this knowledge can only produce a hatred of God as it tells only of death and destruction because of her sinful state, so she flees from God.

While the reprobate only ever gain knowledge of God at this level, the elect human is privileged to receive knowledge at another level, where his conscience is made aware of a true knowledge of God directed to him by the Spirit. His conscience experiences the same dread of death as the reprobate, but the Spirit shows him through the Word in Scripture that God is Creator and Redeemer who, through Christ, provides all good things to him. This knowledge produces repentance, a turning away from sin and a turning to God to cleave to Godself in Christ through the Spirit so as to receive life with God as an adopted son and all the good things it brings. All this is a gift of the Spirit, who not only gives the knowledge to the elect conscience by illuminating the Word in Scripture, but also works directly to produce repentance and faith. Certainly, this change in the elect human will produce outward manifestations in increasing righteousness of life, but the change the Spirit works in this is all internal to the human, and he is informed by his conscience that the change is true. It is his conscience which tells him God provides good things for him, and it is his conscience which tells him that God wants to adopt him, that God has adopted him and that he can now participate with God as an adopted son. A result of what he has learned through his conscience is the faith he now experiences, and it is his conscience which assures him that this faith is true. The testimony of his conscience is central to his knowing that his faith is genuine and not misplaced.[47] Calvin suggests that faith must be confirmed by a good conscience which grows out of sanctification, the growth of righteousness in the believer's life.[48] Nevertheless, because his conscience is a common ground for him and God, the Spirit is testifying to him concerning the truth of all this and that his faith is genuine, but his "part" of the common ground means that there is an aspect in which he, himself, is confronted by the testimony of the

---

47. Zachman, *Reconsidering John Calvin*, 141.
48. Ibid., 246.

Spirit and so must decide whether his faith is genuine or not, in fact whether the knowledge given by God to his conscience is true in itself or not.[49] The question here is, as all this is internal to the believer, how can he be assured of his faith and salvation as it may only be his subjective opinion? Note the issue is not that his faith is his opinion, it can never be that for Calvin, even an opinion formed by the Spirit,[50] but that his assurance that his faith is genuine may be his opinion. Even allowing that his good conscience grows out of the sanctifying work of Christ in him, that still leaves the necessity of judging how genuine his sanctification is.

The Question on Assurance

This question, raised by Zachman's work, can be placed alongside that which arose from Shepherd's work which identified the ambiguity between the Incarnation and election. Zachman is also aware of the latter, noting that there is an instability in Calvin's theology because of "universal reconciliation and limited election" which is evidenced by the possibility of reversal of Calvin's order that assurance of election follows from belief in Christ. That is that it is assurance of election which gives rise to confident faith in Christ, as in fact is present in later theologies.[51] Even if this reversal is resisted, the question posed remains. It is not as if the decree of election is removed by the resistance, it still remains, so while the reversal would raise the question: "Am I elect?", Calvin's order still poses: "Is my faith in Christ genuine in view of the fact of election?" It is, in essence, the same question which comes out of both authors' works, but from different aspects of Calvin's theology. This can be stated as: "Because I must rely on my election and the testimony of my good conscience, what assurance do I have of my faith other than my opinion?"

Calvin, of course, is aware of the question and does address it. For him "God himself is the sole and proper witness of himself."[52] It is the Holy Spirit who is "witness to us of our adoption" and who makes Christ known through the sanctification of the believer.[53] "The very clarity of

---

49. This is not to suggest that there is any synergy between work on the part of the believer and the Spirit, but the believer is involved. See chapter 1.

50. A point made by Shepherd, *Nature and Function of Faith*, 99.

51. Zachman, *The Assurance of Faith*, 246. He gives Beza and the Westminster Confession of Faith as examples of this occurrence.

52. I.11.1, cited also in Zachman, *The Assurance of Faith*, 131.

53. III.2.8. Zachman, *Reconsidering John Calvin*, 246, links sanctification to a good conscience which confirms faith.

[this] truth itself will of itself provide a sufficiently ready refutation" of the Roman doctrine of implicit faith which calls humans to believe what they do not understand (what nowadays might be termed "blind faith"),[54] by which he means that the clarity of what the Spirit reveals will be such that it is self-evidently true. In like manner, "we have a sufficiently clear and firm testimony that we have been inscribed in the book of life [cf Rev 21:27] if we are in communion with Christ."[55] This communion has come about through God's special call to the elect as "by the inward illumination of his Spirit he causes the preached Word to dwell in their hearts,"[56] and it is this experience of adoption that gives assurance of election. If assurance is sought in election, then the result is "harsh torments" or being utterly overwhelmed, but focusing on adoption soothes: "Here true rest is felt. The God of peace renders all things peaceful, and to behold him at rest is to be at rest."[57] For assurance and peace, humans are told to look to Christ. The believer should not enquire into her election at all, but rely upon what she sees in Christ, the revelation of God, shown to her by the Holy Spirit. As she places reliance on Christ, she will experience what Christ gives her: peace, and hence assurance that her reliance is well placed. How does she know this is true? By placing her reliance upon it and living as if it is, by which she will find out it is true. She must be careful not to understand this as her independent choice to place her reliance on Christ, but to know that her desire to do so and her decision which follows are both works of the Spirit within her. Even so, she must still determine whether the result is a genuine faith. She must understand that, by the Spirit, she is in union with Christ, and by living as such she will find that she is indeed in union with Christ which will be the demonstration to her that her faith was and is genuine. This is how she can know she is in communion with Christ and so have a "sufficiently clear and firm testimony"[58] as to her elect status. This is a circular argument which Calvin only resolves in any way by his insistence that all this occurs only by the illumination of the Spirit by which it must be inferred that God can be relied upon to reveal Godself if God chooses. That is, God self-authenticates what God gives. Certainly, Calvin appeals to the Word and sacraments (external to the believer in a way) as means which God uses to authenticate, but in face of the Word

---

54. III.2.3, also cited in Shepherd, *Nature and Function of Faith*, 106.
55. III.24.5.
56. III.24.8.
57. III.24.4. The latter quote is a citation of Bernard of Clairvaux, *Sermons on the Song of Songs* xxiii. 15, 16, *Life and Works of St Bernard* IV. 141 f.
58. III.24.5.

and sacrament, the elect and the reprobate are apparently equally exposed, in the sense that each is physically present and involved. It is only the work of the Spirit which differentiates between the two. As this work is only able to be discerned by its effects in the elect believer (faith and sanctification), Calvin's conception still leaves space for a human response to the question which it begs—is this really the self-authenticating God at work?

Shepherd and Zachman reach the same conclusion. Shepherd notes that "since the Word is both author and object of faith, that Word alone can authenticate faith; that is, faith is self-authenticating as it embraces the Word."[59] For Calvin, the Word can never be separated from Scripture,[60] so the same thought is echoed when he says "according to Calvin God authenticates Scripture to us as he authenticates himself to us through Scripture."[61] The same self-authentication is effected by the Spirit concerning the result of the decree of the electing God: "everyone is made sure of his own election by the testimony of the Spirit."[62] As God acts on elect humans they are returned to their true humanity and here there can now be a human activity, which Shepherd calls "affirmation," by which the elect human responds. He suggests that there is a real human response which confirms faith, and is "essential to faith's being faith," a faith which ratifies election.[63] Because true faith must mean election, and this is a decree "behind" Christ so to speak, eventually, Shepherd says, despite attempts to the contrary, Calvin concedes that believers are the arbiters of the truth of their calling, and hence their faith.[64]

Zachman says that "God is the sole and proper witness of himself,"[65] for Calvin, and that "It is Jesus Christ himself who forms the primary foundation of the assurance of faith."[66] This "assurance of faith is primarily founded on the assurance of the conscience that Jesus Christ dwells in us and we in Christ" so that the wonderful exchange can take place.[67] He goes on to quote Calvin: "There is nothing of Christ, then, in him who does not hold the elementary principle, that it is God alone who enlightens our minds to perceive His truth, and who by His Spirit seals it on our hearts, *and by this sure attestation to*

---

59. Shepherd, *Nature and Function of Faith*, 208.

60. Ibid., 19.

61. Ibid., 233.

62. John Calvin, *Comm 1 Pet* 1:1, cited in Shepherd, *Nature and Function of Faith*, 60–61.

63. Shepherd, *Nature and Function of Faith*, 82–83.

64. Ibid., 92–93. He bases this on Calvin appealing to introspection by believers when seeking assurance of election, taking note of the "inner call" (III.24.2).

65. Zachman, *The Assurance of Faith*, 131.

66. Ibid., 162.

67. Ibid., 176.

it confirms our conscience."[68] But, to be "fully assured of salvation," the elect human must trust and *know* she trusts in Jesus Christ, must have confidence in God's mercy and also know herself to be a believing sinner to whom God shows mercy.[69] These are things she must find within herself,[70]—a knowledge she trusts Christ, a confidence in God's mercy and a knowledge that she is one to whom God shows mercy, assisted by the Church, of course. It seems that Calvin does not conceive of the possibility that one who is elect might examine herself and judge, herself, whether she truly holds these things. Even if he does consider the possibility, "he does not trust the individual to stand alone before God in conscience, for he does not think we will learn what we need to know."[71] For him, the "inner call ... is a pledge of salvation that cannot deceive us"[72]—the mere existence, to whatever extent, of a trust and a knowledge that she does, indeed, trust Christ is sufficient. The work of the Spirit ensures that the believer will be assured of her faith, something bolstered by the evidence of the Word preached and sacraments shared for the believer. This does not exclude doubt, but any faith is the work of the Spirit, and the existence of faith, however tenuously felt, is sufficient for salvation and hence assurance.[73] There is no consideration of the possibility that she might "ask herself," with some dispassion, whether this trust and faith she has is actually genuine—such dispassion in respect of godly things cannot exist independently of the Spirit, for Calvin. While she must look "especially" to her conscience in which God has worked for assurance, and even find it in the groaning of her conscience at her burden of sin,[74] this is nevertheless the same introspection that Shepherd noted, and must contain within it the possibility, at least, that it is *her* trust and confidence which is in view and crucial. Zachman recognizes this, noting that "The possibility of the testimony of a good conscience founding the assurance of faith cannot in principle be avoided."[75] This being so, because the conscience is an arena shared by God and the human, the door is wide open to the necessity of a human attestation to genuine faith. Thus, Zachman concludes

---

68. *Responsio as Sadoleti Epistolam*, C.O. 5:405; *A Reformation Debate*, 78–79, cited in Zachman, *The Assurance of Faith*, 187 (emphasis his).

69. Zachman, *The Assurance of Faith*, 220 (emphasis his).

70. Zachman, *Reconsidering John Calvin*, 141.

71. Ibid. Zachman means here that Calvin feels the need to teach people what state they are in—their fallenness and corruption "to reveal to you what is wrong with you." He is not directly addressing the issue I am discussing here, but the comment is applicable to the discussion.

72. III.24.2.

73. III.2.20.

74. Ibid.

75. Zachman, *The Assurance of Faith*, 221.

"it is impossible for . . . Calvin . . . not to add some form of self-testimony of the conscience to the testimony of Jesus Christ."[76]

This highlights the different thought environment Calvin occupied compared to our own. Another century was to pass before the rise of the scientific method, where dispassionate observation of phenomena and the application of reason to propose and then test hypotheses could lead to understanding the truth of things. This contained within it the possibility that the same approach could be applied to theology and matters of faith—that is, that one's faith could be examined dispassionately. One could attempt to think about one's faith position from an objective standpoint, evaluating the basis for beliefs held. That is, while the individual certainly held a view from within his faith, he could also contemplate a view from outside his faith.

This latter view did not form part of Calvin's thought world. For him, there were things outside the individual to which he could appeal: Scripture, the sacraments, the piety of life, but these were all contemplated from within faith. In the current thought world, this is valid, but can be augmented by an attempt to step "outside" and ask about assurance from outside faith. This is for the individual to ask: "Putting aside my faith, why is it that I have faith and on what is my assurance based?" Therefore, the self-testimony that Zachman refers to is a testimony made in ignorance of the possibility of dispassionate examination for Calvin, but in current thought can legitimately be a testimony informed also by dispassionate examination. Of course, any attempt at such examination by an individual will not be perfect as the activity will be inevitably colored by the individual themselves, but the arena of investigation certainly exists.

From their different foci, both Shepherd and Zachman reach the same conclusion: in Calvin's thought God is self-authenticating in his revelation and the knowledge he gives of himself, but that there is some human component to the assurance of faith for each believer. That is, the knowledge that this is really God at work is dependent, to some extent, on the believer's own assessment. This is a difficult acknowledgment for Calvin to accommodate, but at least the believer's assessment is done in the presence of the efforts of the self-authenticating God in Christ working in him through the Holy Spirit by the Word, written and preached. For Calvin this is an overwhelming encounter which can have only one result. Only one external anchor exists to which to moor one's faith: God, revealed in Christ.

---

76. Ibid., 223.

An Anchor for Faith: Pentecostals

Pentecostals for their part have little difficulty with the believer making his own assessment, but in Spirit release also point to the self-authenticating God working in the believer in an overwhelming encounter which leads, inevitably it seems, to a deep affirmation of faith, a conviction that this is God in the Holy Spirit drawing him close. As Hocken identified in his work, the early Pentecostal testimony concerning Spirit release made it clear that the character of the encounter was such that while the powerful presence of the Spirit was affirmed, the work of the Spirit also included a greater and deeper revealing of Jesus Christ and the Father in a way which did not ascribe a subordinate position to any of the divine hypostases. A more extensive review of Hocken's papers is now called for.

The Full Content of Spirit Release

In his 1983 paper, he notes that the focus on Spirit release as an endowment of power in Pentecostal doctrinal statements represents the third step in development of comment on Spirit release, a development which robbed the occurrence of much of its richness. The first step is represented by the personal testimony of Pentecostal witnesses; the second by teaching given by Pentecostal preachers "prior to the formulation of any declarations of faith"; and the third step the content of doctrinal statements themselves.[77] In the later paper he posits four steps: the actual experience; personal testimony of the experience; how it was schematized in teaching; and statements of faith by which the teaching was made official. This is a similar description of the same process outlined previously and here he characterizes the process as "narrowing" the content of Spirit release.[78] He further notes that "Accounts of baptism in the Spirit which focus on power without specifying any relationship with the person of Jesus lead readily to presentations of the spiritual gifts simply in terms of power and without specific reference to Jesus Christ."[79] This is precisely what has happened within doctrinal statements and at least some Pentecostal practice as the wider divine content of Spirit release has been shorn from it in the development of doctrine. He thinks "almost always" the definition of Spirit release is restricted to "an

---

77. Hocken, "Jesus Christ," 3. He refers to the steps as "levels" and clearly thinks of the process as a decline through three levels. Chan, *Pentecostal Theology*, 21, makes the same point.

78. Hocken, "Meaning and Purpose," 125.

79. Hocken, "Jesus Christ," 3.

endument (sic) of power for ministry and witness."[80] The true full content of Spirit release in the early Pentecostal encounters needs to be recovered, where it will be discovered that, true to the New Testament witness, "More of the Spirit means more of Jesus Christ."[81] He asserts that "there are countless references in early Pentecostal teaching to show that baptism in the Spirit brings a fuller knowledge of God and of his Son," and gives a number of examples.[82] The most useful is the "'London Declaration' concerning 'The Baptism in the Holy Ghost' of November, 1909 . . . signed by virtually all the leaders of the Pentecostal meetings on Britain at that time."[83] It includes seven "Results" of Spirit Baptism:

1st The Consciousness of the Deity of our Lord Jesus Christ (John xiv., 20).

2nd The Consciousness of our 'Dwelling in Him' (1 John iii., 23, 24) and He in us (Eph iii., 17).

3rd Divine Illumination concerning His Word and Will (John xiv., 16, 17).

4th 'The Testimony of Jesus' (Rev. xix., 10; John xv., 26, 27).

5th The Three-fold Conviction of the World by the Spirit in us. ('I will send the Comforter to you, and when He is come He will reprove the World of Sin, of Righteousness, and of Judgement'— John xvi., 8–11).

    1. The great Sin of fallen man (his unbelief).

    2. The need of the Righteousness of Christ (now with His Father).

    3. The Judgement of the Devil (Heb. ii., 14, 15). [The Prince of the World is already condemned].

6th Our continual guidance into the deep things of God (John xvi., 13; 1 Cor, ii., 9, 10).

7th The continual glorification of Christ (to the exclusion of self). John xvi., Eph i., 17–23; Col ii., 15, iii., 3).[84]

---

80. Hocken, "Meaning and Purpose," 125.
81. Hocken, "Jesus Christ," 4.
82. Ibid., 5, 6.
83. Ibid., 6.
84. *Confidence,* December 1909, cited in Hocken, "Jesus Christ," 6–7.

The remarkable thing about this declaration is that these points focus on the work of God *in toto*, so to speak, with each of the hypostases in view in the context of what God is doing in the world and in humans, and the benefit of that to each human in their apprehension of the triune God. There is no specific mention of power for witness or work here, and it is "not singled out" within the entire declaration according to Hocken.[85] Rather, there is the consciousness of the deity of Christ and his dwelling in us; illumination (by the Spirit) of God's Word (Christ, hence the Father's Word) and his will; the testimony of Jesus, the Son; the conviction of the world by the Spirit; guidance into the "deep things of God" which must encompass God in entirety as Father, Son and Spirit; and finally the glorification of Christ as self is put aside. These speak of a new and deeper apprehension of God in triune fullness, and so a new and deeper relationship with God in Christ through the Spirit. Taken together, this is a startling affirmation of the triune God to the believer. As Hocken notes, for the "truly" Spirit released, the "Trinity ceases to be a merely theoretical construct . . . but is the truth about God as he reveals his inner being."[86]

Theologically, this must be so. If the act of one hypostasis within the triune God is the act of all, then the action of the Spirit in Spirit release cannot be isolated from the other hypostases. More specifically, the being of each hypostasis within God is defined, in part at least, by their intra-trinitarian, perichoretic relations with each of the other hypostases. This being so, to deal with the Spirit is to deal with an entity who is distinct from the other hypostases, but whose being includes the being of the Father and the Son in some way via the perichoretic relations, so it is impossible to encounter the Spirit without the other hypostases also being involved. It is then entirely to be expected that the content of an encounter with the Spirit will include the Father and the Son also. This, of course, could be so without the believer being aware of it, but the early testimonies are clear and consistent: what the Spirit brings when manifested in Spirit release is new and deeper knowledge of the Spirit, *and* the Father *and* the Son. That is, the believer is very aware of the Spirit, but is also made more aware of the Father and the Son through what the Spirit does. However, some care is required here. It is not that the Spirit adds anything to God's revelation in Christ, there is not new, "extra-scriptural," information, rather the new knowledge consists of a deeper understanding of the already fully revealed Christ. Nothing less than the fullness of Christ dwelt within the believer prior to Spirit release and that same fullness remains after. But it is a fullness with which the believer

---

85. Hocken, "Jesus Christ," 7.
86. Hocken, "Meaning and Purpose," 130.

has a more intimate relationship, where the union she enjoys with Christ penetrates her being more deeply and so changes her.

In the light of all this, it is clear that Pentecostal statements of faith which restrict the definition of Spirit release to an endowment of power miss the mark—Hocken suggests they identify the *purpose* of Spirit release (legitimately to provide power for service) not its *meaning* which he calls "revelation", but which I refer to as a "new and deeper knowledge." This knowledge leads to a deeper relationship or a deeper understanding of the existing union in Christ and its possibilities and is itself a more basic category than power.[87] In other words, the content of Spirit release is new knowledge which draws the believer into new possibilities in God, one of which is power for service.

The Pentecostal assurance of faith informed by Spirit release is therefore not based on an ecstatic experience as the Spirit alone is encountered, but is based very much on the self-authentication of God who is Father, Son and Spirit and who reveals Godself as such in Spirit release. Spirit release occurs for those who are already in Christ, so the concept of the triune God is not foreign to the believer. Rather, through Scripture and its proclamation the believer is already aware of the one God in three hypostases so what the Spirit reveals concerning the other hypostases builds upon knowledge already held by the believer. At its base, Spirit release is a numinous experience in which God self-authenticates, but this occurs in the light of previous influences which assist in this authentication for the believer. Each believer has been exposed to the Word and its preaching within the church, and the sacraments. He has also made some progress in sanctification and can identify some fruit of the Spirit's work in his life. In the same way in which Calvin appeals to these elements, the believer has true knowledge ("saving" knowledge) of God through God's revelation, Jesus Christ. His salvation has been effected by Christ and his Christian journey to date has been mediated by Christ. It is from this position that he understands his Spirit release. Through the action of the Spirit, the previous illumination of Christ and the Father is made much brighter, so he can testify as to true knowledge of the triune God and his saving action for him.[88]

---

87. Ibid., 128, 131–32.

88. This will not necessarily apply to the person who receives Spirit release in the sense I am using the term at the time of Christian initiation. While such a person may well have been exposed to preaching and Scripture and so have some knowledge of God as Father, Son and Spirit, the possibility is open that this is not the case so there is no knowledge to build upon. This does not weaken the argument as in the Pentecostal position the order and prior knowledge will be the vastly predominant situation. For the small minority of instances where this may not be the case, appeal can be made to the fact that salvation is contained in the work of Christ and it is illumination of that by

A useful analogy can be drawn with the biblical account of the so-called conversion of Paul. He had been enthusiastically persecuting Christians and he was doing so as he viewed the faith as inimical to the knowledge of God in which he was steeped (Acts 22:3–5). His encounter on the road to Damascus (Acts 9:1–22; 22:6–16; 26:12–18) incorporated a bright light and a voice who identified himself as the very Jesus whose followers he was persecuting, something he identified as persecution of himself. The change in Paul because of this encounter was dramatic and immediate: he was baptized and started preaching Christ in Damascus. Paul himself refers to this experience as how God revealed God's Son to him (Gal 1:15–16); here is a numinous experience in which the God whom Paul already acknowledged imparted further knowledge as to the person of his Son. We can say little more than this about the actual occasion, but it was dramatically life-changing for Paul. The Pentecostal experience of Spirit release is closely analogous in that one with previous knowledge receives new knowledge which has a dramatic, transforming impact within the believer and her Christian witness.

It is not that what the Spirit does in Spirit release is merely consistent with the Word in Scripture or the triune God in entirety; it is that what he it *contains* testimony concerning the Father and the Son, and contains it in a way which acts directly on the believer to draw him more deeply into his union with Christ and participation with the triune God's communion. The Spirit is certainly not anonymous in this encounter—being revealed to the believer along with the companion hypostases—but the links the Spirit creates, or renews, or strengthens, are with the Spirit, and the Father and the Son. The Pentecostal is willing to assert that his faith (that is, that part of his faith identified with him, rather than what may have come from God) plays a part here as he receives this new knowledge and judges it to be true. But it is a faith overwhelmed, a faith confronted by the glory of the triune God such that it must only proclaim the truth of what is apprehended and respond with praise and new enthusiasm and power in service for his Lord.

Affinities

There is significant similarity between the respective positions of Calvin and the Pentecostals. In both there is a life-changing encounter with God which changes the very being of the human. For Calvin, it is the occasion of conversion, where the believer realizes she is elect and becomes subject to the work

---

the Spirit which is crucial in Christian initiation, so the following Spirit release occurs with that knowledge already sealed for the new believer. Even here, then, there is some prior knowledge to build upon.

of the Spirit in her as she receives faith, is justified, and regenerated. She is transformed into a new creation in union with Christ and it is her knowledge of this union through faith which informs her of the transformation. For the Pentecostal, it is the occasion of Spirit release which occurs in one already converted, who already has faith, who receives a deeper insight into the fullness of the God who is Father, Son and Spirit and who experiences a new release of the Spirit within her who acts to move her in new ways of praise and witness. She is truly transformed by the work of God within her. For Calvin and the Pentecostal, there is encounter and transformation.

The differences between each are less significant than may at first appear, and, I suggest, much less significant than the similarities. If a hypothetical "Calvin disciple" is considered alongside his "Pentecostal" counterpart, the most obvious difference between the two is that Calvin is talking of Christian initiation for his disciple, whereas the Pentecostal is not. This is a clear difference which must be conceded, but this is only an issue of timing for the respective disciples.

A second difference is that Calvin is clear that this conversion and journey occurs within the church and because of the church. It is the proclamation of the Word by the church which God, through the Spirit, uses to bring the disciple to faith and union, and the continual exposure of the disciple to the proclamation which the Spirit uses to produce regeneration. This is not the only means, as the sacraments ministered by the Church (particularly the Lord's Supper) play an equally important role in regeneration. The Pentecostal disciple has the same journey of regeneration which she will call sanctification, at and following her conversion, but there will be a step-change in transformation at the point of Spirit release which can be viewed as a brief period of acceleration (however remarkable) in her regeneration. She will recognize that the church has a role in her conversion, because it is a place where the Word is preached, and its members proclaim the Word beyond its confines. The role of the sacraments, while acknowledged, is likely to be muted. But she will understand that her conversion, sanctification, and Spirit release are primarily founded on the direct work of the Spirit with her, the church playing a supporting role.[89]

Once past Spirit release, for the Pentecostal, each disciple can look back on a journey of Spirit-generated transformation (albeit with different views or emphases on the means utilized by the Spirit). For Calvin's disciple it is a single step-change followed by gradual regeneration under the ministry of

---

89. This, of course, carries the possibility that she may conclude she has no need of the church and can journey with Christ without any church affiliation or participation. Such views are not unknown, if mistaken.

the church, while for the other there are two step-changes, one at conversion and one at Spirit release, with ongoing regeneration or sanctification.

A third difference is that for Calvin it is the elect who is transformed as faith arrives through the Spirit, whereas for the Pentecostal it is one who already has faith who is transformed further by the work of the Spirit. But how different are the positions of the respective disciples in reality? Calvin's disciple who comes to faith, and the Pentecostal disciple who has faith before Spirit release both share salvation prior to the coming of the Spirit they each recognize. Calvin's disciple has salvation because of his elect status, even though he doesn't know it. The Pentecostal disciple has salvation because she has already entered into union with Christ prior to Spirit release,[90] so the positions are linked by the salvation shared in common. The difference resides only in the respective knowledge each disciple has prior to the respective encounters with the Spirit which are the subjects of this discussion.

A fourth difference is in the apprehension of the Spirit. There is a marked contrast here, where the Pentecostal wants to say she has encountered and recognized the Spirit directly and personally, whereas Calvin's disciple wants to declare that it is definitely the Spirit who has worked in him, but he can only detect that by the Spirit's impact in the faith in Christ which is produced.[91] He is at pains to insist that the Spirit works in secret so as to ensure that Christ, the revelation of God, remains utterly unobscured by anything of the person of the Spirit. However, the contrast is not as stark as this. The Pentecostal also wants to say that, in Spirit release, there is a new and deeper revealing of God in Christ, and God the Father, which evinces praise and a deepening of faith. Far from acting to conceal Christ in any way, the very "visible" Spirit enhances the appreciation of Christ as the revelation of God. Certainly, the action of the Spirit in ensuring visibility carries with it the risk that the disciple will not "see past" the Spirit to Christ and the Father. If the disciple succumbs to this possibility, then she is isolating the Spirit from the triune community in God and the Spirit's work in her reduces to an empowerment which is unmediated by Christ and can produce unfortunate results. This can come about through the actions of the believer in response to what she believes is empowerment by the Spirit. If she wishes to be entirely Spirit-directed (a laudable aim), then she will attempt to discern what the Spirit is saying to her directly. What she recognizes as Spirit utterance may not be, so if she proceeds as "directed" without allowing any mediation by Christ, she

---

90. A priority which may not be obvious if Christian initiation and Spirit release occur together.

91. Although note the means used discussed under the second difference.

is acting in isolation from Christ and so likely pursuing a "non-christian" agenda.[92] This is problematical enough at an individual level but is much more so if she is in a church leadership position with some authority, where she can use such "direction" to lead a church community to "unchristian" ends. Thus, the difficulties occur, not because the Spirit is empowering independently of the Father and the Son, but because the believer looks only to the Spirit as empowerment and responds to influences which are not the Spirit. This is, of course, the issue previously identified surrounding how the believer can know the influence is actually the Holy Spirit and also introduces complexities around actual divine activity as, in freedom, God may choose to actually empower a believer who is looking only to the Spirit. I do not want to pursue such complexities here, but it is important to note that understanding the power of the Spirit as isolated from the other hypostases is inappropriate and carries dangers.

As I have already identified, this can not only occur within the disciple at the time of Spirit release, but has effectively occurred in the process of the development of Pentecostal statements of faith where the original content of Spirit release has been progressively pared away to reduce it to the endowment of power for service. This has created a situation where a modern disciple experiencing Spirit release in a Pentecostal environment is most likely taught that what has occurred is restricted to an endowment for service, thus denying its accompanying trinitarian convictions. The risk of isolating the Spirit has become the almost inevitable outcome. It is to be hoped that the move to recover the full content of Spirit release will lead to a broadening of statements of faith and hence teaching on the subject within Pentecostalism so that this path to the isolation of the Spirit will be closed.

Returning to the full content of Spirit release, while there is a contrast between the view of each disciple on the "visibility" of the Spirit, what comes with the work of the Spirit in each case is the same affirmation concerning Christ. There is a much greater degree of agreement theologically than first appears.

But it is not agreement that is being sought, even though there is agreement among the differences. What is being sought is affinity between the positions, or links, and I suggest that there is a strong affinity between

---

92. A personal experience may serve to illustrate better what I am suggesting. On one occasion, a woman told me information about my situation which she claimed the Spirit had told her and which, she imagined, would be useful to me (a "word of knowledge" as Pentecostals would understand it). Unfortunately, I knew the facts of the situation and knew the information to be false. To apply a standard of truth as Christ would teach, what she averred was wrong. When I subsequently told her that the information was factually incorrect, she would not accept that, as she was confident that she knew when God, by the Spirit, was revealing things to her.

Calvin and Pentecostal thought in the transformation which occurs in the believer when the Spirit comes. This affinity is heavily emphasized by the ground for assurance of faith in both positions. Each has some element of human appraisal, very muted for Calvin but obvious for Pentecostals, and each relies on the self-authenticating God to give assurance of faith, albeit in the "external" context of the Church for Calvin. This represents a strong affinity between the respective theologies.

I suggest this affinity is made more obvious by considering whether Spirit release can offer anything to Calvin's thought by way of useful extension. I am not considering here an attempt to incorporate Spirit release within Calvin's thought,[93] but that it may be useful to explore its impact if the truth of the experience is admitted. For Calvin, the believer's faith is a concrete knowledge he holds beyond any simply intellectual acceptance of the truth of doctrine, founded in the work of the Spirit. The believer must therefore rely on something beyond himself to be assured of his faith. This is provided, at least substantially, by the Word, read and preached in the church, and the sacraments. Nevertheless, this is a somewhat uncomfortable position as his faith, to be genuine, must rely on his election, something he can know nothing about. But he has his conscience, an arena within him where God can work to produce a good conscience, something that only occurs in the elect. However, there is a considerable human influence in evaluating whether his conscience is "good," so some uncertainty remains as it relies in part on him, not God. If this believer, wondering about the certainty of his faith, were to experience Spirit release as Pentecostals understand it, what are the consequences for his assurance of faith?

What he would perceive is the Spirit; that which he would consider to be secret is now revealed. This by itself may prompt him to doubt the validity of the experience as he questions whether such a Spirit could possibly be revealed in such a way. However, through this encounter he is shown the Father and the Son, or he is drawn more deeply into Christ so that he gains new knowledge of him and finds his union with him deepened and strengthened alongside a new and deeper conviction of the reality of the Trinity. The appearance of the Spirit has given him new glimpses of the object of his faith, the God who is Father, Son and Spirit. Beforehand, he determined that Christ is the revelation of God, now he finds that within this experience *is* the revelation,[94] Christ himself. This can do nothing other

---

93. Which founders on Calvin's insistence that the work of the Spirit is secret for one thing. See the discussion on this subject in chapter 6.

94. Hocken, "Jesus Christ," 4, uses this phrase without the emphasis, but he is using "revelation" to mean the extra knowledge granted in Spirit baptism, not in Calvin's sense as I use above.

than strengthen and affirm his previous understandings about Christ and so bolster his assurance of faith. The foundation for his assurance has been made much more secure, although he will find that he is still relying on the self-authenticating God coupled with his own evaluation. But this has been a significant experience testifying of the truth in Christ, and it opens the way to further acknowledged work of the Spirit in him, so increasing his assurance. Theologically, it would be challenging, but he need only admit that the Spirit can work "in the open" as well as secretly for there to be no inconsistency. Once this is accepted, the experience could become an important and useful confirmation of what he understands in faith and so represent a more than useful advance building upon Calvin's thought.

Calvin, of course, would not agree and would look upon such a believer with some horror, concerned that he is claiming a visibility for the Spirit which detracts from God's revelation of Godself, indeed suggests that Christ is not the complete revelation of God. The very visibility of the Spirit claimed in Spirit release is sufficient for Calvin to shy away from the experience. He is critical of the Libertines who exalted the teaching of the Spirit above Scripture,[95] thus isolating the work of the Spirit. He goes on to assert: "Therefore the Spirit, promised to us, has not the task of inventing new and unheard-of revelations, or of forging a new kind of doctrine, to lead us away from the received doctrine of the gospel, but of sealing our minds with that very doctrine which is commended by the gospel."[96] His position is that the Spirit is inseparable from Scripture and so the one who has dispensed the Word completes his work "by the efficacious confirmation of the word."[97] It is obvious that he would consider as spurious any claim that the Spirit has done something apparently separate from Scripture, even if consistent with it. Far from building on his thought, Calvin would likely consider Spirit release to be an unjustified departure from his theology and, in fact, from Christ himself, which could not give any increased assurance of faith.

This view, of course, is based entirely on Calvin's thought, and it may be that the man himself would prove to be more open to a positive reception for Spirit release. Whether this be true or not, there is clearly more potential for the Pentecostal to look favorably upon Calvin. Spirit release is understood by Pentecostals to be a direct encounter with God in which through the Spirit (sent by Christ), God acts to draw the human to a deeper appreciation of the fullness of Godself, where there is a real drawing in of the human by the Spirit thus increasing the intimacy of the union between

---

95. I.9.1.
96. Ibid.
97. I.9.2.

the believer and Christ and strengthening the bond which holds the union together. The human certainly experiences this as God coming to her, but this is an action reciprocal to God's drawing in. It is helpful, I suggest, to the Pentecostal's understanding of what has happened to her to consider Calvin's account of the union, the work of the Spirit in it, and the resulting participation in God. His account will give her a good foundation on which to understand her Spirit release and its effect on the strength of her faith. She need only put to one side Calvin's insistence on the secrecy of the Spirit's work, or, better perhaps, make an extension from Calvin's indirect experience of the Spirit via faith and godliness in the believer's life. This will come easily to her in contrast to a Calvin disciple, and the rest will sit comfortably with her on Calvin's shoulders as it were. For her, Calvin's thought offers a rich resource in her exploration of the meaning of Spirit release and the examination of her faith.

4

Providence and Guidance

There is a broad diversity of views within Pentecostal theology, as was noted in chapter two, which makes it difficult to identify what it is that makes Pentecostal theology distinctive, if indeed this is possible at all. Alister McGrath suggests that "The feature that both characterizes and distinguishes Pentecostalism from all other forms of Christianity is its insistence and emphasis upon an immediate encounter with God through the Holy Spirit and the ensuing transformation of individuals."[1] This is a direct apprehension of God within the believer and her life which he goes on to contrast with a Protestantism where knowledge of God is limited to what can be known from the Bible, accessed by reading it or hearing it expounded in preaching. Such a traditional Protestantism is wary of a direct knowledge of God and questions its truth, whereas Pentecostalism allows God "an impact upon the totality of existence" and "injects the presence of God into everyday life."[2] The encounter he refers to is, of course, Spirit release, an occurrence common to almost all Pentecostalism, so his assertion can be comfortably affirmed.

But McGrath's treatment goes beyond the experience of Spirit release itself and extends not only into the transformation of the believer, the ongoing process of sanctification, but also every aspect of life itself. What this means is not that sanctifying actions can be neatly separated from other occurrences which are not sanctifying, but that God is involved with the believer in the whole of her life, not just those occasions which are obviously God-focused. So, attending worship and hearing Scripture expounded can be appreciated as an obvious sanctifying activity (whether or not it is efficacious to the believer at the time), whereas finding a car park is not obviously sanctifying (although the Spirit could well use it as such). The "totality of existence" and "everyday life" are expressions which exclude no

---

1. McGrath, *Christianity's Dangerous New Idea*, 424.
2. Ibid., 429–32.

part of the believer's life—God is involved with every task, every choice and every happening for the believer. He can look to God for guidance and assistance everywhere, even for help in finding a car park. While retaining a free will in making his choices, the believer is never left alone when faced with them, however minor they may be; God, through the immediate activity of his Spirit, is ever willing to direct the believer's choices. Duffield and Van Cleave echo this close involvement with the believer in their very brief discussion on providence, noting that God supplies believers' "needs and wants" to the smallest details.[3]

This offers a continuation of what occurred for the believer at Spirit release. There, through the Spirit she encountered the triune God in such a direct and overwhelming way that her union with Christ and apprehension of who God is was greatly enhanced and the further release of the already indwelling Spirit changed her such that her future life would be transformed. The new immediacy of the Spirit to her is not something to be visited on occasion, it is something to be lived with every day. Thus, the Spirit is involved all the time; it is as if the Spirit is imposed on every aspect of her existence. What has started at Spirit release continues, albeit in what might be said to be a more controlled way, every day which follows. This does not mean that the Spirit is at the believer's disposal, available to assist him in achieving what he wants to achieve (despite Duffield and Van Cleave's assertion that God provides his "wants"), the very experience of Spirit release where the believer finds himself in the overwhelming presence of another shows that God's involvement is for God's purposes, not the believer's. Thus, while the believer will seek the Spirit's influence in every part of his life, it will be in the context of his seeking to be obedient to God's guidance through the Spirit, not to seek personal advantage for himself. Of course, this does not exclude human sinfulness wherein God's help will be sought for personal advantage.

It is this individual attention to all the details of a believer's life which will be the focus of this chapter, what might be called the personal providence of God. God's providence, of course, is of cosmic proportions, but I have deliberately limited the discussion to this personal providence and will avoid consideration of a wider providence,[4] as to do so will reduce to a recitation of the agreement between Calvin and Pentecostals on general providence.[5] I will also further limit the discussion, in general, to the providence

3. Duffield and van Cleave, *Foundations of Pentecostal Theology*, 87.

4. By which is meant God's providential care for the whole universe in contrast to his attention to the individual.

5. Williams, *Renewal Theology*, 1:117–39, makes this evident in his discussion of providence.

of God for the individual and how her union with Christ and the work of the Spirit in that bears upon what I term her personal providence. Of course, the church plays a crucial role in the establishment, health and development of the union between Christ and the believer and hence in the providence of God, particularly for Calvin. However, there must be some limitation on the scope of the discussion to allow an exploration in sufficient depth within the available space. This choice also remains truer to the character of Spirit release and the Pentecostal's understanding of the relationship she enjoys with Christ so is a more fruitful space to explore.

In the light of the above brief discussion, what is striking is the similarity between the extent of the involvement of God in the believer's life for Pentecostals and Calvin. The latter would agree that the Spirit is at work at a personal level, involved in everything that happens to an intimate degree, but his view on the secrecy of the Spirit's work means that he would not agree that the Spirit can be sought for guidance in the way Pentecostals claim. There are also fruitful grounds for discussion in examining what each says about free will and God's purposes, having some regard to how they relate to predestination. For example, a first glance at Calvin's doctrine of predestination might suggest that God directs everything that happens, leaving the believer little more than a pawn in his hands, whereas the Pentecostal has no difficulty in asserting some separate contribution from the believer which seems to give value to divine guidance in a way which Calvin does not. However, the situation is more complex than this and requires exploration to ensure we have the respective positions correct. A suitable starting point is Calvin's view on personal providence and how it sits with these other aspects of his thought.

Calvin on Providence

There is no doubt that Calvin views every action and happening in the world as not only under God's control, but also as caused by God[6]—whatever happens to us comes from God.[7] Thus God "sustains, nourishes, and cares for, everything he has made, even to the last sparrow";[8] "all events are governed

---

6. Even accidents, Parker, *Calvin*, 44–45; I.8.8.

7. Zachman, *Image and Word*, 74. In this work, Zachman notes that prior to 1550 Calvin's focus on providence was "on the special care of God for the pious" and after the "protection and preservation of the church throughout history." As my concern is the individual rather than the church, this and other references to this work refer to the pre-1550 Calvin.

8. I.16.1.

by God's secret plan";[9] and God's omnipotence is "a watchful, effective, active sort engaged in ceaseless activity . . . directed toward individual and particular motions."[10] Equally, "nothing happens except what is knowingly and willingly decreed by [God]"[11] and "nothing at all in the world is undertaken without his determination,"[12] so much so that if anything could happen without God ordaining it, "it would then happen without any cause."[13]

There are no exceptions to this: what is good happens because God directs it, but the same is the case for what is evil. It is attractive to try to resolve this uncomfortable position by removing God from the scene somewhat and making a distinction between actions which God positively and directly causes and those for which God merely gives permission. That is, the suggestion that some things happen, not because God causes them, but because God does not intervene to prevent them and so permits them. Calvin will have none of this, being emphatic that mere permission for evil happenings is not how God acts: "they babble and talk absurdly who, in place of God's providence, substitute bare permission."[14] Calvin's answer to this is entirely scriptural—he makes no attempt to address the logic of the situation. He gives numerous examples which declare that deeds which, on the face of it, are evil, but which are declared to be God's doing. One of more than a dozen references is Absolam sleeping with David's concubines (2 Sam 16:22) which God brought about (2 Sam 12:11-12).[15] Such things occur because God causes the impulse in humans to engage in such acts. Among a further extensive clutch of scriptural examples he gives are the occasions of God causing Pharaoh's heart to be turned against the release of the Israelites (Exod 9:12; 10:20, 27; 11:10, 14:8).[16] He also disposes of the charge that God must have two wills in this—one clearly seen in what he forbids and a second, secret, will where he decrees that which contradicts what he has forbidden. Instead, scripture makes it clear that God is open about what God wills, even things which include or comprise actions forbidden to humans.[17] However, here he does hint at the possibility that God may be more removed from evil actions than good ones: "in a wonderful

9. I.16.2.
10. I.16.3.
11. Ibid.
12. I.16.6.
13. I.16.8.
14. I.18.1.
15. Ibid.
16. I.18.2.
17. I.18.3.

and ineffable manner nothing is done without God's will, not even that which is against his will. For it would not be done if he did not permit it; yet he does not unwillingly permit it, but willingly."[18] There is here the concept of a willing permission—God is not sitting aside from the action, merely allowing it to occur; rather God is contributing to the action by a permission given which has a sufficient causal effect, but not necessarily a direct causal effect. It may be that such actions may be ascribed to God, but that responsibility for them can be pinned on someone else. This is an important point which requires discussion.

Before doing so, there is left the clear assertion that God wills all, good or bad. The apparent contradiction inherent in this—that God wills what is opposed to God as well as what is not—is left unresolved because Scripture clearly teaches that all is directed by God, for Calvin. However, the contradiction is not left unaddressed. Calvin's response is simply that "on account of our mental incapacity, we do not grasp how in divers (sic) ways [God] wills and does not will something to take place." Equally, it is not beyond God to ensure that good comes out of evil. Finally, it is impious and profane of humans to apply their judgement to the apparent contradiction because not only does that set them against Scripture, but they are also presuming to apply their puny understanding from a position of complete unworthiness in God's eyes to an issue God has determined.[19] It is presumptuous and wrong to try to understand God's reasoning where that understanding is not given in Scripture. Paul Helm summarizes this neatly: Calvin rejects using commonsense—the norm is that we can know *that* God acts this way, not *how* or *why*.[20] What this leaves, for one attempting to puzzle out how Calvin's position works, is a gap. God wills all and it is easy to affirm that he wills good things, but to acknowledge that he also wills evil things in contradiction to his revealed nature is to say something different. Between the two there is a gap which is obvious to human eyes, but which can only be crossed by God—it is not given to humans to know why the gap exists for us or to know how God bridges it.

The gap is emphasized by the responsibility humans bear for sin so that God legitimately holds them accountable for it. This is certainly clearly taught in Scripture,[21] but Calvin puts the issue in stark relief when he says:

> I grant more: thieves and murderers and other evildoers are the instruments of divine providence, and the Lord himself uses

18. Ibid.
19. Ibid.
20. Helm, *John Calvin's Ideas*, 104 (emphasis his).
21. I.17.3; I.18.4.

these to carry out the judgements that he has determined with himself. Yet I deny that they can derive from this any excuse for their evil deeds. Why? Will they either involve God in the same iniquity with themselves, or will they cloak their own depravity with his justice? They can do neither.[22]

The only ways he sees that humans can evade responsibility for their sins are to say that they are godly acts, and so not sin at all, or claim that God approves of their sin. While the logic of the situation may appeal to humans looking to absolve themselves, neither option is permitted by Scripture, making both unavailable to sinful men and women. Both these points amount to the view that as every action is directed by God, humans have no say in anything which occurs, they are merely pawns on the board; together the universe God plays with. Calvin rejects such fatalism and in holding humans responsible clearly holds that human sin is *their* sin. This means that he must show some human involvement in their sinful actions—if it is not solely God's determination that a particular evil act is perpetrated, then the human indulging in the act is determining that the act occur. Logically, the direction of the act could be entirely the human's determination without any influence from God, or there could be a combination of human and divine determination in the same act. Calvin's doctrine on providence will not allow the former as it would place some acts entirely outside God's control, so the latter must prevail. This is the realm of primary and secondary causes for particular acts, where both may be at play in what occurs.

Thus, if we consider an evil act by an individual, it has a primary and a secondary cause for Calvin. The primary cause is provided by God who is causally involved in everything which occurs, so must be causally involved in this act also. As it is an evil act committed by an individual human, that human is also causally involved, but there is a difference in character between the causal actions. The divine causal action is a necessary action to ensure the act occurs, but by God's decree is not sufficient to ensure the act occurs. The human causal action is also necessary but not sufficient to ensure the act occurs; if the human causal action was not present the act would not occur. As Zachman expresses it, human actions come about through their own deliberation and events are experienced as "contingent and even fortuitous" but all is under God's control.[23] Both divine and human causal actions are required to ensure the act occurs. However, the situation is further complicated by the fact that the insufficiency of God's causal action is only such because God decrees that the human causal action is necessary;

22. 1.17.5.
23. Zachman, *Image and Word*, 82–84.

ultimately the act occurs because it is within God's providential decree. In contrast, for godly acts, the causal action of God is both necessary and sufficient, and may be the only cause at work; certainly this is so for the reprobate. In their case, they have no capacity for godly acts of themselves, so any godly act is entirely due to God's causal action. However, for the awakened elect, there may appear to be human causal action, but the desire and ability to exercise it arises entirely from God through the Holy Spirit, so the human action may be necessary but is not sufficient. Helm notes this difference between regeneration and the "hardening" of the reprobate. He calls it an asymmetry where humans are left to themselves in hardening whereas the Spirit works in them in regeneration.[24]

Calvin doesn't address the issue in these exact terms, but perhaps his most concise statement is "that God's providence does not always meet us in its naked form, but God in a sense clothes it with the means employed."[25] God can, and does, engage in direct causal action without human involvement, but also uses means separate from him to achieve his ends. Thus, some action he desires is caused by him influencing a human who is the means by which the action occurs—the human is required to apply what causal action is available to him to ensure the act desired by God occurs. It is in this arena that Calvin's concept of a willing permission operates and it is profitable to give it some brief consideration.

Willing Permission

This concept of willing permission Calvin borrows from Augustine, as he makes clear,[26] and he does little more than mention it as far as I am aware. Nevertheless, it does represent some movement towards closing the gap in understanding between good and evil acts: each is willed by God in whom there is no evil at all. The gap cannot be explained by mere permission as Calvin rejects that position on scriptural grounds. But willing permission implies some involvement beyond a passive permission-giving on the part of God. A particular evil act is obviously permitted as its occurrence shows, but God is somehow active in the permission-giving so that God contributes in some way to causing the act. The case of Job (an example used by Calvin himself)[27] is perhaps useful in teasing out what willing permission might be.

---

24. Helm, *John Calvin's Ideas*, 116.
25. I.17.4.
26. I.18.3.
27. I.18.1.

Satan presents himself to God on two occasions (Job 1:6–12; 2:1–6) where God extols the virtue of "my servant Job." Satan suggests that Job's virtue is due to his comfort, so God invites Satan firstly to afflict everything and everyone around Job but leave him untouched (1:12) and secondly to afflict him with disease but not kill him (2:6). The result is that Job loses all his possessions, family (apart from his wife) and his health, a series of evils which he correctly attributes to God (1:21, 2:10) and which are later explicitly attributed to God (42:11). Undoubtedly, God has a purpose in what happens to Job, and undoubtedly the testimony of the text is that it was God who brought the evil upon Job. But it is equally true that Satan has also done what he wanted to do by afflicting Job—there are two causal agents involved in the activity. The key to trying to grasp the active involvement of God comes in 1:12 and 2:6. In the former, God specifically places Job's possessions at Satan's disposal: "Very well, all that he has is in your power; only do not stretch out your hand against him!" In the latter it is Job himself: "Very well, he is in your power; only spare his life." It is not God who has directly afflicted Job: Satan has done so and can be held responsible for his action. However, God, by a deliberate act, placed Job at Satan's disposal with knowledge of what would happen.[28] This is an active permission-giving, emphasized by the placing of conditions on the permission. God has, in effect, placed Job in Satan's way knowing full well what will happen: it is akin to placing something on the rails immediately in front of a train—the result is inevitable and the placer is the primary cause with the train only secondary. This is the sense of willing permission—there is an active, knowledgeable participation by God in a way which ensures God's "fingers" are all over the resulting acts without God's participation ever being a willing endorsement, yet God can legitimately remain God and hold the secondary causal agent responsible. The gap remains, but it doesn't yawn as wide when willing permission is considered.

God's Will and Human Wills

The gap is also closed somewhat if Calvin's view of free will and the operation of God's will and human wills are considered. The modern colloquial understanding of free will is the freedom of choice that a free moral agent has to choose her courses of action, but this is not what Calvin means by free will. He emphatically denies that humans have a will which is free in that sense at all. Rather, he has no objection to free will in the sense

---

28. This is Calvin's argument in I.18.1, but I have expanded it considerably.

of the choice being made without coercion.[29] He goes on to identify four qualifiers of will:

- *Free*—understood to mean having the power of choosing good or evil;
- *Bound*—a corrupt will which can only choose evil;
- *Self-determined*—a will which directs itself without external influences; and
- *Coerced*—a will forced by external influence.

It is sufficient here to note that, for Calvin, humans do not have a free will in the modern colloquial sense,[30] but that they do have the power to choose between alternatives without external influence—a self-determined will, one which is not coerced.[31] This does not mean that this will is not bound—faced with two alternatives, a bound will can make a self-determined choice, but it will choose only evil if given an evil and a godly choice. The human condition after the Fall is that the will is oriented "to serve the creature rather that the Creator," so that while genuine choices can be made, they are motivated by the creature and so cannot be good.[32] With the exception of the awakened elect, humans live with their backs to God, able to see only the evil possibilities and choose between them; the possibilities which represent obedience to God are not perceived at all. This condition has not been imposed on humans, but results from original sin chosen in deliberate disobedience of God's instructions for which humans are responsible. It is not a condition imposed on them, but is one willingly chosen. Hence, even in making choices blind to the godly alternatives, humans are doing so themselves in an un-coerced manner.

Justification changes things for the elect. Once justified, the human is made aware of what represents obedience to God and, through the work of the Spirit, has a will to be obedient by the grace of God through the union with Christ each believer enjoys. This access to obedience is always provided by God, but the human is still aware of evil or disobedient possibilities so is presented with a choice he must make. He is guided in his choice by what he has learnt from Scripture, illuminated by the Spirit, so God's involvement in the particular choice operates at two levels: first the way of obedience is revealed to him, and, second, God has educated him

---

29. II.3.8; Calvin, *The Bondage and Liberation of the Will*, cited in Helm, *John Calvin's Ideas*, 159.

30. *Bondage*, cited in Helm, *John Calvin's Ideas*, 69.

31. Helm, *John Calvin's Ideas*, 160.

32. Ibid., 161. Helm notes that Calvin did not express this idea in this manner.

so as to be able to properly identify what obedience is in general and *the* appropriately obedient choice in particular. Whether the latter is adopted or not *is* a decision of his will.[33]

Still, God exercises "providential control over every action taken,"[34] so no single event occurs unless it is willed by God. So, in any action involving a human there are two wills at play. On God's side of the gap, so to speak, is God's will exercising overall control and a specific control which ensures the divinely willed outcome occurs. At the human side, there is a human will exercising a freedom to choose which is un-coerced, but not free to make independent moral choices. Because it is un-coerced, the human does not perceive God's direction but sees her choice as her own, without external involvement. If she is an awakened elect, she can see godly choices as well as evil ones by the grace of God. Still, because the work of the Spirit is secret, her decisions, even though entirely the work of the Spirit (as they surely are for godly actions), will appear to be hers, albeit one in union with Christ. "[She will] penetrate to God's providence by . . . [her] faith" but experience events as if they were "strictly contingent and even fortuitous."[35] There is thus an interplay between God's will and human wills across the gap to give effect to the choice which satisfies both God's intent and the freedom of the human to choose. Just what this is and how it operates is not given to humans, but in Calvin's thought it clearly exists so as to give meaning to the human choice.

The Spirit in Providence

For the awakened elect, these choices are not uninformed choices, however. Her status in union with Christ and indwelt by the Spirit means that not only is she now aware of godly choices, but that the Spirit works in her so she is able to adopt them. She does not select the godly option all the time, but the hope is that as her regeneration proceeds she will do so more frequently. Analysis of Calvin's account of the ongoing component of regeneration shows that it involves the Spirit in three related roles.

The first is a teaching role through the illumination of Scripture. This is *the* way in which the believer learns godly ways which he can apply to his life and situations he faces. This occurs as Scripture is expounded in

---

33. Billings, *Participation and the Gift*, 49. Good human acts arise from the activity of the indwellng Spirit, but in a way where the acts are the human's and the Spirit not coercive—the Spirit works so the good acts are voluntary.

34. Helm, *John Calvin's Ideas*, 168.

35. Zachman, *Image and Word*, 82.

preaching or read directly, when the Spirit operates in the interaction of words and reader, or words, preacher, and listener to make the word the Word of God. This Word the hearer or reader can perceive and, by the operation of the Spirit, take into his being so that it is learnt in a manner which will now affect his future choices and behavior. Armed with this knowledge, and by the power of the Spirit, he can make choices in which the godly choice is now not only known to him, but can be taken—his knowledge in the Spirit shows which are the evil choices and which are godly. This is an indirect function of the Spirit,[36] but because of the secrecy of the Spirit's work for Calvin, the believer will not be directly aware of this functioning. The believer may see two choices before her and recognize one as an evil choice and one as a godly choice, but will perceive that this is simply knowledge she now has. She will not perceive the direct activity of the Spirit showing her which character belongs to which choice, although she may acknowledge the activity of the Spirit in giving her this knowledge. Now, in exercising the choice, she perceives it as her choice, even if it is informed and effected by the prior and present work of the Spirit.

This present work of the Spirit points to the second role the Spirit plays. Within the union, in which the Spirit forms the bond by which Christ and the believer are joined, what Christ perceives in a particular situation must also be available to the believer because of the intimacy of the union, at least on occasion. As the bonding agent, the Spirit is involved in the intimate exchange which characterizes the union and hence is involved in the sharing of perceptions in any situation. That is, the Spirit ensures the believer knows the mind of Christ. While this is so, the believer, even now possessing in one sense the mind of Christ on the matter, may not take the godly alternative, but her old nature may assert itself and the evil alternative be adopted. This is so because her will is un-coerced; by definition she must be able to adopt the evil alternative. Although it is to some extent a circular argument, it is worth noting that, from another perspective, history demonstrates that the believer has an un-coerced will. While she is a new creation in union with Christ, observation of her behavior will show a series of evil behaviors which she has chosen. The very fact that she makes evil choices indicates that even in the most intimate contact with Christ her will is not coerced and hence she is so involved with her choices that she can be held responsible for them.

However, the expectation is that over a believer's life in Christ, her choices will mean that her disobedience decreases as her obedience to

---

36. Indirect since the knowledge has previously been imparted by the Spirit, but there is also a direct component as the Spirit enables the godly choice to be made.

God increases. This is the third role of the Spirit: regeneration whereby the believer becomes more godly as his life proceeds. Not only is the Spirit enabling the godly choices to be evident to the believer, but as life proceeds and more godly choices are made, the Spirit operates to change the character of the believer. Within the new creation that he is, the creaturely nature recedes and the nature of Christ becomes more dominant. The Spirit's activity in identifying godly choices has a dynamic character whereby a shift is promoted between the natures within the believer as time goes on. The believer is shifted along a continuum in which his character moves towards godliness and away from sinful creatureliness; a movement promoted by the Spirit and aided, in part, by each choice made along the way for a godly alternative over an evil alternative. Of course, it is hindered by evil choices made over godly ones, but for the elect the movement will be toward God once they are awakened.

In sum, the Spirit works in three ways in personal providence or guidance for the believer. They are teaching what godly behavior is; revealing godly alternatives and giving effect to the godly choices the believer makes; and drawing the character of the believer ever closer to the divine nature of Christ within, as the believer lives life. The believer will apprehend his learning and the exercise of his choices and the growth towards God that results as his because of the secrecy of the Spirit in this work. Nevertheless, his faith means he will properly be able to assert the providence and guidance of God for him. All this is only possible because of the union which exists between the believer and Christ; while this sanctifying union cannot be said to be the "main hinge" on which Calvin's religion turns, it is of the highest importance within his thought and certainly the hinge on which personal providence turns. The work of the Spirit in individual guidance is pervasive and is only possible because the union exists as a medium by which this benefit of Christ can be transferred to the believer.

Providence and the Union

The importance of the union cannot be understated. For the believer, in the interplay of God's will and human wills involved in any choice (and certainly, at the ultimate, in every choice), she can only be aware of the godly alternative if the union exists. It is through the union alone that the Spirit can regenerate the human, illuminating, instructing, and empowering in the believer's life and actions; without the union, these "higher" actions of the Spirit[37] are not possible in any human. Equally, there can be no limit to

---

37. As contrasted with the "lower" action of the Spirit with the reprobate II.4.1; III.2.13.

the Spirit's work with the believer—the union is total, involving the whole being—so God through the Spirit can be, and is, involved in every aspect of the believer's life, however intimate. But, while the union is exclusive for the individual believer, Calvin does not conceive of this working being in any way entirely between God and the believer without the necessity of external moderators. Far from it, as to do so is to allow the believer to be led entirely by what she believes God is saying to her independent of the means which Calvin believes to be necessary—Scripture and the church.[38] The reality and necessity, for Calvin, is that Scripture must be present through which the Spirit might instruct the believer, and this can either be received through preaching in the church or direct reading. For those who are illiterate, the former is the way in which Scripture can be present for them. This work of the Spirit is furthered in the church through the sacraments which act to seal the promises contained in the preached word. Hence, while the guidance of a person is individual to them via the union, this occurs to a large degree through the ministry of the church, where exposition of Scripture and the sacraments are present, and the Spirit can work. Other influences by the Spirit are possible, of course, but the believer will not recognize them as such without the knowledge he has gained, through the Spirit, from Scripture. The believer will perceive that he is receiving divine guidance and will understand that God is acting providentially towards him through what he perceives and learns in the church, which will be providing a necessary moderating influence on his behavior.

The gap between God's willing on one side and the willing of evil together with human responsibility for it on the other in respect of any human act is narrowed somewhat by the concept of God's willing permission and the interplay of wills which occurs for the elect in their choices, but it still remains. However, the union between the believer and Christ means that there is no *actual* gap between the two beings, rather it is a gap of understanding how the contrasting positions on each side can hold: it is a conceptual gap. What the mystical union means is that the believer can be confident that the gap can be crossed; that life can be lived in ignorance of how the gap is crossed, reliant on God's providence and guidance. Such confidence is not available to the unbeliever who does not enjoy union with Christ, of course. But, enjoying the confidence of Christ, the believer can look forward to a lifetime of God's guidance through the secret work of the Spirit as she applies herself to the obedience to him taught in Scripture, ensuring a rich providence for her in all aspects of her life, whatever circumstances may befall her.

38. I.9.1–3.

Pentecostal Providence

The somewhat different Pentecostal view is informed not only by the experience of Spirit release, but also by the theological context which dominates. Roger Olsen comments that "Today, semi-Pelagianism is the default theology of most American evangelical Christians,"[39] a comment easily extendable to Pentecostals who share a theological heritage with evangelicals. The author's observations within Pentecostalism in New Zealand serve to confirm a similar position there.[40] However, where theology is formalized the semi-Pelagian nature tends to disappear. Thus, the Acts Churches New Zealand Statement of Belief includes:

> 3. . . . the necessity of repentance and regeneration by grace and through faith in Christ alone, and the eternal separation from God of the finally unrepentant.
>
> 5. The justification and sanctification of believers through the finished work of Christ, their security as they remain in him, and their future resurrection in an incorruptible body.[41]

These statements are not semi-Pelagian with their insistence on repentance and regeneration by grace alone and justification through the finished work of Christ. Rather, they are Arminian, with the damnation of the "finally unrepentant" and the security of believers as they remain in Christ departing from a Calvinist position. More general observations are made by Railey and Aker, who aver that most Pentecostals are Arminian;[42] Grudem who thinks both Calvinist and Arminian persuasions exist in Pentecostalism with the latter dominating in Pentecostal denominations;[43] and Olsen who states that all Pentecostals are Arminian.[44] It is thus not unfair to adopt Arminianism as a representative Pentecostal position and it seems likely that it is the dominant one.[45] As there are marked differences

---

39. Olsen, *Arminian Theology*, 30.

40. These are mostly within Acts Churches New Zealand (formerly the Apostolic Church Movement New Zealand), the denomination with which I was associated. As an example, the "vision statement" of the Dunedin City Apostolic Church (with which I had an association), which was "Living to See Many Others Turn to Follow Jesus," reveals a semi-Pelagian nature.

41. Acts Churches New Zealand, "Statement of Belief."

42. Railey and Aker, "Theological Foundations," 50.

43. Grudem, *Systematic Theology*, 338.

44. Olsen, *Arminian Theology*, 14.

45. While the observation on semi-Pelagianism holds true, when the issue is explored and the implications of semi-Pelagianism pointed out to individuals, my

in the Arminian view of providence compared to Calvin, it needs to be explored in some detail.

Arminianism and Providence

Arminianism is named after Jacob (or James) Arminius (1560–1609), a Dutch theologian who proposed a synergistic form of salvation in contrast to the monergism of Calvin.[46] Arminianism has a different view of providence from Calvin, not because, as often supposed, it denies the sovereignty of God, but because it views Calvin's doctrine as making God the author of sin and evil,[47] something it cannot countenance as it sees that as antithetical to God himself. Arminius writes:

> God can indeed do what He wills with His own; but He cannot will to do with His own what He cannot rightly do, for His will is circumscribed within the bounds of justice;[48] and

> God is good by a natural and internal necessity, not, *freely*.[49]

That is, God can do whatever he wants, but acts contrary to God's character are inconceivable. It is not that God can do anything but chooses to be good, it is that God's nature means that God will always be good. This being so, he cannot be the author of sin. This is not a conclusion reached by means of reason *contra* Scripture but rather follows Scripture; for Arminians the paradox of an unconditionally good God who is the author of sin "is not taught in Scripture," so their position is entirely scripturally based.[50] The examples that Calvin adduces from Scripture to show that God ordains evil, the Arminian sees differently. Rather than being ordained, evil is permitted:

---

experience is that almost without exception they readily agree that their position is Arminian.

46. Stanglin and McCall, *Jacob Arminius*, 152. They note that there are those who disagree. Olsen describes Arminius as a "theologian who wrote numerous works . . . defending an evangelical form of synergism . . . against monergism" (Olsen, *Arminian Theology*, 13).

47. Stanglin and McCall, *Jacob Arminius*, 23, 116, 129–31; Olsen, *Arminian Theology*, 118.

48. Arminius, "Friendly Conference with Mr Francis Junius" cited in Olsen, *Arminian Theology*, 119 (emphasis in the original).

49. Arminius, "Certain Articles to be Diligently Examined and Weighed," cited in Olsen, *Arminian Theology*, 102 (emphasis his).

50. Olsen, *Arminian Theology*, 100.

> [God] neither wills sin to happen, nor wills it not to happen. For permission is the act of a relaxed will; which relaxing of the will here was fitting in God, because he made man with a free power of choice, that he might test his free and voluntary obedience; which he could not have done, if he had placed any insuperable obstacle in man's way.[51]

Nevertheless, this does not occur in isolation from God, unaffected by God; rather it occurs with his concurrence—that is, God cooperates to effect the evil.[52] This is a strong position as Arminius sets out:

> The Concurrence of God is not his immediate influx into a second or inferior *cause* but is an action of God immediately flowing into *the effect* of the creature, so that the same effect in one and the same entire action may be produced simultaneously by God and the creature.[53]

Concurrence is necessary for any creature to do anything at all, but God's involvement is such that the creaturely cause determines the outcome, so the creaturely action is its own and free.[54] Thus, Arminius does not mean a "relaxed will" is passivity on the part of God, instead it is a "middle act between willing and not-willing."[55] This is a permission in which God is somehow involved—he is "designedly and willingly" permitting evil, as Olsen puts it.[56] He further comments that "God never denies concurrence to a rational and free creature" and "when God decided to permit an act, even a sinful one, he cannot consistently withhold the power to commit it."[57] Thus concurrence works by the free creature deciding to commit an evil act, something which can only happen if God allows it and, having allowed it, God will always provide the wherewithal to the creature to ensure the act occurs. The responsibility for the act remains with the creature, as he has made the free decision to commit it.

If the passages from Job considered above (1:6–12; 2:1–6) are revisited in this light, then a different construction can be taken from them than previously. When Satan presents himself, he is given permission, but limitations are placed on what he is to do: Job is in Satan's power but he may not afflict

---

51. Arminius, *Works*, cited in Stanglin and McCall, *Jacob Arminius*, 74.

52. Stanglin and McCall, *Jacob Arminius*, 96–97.

53. Arminius, *Works*, cited in Stanglin and McCall, *Jacob Arminius*, 96–97, also Olsen, *Arminian Theology*, 122.

54. Stanglin and McCall, *Jacob Arminius*, 97.

55. Arminius, "Exam. Perk," cited in Stanglin and McCall, *Jacob Arminius*, 99.

56. Olsen, *Arminian Theology*, 120.

57. Ibid., 122.

him and, later, he may not kill him (1:12; 2:6) The evil is permitted with strict limits, and the reader is given a broad hint that this is giving effect to God's purposes. With permission it is now Satan's free choice to afflict Job, but concurrence is necessary to actually allow him to inflict the evil upon Job that he desires. In some way, God assists Satan to give effect to Satan's free decisions. Job's references to God giving and taking away (1:21) and receiving the good and the bad at God's hands (2:10) are references to God's permitting what has happened and hint at God's concurrence in the events. The writer's comment on God bringing evil upon Job (24:11) is also seen the same way; it is true in light of God's concurrence and permission. While such an analysis seems more forced than the earlier one, it does have the positive attribute of not cutting across the numerous other Scripture attestations to the goodness of God and God's love for humanity.

However, this view of evil and sin does not impinge on the sovereignty or providence of God, for "nothing happens by chance or accidentally."[58] How this can be without making God the author of sin Arminius explains:

> Nothing is done without God's ordination: if by the word 'ordination' is signified 'that God appoints things of any kind to be done,' this mode of enunciation is erroneous and it follows as a consequence from it that *God is the author of sin*. But if it signify, that 'whatever it be that is done, God ordains it to a good end,' the terms in which it is conceived are in that case correct.[59]

That is, God controls everything "*in the sense that* he points it to a good end," and his "intimate and direct involvement in every event of nature and history" is affirmed, but authorship of sin and evil is excluded.[60] Thus, God is self-limiting in history—much that happens is permitted by him but is contrary to his antecedent will (see below). This self-limitation is "to allow for genuine human free agency (for the sake of genuine relationships that are not manipulated or controlled)";[61] without it, human free agency in Arminian terms cannot exist, so it must in some sense generate or guarantee free agency.

---

58. Arminius, *Works*, cited in Stanglin and McCall, *Jacob Arminius*, 96. They note that in the original Dutch and Latin the terms "may bear a negative and positive connotation, respectively. Thus, the meaning is that nothing bad or good happens by chance," n. 7. Hence the phrase is meant to specifically encompass both good and evil occurrences rather than simply being a general observation.

59. Arminius, *Works*, cited in Olsen, *Arminian Theology*, 120 (emphasis in the original).

60. Olsen, *Arminian Theology*, 120; 116 (emphasis his).

61. Ibid., 38, 39.

Williams echoes just these views in his comments on providence and human liberty. He defines providence as "the overseeing care and guardianship of God for all his creation" which extends to a particular care for each individual, even the least: God is holding all together and ensuring it works.[62] God is present in creation, directing it to ensure that his *purpose* is fulfilled, but this does not deny the freedom of human action nor the evil of human intent.[63]

Thus, for Pentecostals, reflecting the Arminian view, God is providing for creation at every level, ensuring it continues to work and also that it continues to move towards God's purposes. This concern excludes nothing, so God is involved in every action of every human, believer or otherwise. However, God does not determine every action of every human; while God may be the prime cause of any good action, God is neither the prime cause nor uses secondary causes to bring about any evil action, as to be so would make God the author of sin. Rather, God permits evil actions and concurs in them by providing whatever is necessary from Godself to ensure the evil action occurs, but does so in a manner that imposes limits on the action to ensure that God's overarching purposes are not frustrated. Evil actions occur due to human decisions in exercise of the freedom which God allows humans, a freedom necessary to ensure humans can enter a genuine relationship with God. In this account, a relationship can only be genuine if it comprises two beings who are at liberty to choose to enter the relationship, not if it stands on the unilateral determination of one of the parties (as Arminians say it would for Calvin).

In this conception, there are things which occur which God does not determine, although they are never uncontrolled. In its broadest sense, God wills that all will be saved (1 Tim 2:4), but some refuse the gift (Matt 23:37–8) and God wills that these shall not be saved. There is something to be distinguished in the will of God here, and Arminus recognizes this, holding to the ancient distinction between the antecedent and consequent will of God.[64] God's antecedent will is that will (exercised before creation) that God's good purpose will occur. God's will ensures that all remains under his control in the sense that God's overarching purpose and destination for creation will come to pass. God's consequent will cooperates with the sinner in history to allow the sin and determine that unrepentant sinners are condemned. The operation of both wills ensures that God's purposes are not frustrated, yet the freedom of his creatures is respected

---

62. Williams, *Renewal Theology*, 1:117–19.
63. Ibid., 1:121–24 (emphasis mine).
64. Stanglin and McCall, *Jacob Arminius*, 71–72.

and God does not predetermine their actions so as to allow genuine relationships to develop with them.[65]

The final consideration in Arminianism before examining its impact in personal providence is its attitude to human will. Arminius clearly understood humans to have a libertarian free will, by which is meant an incompatibilist free will (to use modern terminology); a will which is not compatible with determinism.[66] This is not the free will of an independent moral agent but is a self-determined will. This is not the same as what Calvin would describe as self-determined, rather it is somehow constrained without being coerced. Humans have the uncoerced freedom to choose a particular action or not: anything else would do violence to the quality of relationship God desires with them.[67] However, this occurs in a context where God has foreknowledge of the results and here is encountered a concept which Keith D. Stanglin and Thomas H. McCall suggest is relied on "quite heavily" in the theology of Arminius:[68] that of middle knowledge.

In the doctrine, middle knowledge is one of the "three logical moments within the divine knowledge, the first two of which were common to most scholastic accounts."[69] The three are:

1. God's *necessary* knowledge, God knowing all that *must* be and *could* be;

2. God's *free* knowledge, God knowing all that *will* be; and

3. God's middle knowledge, God knowing all that *would* be.[70]

Middle knowledge allows that God knows what any individual would do in any circumstances. This opens an attractive way of reconciling a strong doctrine of divine providence with human freedom: "Because God knows precisely how every individual would respond in any set of circumstances, God then actualizes a particular world with a particular set of individuals and set of circumstances in which they make free choices."[71] It is this which provides the constraint on human free will; while it is uncoerced and so free, it can only operate in the context in which it is placed, a context which acts to place limitations on the choices before the individual human. Thus Olsen

---

65. Olsen, *Arminian Theology*, 123.
66. Stanglin and McCall, *Jacob Arminius*, 117.
67. Ibid., 101.
68. Ibid., 69.
69. Ibid., 65.
70. Ibid., 65–67 (emphasis theirs).
71. Ibid., 67.

can comment that nothing outside influences the human will, but that it is always "influenced and situated in a context."[72]

Human Will for Pentecostals

It is this construction which allows Williams to give his account of who is acting in the Fall. Humans were "granted the freedom to decide in relation to God's will" with no compulsion in respect of the direction their choices would take them—toward God or away. To be genuine, such freedom "*must contain within itself a genuine decision*." However, this was a freedom within the context of human orientation towards God; any choice to move away from God would be contrary to unfallen human nature.[73] Despite this latter point, in an exercise of the freedom given them, the humans did choose the evil option: "The action was wholly contrary to God's command, and done in the freedom God had granted." Hence the humans were responsible for the entry of sin into the world.[74]

Williams describes this as having occurred with God's permissive will. God permitted the action, but also "God's will was actively involved in what transpired." Although the sin was "contrary to God, He willed to fulfil through it His own purpose," and it is this permissive will which "stands behind the sin and fall of mankind."[75] He notes a "strange paradox here. God surely did not will the sin of man (sic), else He would have been the author of evil; yet He did will that through sin and the fall His purpose should be fulfilled."[76]

The two wills of God lie behind the resolution of this paradox (to the extent that it can be resolved).[77] God's antecedent will means that history will proceed to the goal God has established for it and God's consequent will means that God adjusts to events as they occur through the exercise of human freedom (events which occur in the context of God's middle knowledge and of which God has foreknowledge). So, it is not quite as Williams states it; rather God's consequent willing to ensure that despite sin God's antecedent willing remains secure is to some extent a response to the exercise of human freedom.

---

72. Olsen, *Arminian Theology*, 75.
73. Williams, *Renewal Theology*, 1:217–18 (emphasis his).
74. Ibid., 1:229.
75. Ibid., 1:229–230.
76. Ibid., 1:229.
77. God's concurrence plays a role as well, of course.

Within this framework, as God acts providentially for all without exception, the Pentecostal believer can be confident that he can rely on God's personal providence for him. However, he enjoys a significant degree of freedom in the exercise of his will as he has been given the liberty to choose for or against God; he has a true liberty to determine his course by the exercise of a free will which is "more" free than Calvin would care to admit. What has occurred for him at conversion is that the operation of God's prevenient grace has restored a moral will so that he is now able to accept the free gift of salvation, rather than be constrained to reject it as he would without God's grace.[78] Previously, his context was one of being bound by original sin, but now God's grace has set him free—so Olsen can say that the exercise of will at conversion is more an exercise of *freed* will than free will.[79] Now, having accepted God's offer, the believer is aware of the godly and evil alternatives before him, and can choose. Here, his "free will . . . is situated freedom under the influence of the call to the good *and* the pull of the fallen nature."[80] That is, he lives life now equipped to see the godly choices, and under the influence of the Spirit to adopt the godly choice, but his free will still exists so he is also able to see and adopt the evil or sinful choice.

There are thus three wills in operation in any decision between alternatives: in order of impact on the universe, God's antecedent will, God's consequent will, and human free will. God's antecedent will means that the outcome of the history of the universe which God has decreed is preserved and the decision will not affect that, although the shape of history before that end may be affected. God's consequent will means that God notes and responds to the decision, in a way assisted by God's foreknowledge of the decision, so that effect is given to the decision; the outcome required by the decision is assured by the activity of God. This consequent will acts in a way which may or may not impinge on the will of the human; it may be necessary to alter or affect the context of the decision so that the human cannot decide in a manner which frustrates God's antecedent will. The human free will is truly free in making the decision, and God respects the exercise of this free will so as to make it so. However, it is not free in the sense of being that of an independent moral agent, it cannot be that as the exercise of such a free will would threaten God's antecedent will. Rather, the human will is free within the context God has set in God's antecedent and consequent wills and God's possession of middle knowledge. It may be, for example, that in God's consequent will God has manipulated those factors which

---

78. Stanglin and McCall, *Jacob Arminius*, 158; Olsen, *Arminian Theology*, 75.
79. Olsen, *Arminian Theology*, 164 (emphasis mine).
80. Ibid., 174 (emphasis his).

have an influence on the alternatives so that only certain alternatives are on offer, and that the alternatives offered have features that constrain them to be of a certain character. That is, that only alternatives which lead history on paths acceptable to God's antecedent will, or which have been influenced by God so as to eliminate characteristics which may place them in conflict with those paths, are on offer. Of course, these paths may change after the decision is made due to the influence of other humans exercising their free wills, but for the instant of decision, the alternatives lead to certain paths. The human will is free, then, in that it can choose between *these* alternatives without external influence. It is not free to choose between *any* alternatives, as it would be if it were the will of a free moral agent, it can only choose between those alternatives presented.

The exercise of this free will on the part of the believer is something which truly belongs only to her. Certainly, it is an exercise within a context and will be influenced by that context. Equally, while God permits her exercise of her free will, he does so in a way which ensures God's purposes are not frustrated by her decision. But he allows her a freedom of choice in which he does not determine the outcome in any way, or, at the least, does not wholly determine the outcome if he chooses to constrain her choice in some fashion so as to protect his antecedent will. *She* determines her choice, to some extent at least, and God leaves that to her. This means that, faced with a choice between two alternatives she can choose the one that God would rather she didn't. Objectively, this seems an uncomfortable possibility for the parties; God sees a believer making a choice contrary to God's desires and the believer, if she knew it, can make a choice contrary to the desire of the God to whom she is committed. It is, nevertheless, parallel with the Pentecostal view on salvation, where God's desire is that the individual be saved, but this can only occur through a synergism of God's grace and the faith of the human. Confronted with this situation, God is equipped to deal with it as God foreknew the result and will deal with its outcomes to make sure God's purposes remain unthreatened. The believer, on the other hand, may well be horrified that she has made a choice contrary to God's desire. For her, it is one thing to know that God's providence extends to her and all situations she will meet, it is another to know what God's desire is in any given situation. If she is striving for obedience, she will be greatly concerned to know God's desire in any situation so that she may choose correctly (or, if she desires to be rebellious, incorrectly!). That is, God's providence for her through specific guidance in any given choice is very important to her.

Personal Guidance

This guidance is available to her in a number of ways. In a parallel manner to Calvin's thought, the Spirit has come to indwell her at her conversion and established a union between her and Christ, which she will express as the establishment of a relationship with Christ. The Spirit has cleansed her at conversion and now engages on a progressive sanctification, transforming her righteousness as she lives in union with Christ and pursues her sanctification in obedience to him. Alongside and contributing to this process, the Spirit has convicted her of the truth of the witness of Scripture to the nature of Christ as her savior, and continues to reveal that truth more fully (or promotes a deeper knowledge of the realities of God) as she reads Scripture, and hears it preached and taught by others. Although she may be aware of particular insights as insights when they occur, a broader knowledge of Christ and his call on her is being built as she acquires this knowledge and she is being equipped with better knowledge about what it is to be godly—some of it directly scriptural, some of it derived from what she has learnt. She may or may not directly recognize the Spirit in activity in these areas, but the impact on her actions will be real. Thus, faced with a particular situation, her decision on how to respond will be informed by what she knows at the time. It may be that she knows that *this* is how she is to act because of the state of her general knowledge, or it may be that she is led by some specific point she has been shown from Scripture—in either event she will be guided by the knowledge she has gained from the activity of the Spirit in her. As time goes on, and her sanctification proceeds, the depth of her knowledge increases so that the extent of the situations in which she can rely on what she knows grows. To summarize, she becomes more mature and can respond appropriately in a broader range of circumstances. Thus, the Spirit provides guidance in a manner which can be almost anonymous to the believer, but which is nevertheless real and of material benefit.

This process is certainly indirect in much of its impact, and even when it is direct it can appear to leave the believer isolated. By that I mean that he is faced with a choice, but can only weigh the options in the light of the knowledge he has—and this knowledge appears to be his from his perspective. He could easily feel that a perhaps very important decision confronts him and God seems to have absented Godself, leaving him to grapple with the issue on his own. This is where the Pentecostal believer can claim that Spirit release has opened up an entirely new, additional, avenue for guidance through the direct apprehension of the Spirit and his availability to assist him through the enhanced relationship he now enjoys with Christ. This doesn't devalue any of the work of the Spirit in sanctification or illumination of

Scripture—in fact it has the effect of enhancing the work, as the deeper and broader apprehension of the triune God which is the content of Spirit release creates a greater receptivity to these aspects of the Spirit's work. Sanctification proceeds more quickly, and the illumination of Scripture is brighter, so a more godly response is readily generated. Nevertheless, in addition to this enhancement, direct appeal to the Spirit is now available.

Spirit release is certainly an identifiable, discrete occurrence, but the Spirit remains. Williams states this and goes on to suggest that the "coming on" of the Spirit (referring specifically to the terminology used at Acts 19:6) is that "it signified a *taking possession* by the Holy Spirit," so that "henceforward, the Holy Spirit was to be the controlling factor for their lives and ministry."[81] It can be protested here that this is surely no change for one who has saving knowledge of Jesus Christ, is in union with him and within whom the Spirit dwells, but what is meant is that a fundamental change has occurred within the believer. She has encountered the Spirit in such a fundamentally new and numinous manner that her disposition towards God through the Spirit has shifted substantially towards God and away from herself. That is, the "balance" of the new creation which is the creature in union with God has shifted substantially towards God in a way which means that God has more "say" in her day to day activities and decisions. This is a permanent shift (assuming her perseverance in faith), so Spirit release has given rise to much greater opportunities for influence by the Spirit in her future life. This change is captured well by the understanding of the occurrence I have already adopted as the release of the already indwelling Spirit, rather than a new coming separate from, and of a different quality than, the indwelling which occurred at conversion. Release involves no change in character of the indwelling, but rather speaks of the Spirit now being able to act in the believer in new ways, or in a more extensive manner than previously. It is as if the Spirit, once indwelling but confined within a certain part of the believer, is now released, breaking out of confinement to invade and inhabit more "parts" of the believer, or indeed every part of the believer. Thus, in contrast to his previous limited view, the believer might understand that divine healing is now available and so seek it, or that the Spirit could influence the pace of his journey to work and so look for his assistance if he is running late. Another way of expressing this is to say that the believer who once looked upon the world through post-modern rationalistic eyes (albeit eyes acknowledging the reality of God in Christ, however that might be understood) is now convicted of the supernatural nature of God and the reality of God's activity

---

81. Williams, *Renewal Theology*, 2:197 (emphasis his).

in history and hence the willingness of God to act supernaturally in him, with him, or for him in ways which actually change things.

This sense of a God who can "do things" is intensified when the full content of Spirit release is considered. As an encounter which grants deeper insight and knowledge of the Father, Son and Spirit, it invites the believer to a greater participation in God as it enhances the "accessibility" of God. This greater "ease" of participation allows Christ to actualize his presence in the believer's life more readily than previously which not only hastens sanctification, but also allows the believer to perceive God's guidance more clearly. The synergistic activity of Christ and the Spirit means that the believer has a greater appreciation of the presence and activity of God all the time, so making it more likely that he will seek guidance on any issue and that he will correctly perceive what he is given. Having said this, the most likely perception on the part of the believer is that God is very real, he has directly apprehended the Spirit and is aware that the Spirit can, and does, communicate directly with him. In other words, the Spirit is available to give him guidance on any issue—Duffield and Van Cleave may go too far in suggesting "His guiding makes life a personally conducted tour,"[82] but they do capture the conviction that the Spirit can be looked to for assistance in anything which is not incompatible with godliness.

To this point, when considering personal providence I have considered choices made between godly and evil alternatives, highlighting the providence of God available in the godly alternatives. However, the availability and complete involvement of the Spirit to and with the believer opens the possibility of a more nuanced providence; that it might be available to distinguish the best from several godly alternatives, or that it might act in a way neutral to God[83] but to cause advantage to the believer. Examples of the former may include choices of where to worship; of the latter where to find a car park for a godly pursuit. This is certainly what Duffield and Van Cleave have in mind with their "personally conducted tour." The sovereignty of God and the intimacy the believer now shares with Godself through Spirit release mean that the believer is not entitled to place any limit on the providential activity of God who can be looked to for provision in matters great and small. Seeking guidance, then, is important to the believer not only because

---

82. Duffield and Van Cleave, *Foundations of Pentecostal Theology*, 285.

83. It might be argued, of course, that there is no choice in which the outcome is neutral to God, and Calvin would certainly say so. However, within Arminian thought, it is easy to conceive of a situation where any of the alternative outcomes require no response from God in his consequent will to preserve his antecedent will, but that some alternatives produce better outcomes for the believer. This is what I have in view in envisaging a situation where providence could act in a way neutral to God.

it will identify godly from evil alternatives and assist in her sanctification, but also because it might identify the best alternative for her or provide a direct personal benefit to her. This provides more motivation for her to seek the guidance of the Spirit often, in fact continually.

The immediacy of the Spirit in Spirit release and the continuing release within her mean that the believer can look to the Spirit directly for guidance. This release invites her to look to the Spirit, asking "What is the Spirit saying to me on this matter?" The enquiry needs to be firmly placed within the full trinitarian content of Spirit release to avoid separating the Spirit from the Son and the Father, but the experience of Spirit release and its continuing impact in her life informs her that such direct guidance is available without recourse to Scripture or the teaching of the church. This is because she has been shown that she can apprehend the Spirit directly, so there is little to suggest that she need look elsewhere. This direct guidance is also available with the assistance of others through the operation of spiritual gifts, where its directness is of a different character. The involvement of another believer is certainly the involvement of the church, but it is a matter of the church active in facilitating the direct and specific guidance of the Spirit to the believer. The most obvious gifts which might operate in this manner are the gifts of "the utterance of knowledge" or "prophecy" (1 Cor 12:8, 10), where something is said to the believer by another who is being used by the Spirit for the purpose.

Williams describes knowledge as "an inspired word of teaching or instruction," although limiting it to the context of the gathered community.[84] David Lim says that the gift is "teaching the truths of the Word of God" and quotes Donald Gee as describing it as "flashes of insight into truth that penetrated beyond the operation of . . . unaided intellect."[85] Duffield and Van Cleave describe it as bringing to light "the principles of doctrine that form a basis for . . . action,"[86] a somewhat narrower conception than the other two sources. All of them agree that it is a direct inspiration and is not the result of study. Accordingly, a believer could be informed concerning her future action by the gift of knowledge operating, the insight being given perhaps informing her directly about how she should proceed in the matter at hand.

Prophecy is the declaration of a message from God which has been revealed to the person speaking the prophecy, it is "an immediate communication from God in the common language."[87] Duffield and Van Cleave

---

84. Williams, *Renewal Theology*, 2:356.
85. Lim, "Spiritual Gifts," 466; and Gee, *Spiritual Gifts*, cited there.
86. Duffield and Van Cleave, *Foundations of Pentecostal Theology*, 336.
87. Williams, *Renewal Theology*, 2:382.

take a similar view, prophecy being words given by God to be delivered by an individual,[88] while Lim calls it "Spirit-inspired spontaneous messages in the speaker's known language."[89] It has similarities with knowledge, but none of the sources link it to doctrine or Scripture as they do knowledge. Even more than knowledge, prophecy can therefore be conceived as direct information from God to a community or an individual and can be directed towards providing guidance for a believer in the decisions he faces. He hears the prophetic utterance (or a word of knowledge which he can apply) and experiences it as God speaking directly to him through the operation of the Spirit in the person speaking. Although mediated by the speaker, it is nevertheless a direct communication.

Both the direct discernment of guidance from the Spirit or the operation of spiritual gifts raise the question of how the believer can determine that the direction given comes from God. Even if its context is the church, its direct nature contains within it the possibility of error. Answers can be supplied around whether what is given fits a Christian framework, or how the guidance affects the ongoing quality of the life of the believer, although the latter is more helpful over time than in a particular instance. The most common answer encountered is that what direction is given must be consistent with Scripture,[90] but while consistency must mean that what is given does not contradict Scripture, it does not necessarily mean divine origin as it could parallel Scripture without being at all related. Perhaps a better response is to borrow the Arminian idea of concurrence, so that what is given must be concurrent with Scripture. By this I mean that there is not only no contradiction with Scripture but there is a positive alignment with Scripture. This could mean that what is given has an obvious scriptural derivation but could also mean that it can be clearly linked to scriptural truth. However, this might be understood, what is clear is that Pentecostals must take seriously the scriptural instruction to test the spirits (1 John 4:1–6)[91] so that what is spoken in knowledge or prophecy and what is heard directly is not accepted uncritically, but is considered and a decision made as to its authenticity. There is an acceptance that such testing will not be perfect so that errors will be made, but even those can be seen positively as part of the inevitable failures on the journey of sanctification.

---

88. Duffield and Van Cleave, *Foundations of Pentecostal Theology*, 339.

89. Lim, "Spiritual Gifts," 467.

90. For example, "[Spirit baptism in its full content] verifies, clarifies, emphasizes, or enforces the truths of the Bible" (Railey and Aker, "Theological Foundations," 50–51).

91. The context there appears to be directed at false teaching about the humanity of Jesus, but I suggest the principle is more widely applicable than simply that issue.

The pneumatological soteriology suggested by Yong and Macchia also provides a fruitful framework for ongoing personal providence. Salvation is understood as being a dynamic event, comprising the establishment of a union with Christ through the synergistic work of Christ and the Spirit followed by a life lived reoriented to Christ. There is not the conversion event followed by ongoing sanctification which can be separated by the differing character of each, but rather salvation itself has a starting point at Christian initiation and has a uniform character of a continuing participation in God from and including that point. It is a dynamic living in the Spirit, in which the synergistic activity of the Spirit and Christ produce and maintain a living relationship between the believer and God. A critical part of this is the reorientation to God of the believer brought about by Spirit release so that the believer's decision-making and behavior are driven more and more by the Spirit. This is certainly providential for the believer as his decisions become more God-oriented through the operation of the Spirit. It is different from the discrete guidance just described because of Spirit release, as what is aimed at is not so much instruction on each decision, but godly outcomes without individual instruction. This, at first glance, is the same as that process described for sanctification above, but it has a different character in that it is salvation which is in view, not the perfection of one already saved. It is not that the believer has been reoriented and is now learning how to behave as one reoriented, it is that the reorientation is an ongoing, active process and that the believer is participating in the reorientation every day. It isn't so much that the Spirit is looked to for particular guidance, it is that the general reorientation results in the believer adopting the appropriate direction. In doing this, he is allowing the Spirit to give guidance and he can be confident in the providence of God for him personally.

Affinities

Equipped with the foregoing outlines, we can now attempt to see how they might engage with each other. As a starting point, I have entitled this chapter "Providence and Guidance" and tended to use the two terms interchangeably although they are certainly not synonyms. "Providence" has dominated in the discussion on Calvin's thought to the exclusion of "guidance," while the latter has assumed greater prominence in considering Pentecostal theology and this is not accidental. The difference between the terms necessitates some explanation of my use of them which will also prove useful in considering whether there is any affinity between Calvin and Pentecostals in these areas.

Theologically, providence is the continual activity of God by which creation is sustained, and all events are directed to the goal God has appointed.[92] It has to do with connecting creation with its redemption and its final consummation, encompassing the entire cosmos.[93] Guidance is included within these definitions and is colloquially understood as "direction [or] leadership."[94] There is clearly a relation between the two terms: the foresight and benevolent care of God will certainly involve giving direction or leadership to the humans towards whom God is being provident. That is, guidance is a part of providence. Hence providence is more complete than guidance; it will include not only directing the human, but also the benefit towards which she is directed. To say that God is being provident is to say that he is directing the human and giving her what she requires according to his loving care. Saying that God is guiding the human is to suggest that she is shown what God has provided for her, but that its actual provision may depend on factors other than God.

It is correct then to associate providence in its full sense with Calvin's views on the subject. Everything happens as God intends via direct cause or through secondary causes, so his action toward the human includes both direction and the resulting benefit. Both are in God's gift and the human *will* receive them if God wills that she must. Guidance, on the other hand, sits more comfortably within Pentecostal thought as there God's involvement in providing for creation certainly includes giving guidance for the believer, but whether the believer avails himself of the proffered benefit is determined by the believer's free will with the concurrence of God's consequent will. The determination that the benefit *will* be the believer's does not rest with God; it rests with the believer. God's role is limited to providing the opportunity to partake of the benefit and acting concurrently with the believer to ensure it is given should the believer choose it, neither of which are determinative. Inevitably, then, it is more correct to talk of providence in respect of Calvin and guidance in respect of Pentecostals, and this has been reflected in the discussion so far.

It is obvious that there is a substantial difference between the two views in respect of providence, broadly understood. Both want to assert the loving care of God for creation, and particularly believers, but each sees the care worked out in a different manner. For a particular instance of God providing some benefit for an individual, both want to say that the benefit *is* provided. Calvin's doctrine means that the benefit is provided *and* will be

---

92. Douglas, "Providence," 1292–93.
93. McFarland et al., "Providence," 416–19.
94. Macdonald, "Guidance," 578.

enjoyed by the believer through the benevolent causation of God. However, for the Pentecostal, while the benefit is just as real, it remains provisional until the believer decides to receive it. But God does not leave the believer alone in her decision-making. While it is an exercise of her free will, God has come to her in a direct way through Spirit release and continues in that direct involvement with her through the union she enjoys with Christ. In some sense, while Spirit release occurs in the believer who makes herself willingly available for God to invade, so to speak, invade God does. The experience is so overwhelming that the believer feels left with no choice other than to abandon herself to this God with her. Not only is this the case at Spirit release itself, but it produces a continuing desire to abandon herself to God as the Spirit uses the new and deeper illumination of the triune God to transform her, so she can expect and seek divine guidance and providence for all parts of her life. That means that the approach for guidance in a particular instance is not a diffident request whose result will be dispassionately examined so as to make a "logical" free will decision. No, the approach is made in the conviction that God knows best and a desire for God to reveal the best for her. This is surely apt to produce a presumption on the part of the believer that her best decision is to accept God's benefit. Calvin would not want to countenance such a direct and apparently unmoderated impact from God, but would affirm that abandonment to God is powerfully taught to the elect through Scripture and the ministry of the church in its proclamation and administering of the sacraments. Nevertheless, the conditions God has worked to create within believers through Spirit release mean that the outcome of God's providence for believers is much closer to Calvin's conception than at first appears, although by no means identical with it.

Affinities: Human and Divine Wills and Decision-making

It is possible to deduce a similar relation between the operation of divine and human wills in each occurrence of God's providence. Calvin's disciple, so to speak, is subject to God's will which determines his action, but he also exercises his free will in deciding his course. This will is truly free in that it is un-coerced, but the choice he makes is always in accord with God's will, determined beforehand, but operating through a secondary cause as God makes use of the means provided by the believer's decision. In doing so, however, there is not a direct determination by God of the specific action even by direction of the means. Rather, God is involved by way of willing permission which is more than a passive allowing and less than a divine direction, but just how this can be so is not available to the human. The Pentecostal exercises his free will, which is not that of an independent moral agent but is freer than Calvin's in that it is possible for the believer to make a decision which is contrary to God's provision for him. However, his will is not without constraints as he cannot make a decision which will impede God's antecedent will, determined beforehand in foreknowledge of the believer's decision, but he can decide in a way which obliges God to make a response. But, again, he makes this decision in the context of Spirit release through which God has produced in him an intense desire to be oriented to God and so be obedient to him: in short, he is primed to exercise his will in a way which is entirely in accord with God's antecedent will. Through Spirit release God has caused a shift in the exercise of the believer's will so that he is very much more inclined to align it with God's will. While the operation of God's will and human will are conceived to be different, under the influence of the released Spirit within him, the outcomes could be very similar.

The gap in understanding within Calvin's thought concerning how it is that God controls all outcomes, yet humans have a genuine involvement through the exercise of their wills does not exist within Pentecostal theology. However, there is still a gap of a somewhat different nature. The general approach that God controls all things so that history moves to its predetermined end, yet there is genuine choice inclusive of the possibility that outcomes contrary to God's intent are possible for the human, does not stand close scrutiny as eliminating any gap. This understanding is the Arminian position of the interplay of God's antecedent and consequent wills with God's concurrence in human actions; where the gap lies is how it is that concurrence can contribute to sinful human actions. There is a desire to ensure that God is not made the author of sin in Arminian thought, but concurrence implicates God in sinful actions. The explanation offered that this is necessary to preserve a genuine relationship between God and the human may be entirely correct, but this is not an explanation as to how it is that God concurs in sinful human action but is not the author of it in any way. The gap is placed differently but is of the same essential character. What is not explained in either system is how it can be that God has some relation to sinful actions without ever bearing responsibility for them. There is significant difference between the positions which revolves around the degree of freedom of the human, but at the core they both want to say similar things about God's sovereignty.

The reorientation achieved in Spirit release or a Spirit soteriology offers guidance to Pentecostals in a way different from Calvin. For him the believer learns of God's will and therefore how she should exercise her free will from Scripture, either taught through the church or read directly with the guidance of the church. Therefore, any decision will appear to be an application of what has been learnt from these sources. Of course, this is not ontologically the case, as the Spirit is secretly working in her to illuminate the truth and transform her, reorient her to God, and give effect to God's intentions for her. She will accordingly be becoming more prone to choosing the godly alternative realized by the Spirit active in her, so discovering God's provision for her. This spiritual influence certainly acts in her decision-making. Nevertheless, as the Spirit is not directly apprehended but rather known indirectly through her faith, the choices she makes will appear to her to be her choices made in respect for her faith and in the knowledge she has gained.

For Pentecostals, all this is true also, but as the Spirit is directly apprehended, the potential exists for the believer to identify direct guidance for the decision. It is no longer his alone, he perceives that the released Spirit has given him direction and while it is properly his decision, the choice for God's providence will be recognized as the believer acceding to God's leading. He may well claim that God is providing and he is enjoying God's provision. Curiously, the Pentecostal who wants to claim free will in deciding for God may be more inclined to feel that he is truly being provided for, although the degree of freedom accorded his will places God's provision at risk. In contrast, in Calvin's thought the secrecy of the Spirit may surround the decision in doubt for the believer, but its outcome in reality is never at risk.

Here, Spirit release offers a directly apprehended involvement by God through the Spirit and so provides an additional aid to the Pentecostal believer in his decision-making. Nevertheless, much of the underlying ground is the same for Calvin and the Pentecostals. For Calvin, the believer is one of the elect in whom her election has been awakened—God has determined since before creation that this individual will be awakened at this time to her true place in God and introduced to God's provision for her, ultimately life eternal. What is confirmed in her awakening is a union between her and Christ and through that union she is reoriented to God by the activity of the Spirit; now she will live her life as one of the elect and inevitably she will more and more live oriented to God. As her sanctification proceeds beyond this awakening, she will make more and more godly choices and fewer sinful human ones through the work of the Spirit in her. All this occurs as the entire free gift of God who has determined this course for her, although she may have experienced her awakening as a decision she made, and will also experience her decision-making as her own. Nevertheless, it is God who has provided this for her and who ensures it occurs.

The Pentecostal view is different in that, while her salvation is a gift from God, she is free to refuse the gift. She is saved if she accepts the gift—expressed within Arminian thought, she does not resist the grace God extends to her in offering salvation.[95] Thus her election has not been predetermined by God but she has become part of the elect community of believers by her non-resistance, an occurrence foreseen by God from before creation. While her salvation is not dependent on her merit or any work on her behalf (the "act" of non-resistance not being a work), she does have an involvement in her salvation beyond what Calvin envisages as she could do a work and resist God's grace. This human involvement continues in her sanctification as she makes decisions on her actions, so her salvation and Christian life have not been solely determined by God, but rather by God's act combined with her acceptance. This synergism contains within it the possibility that she will understand that God has done something for her, not only in the sense that she has received salvation as a gift, but also that she is the more important party in the transaction. That is, the possibility exists that she will see that her future life is one in which she is to be assisted by God to achieve her aims and that the providence of God exists for that purpose. In short, she may see that the point is not participation in God, but God's participation in her.[96]

Spirit release, understood in its full content, can function as a corrective to this attitude. The quality of the occurrence is such that there is an overwhelming insight into who God is (Father, Son and Spirit) and God's magnitude relative to the believer. The invasion of the believer by the Spirit is such that he understands that this is God, and that he gains an impression of the majesty of God and a conviction that this is someone he is to serve. It is simply ridiculous to contemplate that the puny human he has been shown to be could conceive of this God being in any way at his service. This is confirmed as the Spirit reveals Christ and the Father in Spirit release, and being shown Christ further illuminates him as God's revelation and directs the believer to Scripture to discover what he is about. There, it is made clear that Christ as the revelation of God calls the believer to follow him and live for him—to be "in Christ." While Spirit release appears a subjective experience, its full content draws the believer to Scripture and so grounds him in the Word. Henceforth, this knowledge should act to ensure that his orientation to God and desire to serve him is entirely dominant within him, and he should be utterly convinced that the released Spirit is there for divine purposes, not those of the human. In this manner, Spirit release may almost dictate that the believer becomes committed to God's purposes and participation in him.

---

95. Stanglin and McCall, *Jacob Arminius*, 158.

96. See Horton, *Christless Christianity*, for an extended discussion on how this possibility is worked out in sectors of the North American church.

Affinities: Union and Discovery

A similar conclusion can be drawn from the operation of the mystical union within the believer. It is through the union that the believer receives the benefits of Christ and avails themselves of God's provision. For Calvin, the extent of God's control over all that occurs means that the vastly predominant activity of the union is Christ working in the believer through the Spirit. Personal providence is provided through Christ to the believer—the "flow" within the union is in this direction. This does not conflict with the union being a mutually inter-penetrating relation between two parties in which there is something real which is from the believer to Christ, but whatever the believer has originates in Christ, so the exchange within the union is heavily weighted towards the Christ to believer "direction." This is so much so that it is fair to characterize the union as being almost one-way.

For the Pentecostal, the union is understood as a relationship within which the believer has the freedom to act sinfully in a way which is not determined by God at all. Certainly, God uses the relationship to provide for the believer, but because of the greater degree of autonomy granted to him, the believer can use it to look to God for that providence (or guidance) in a real way which is different to Calvin's conception. The "traffic" in the union is very much more two-way, with enquiry flowing from the believer and provision from Christ. This understanding is consistent with Arminian thought and may have existed prior to Spirit release, and it carries also the possibility that the believer will see that the access he enjoys through the union is to assist him achieve his aims. He can enquire and receive something from God for his use. The likelihood of this possibility arising is increased if Spirit release is understood solely as the Spirit coming to equip the believer as noted in chapter three. However, understood in its full content as described there, Spirit release can serve as a corrective, the believer being overwhelmed to an extent which drives him to understand that what he is to be about is serving God.

From the believer's perspective, the experience of seeking God's providence is, at one level, the same. Calvin's disciple has her future laid out for her by God's decree, but, while she may acknowledge that God's decree governs, she doesn't know the future and wending her path through it involves what she experiences as hard work on her part.[97] Led and energized by the Spirit, she looks to what she learns from Scripture, through the ministry of the church, so she can apply it in making decisions on her future actions; she looks to her faith, and through it to the secret work of the Spirit to also

---

97. Zachman, *Image and Word*, 82, 84.

inform her as she apparently picks her path. In doing so, she experiences the decisions she makes as *her* free decisions, as a result of which she discovers God's provision for her.[98] And this is a real discovery: she cannot know what that provision is, yet God has made it and as she lives as one of the elect, the Spirit in secret ensures she will discover what God has planned for her, as she receives it.[99] In a similar way, the Pentecostal disciple has guidance from Scripture but also looks to the directly apprehended Spirit as a further source of guidance towards God's provision, but he exercises his free will, and actually affects his future in a way un-coerced by God. Each time he accurately receives guidance he discovers God's provision for him, although he does so before he receives it. The discovery is provisional as he must trust in faith that he has perceived correctly and act accordingly. Then the provisional discovery will be confirmed.

At another level, the experiences are different, because the Pentecostal does enjoy a greater freedom of action and has the direct, perceived influence of the Spirit to assist him. He will likely feel that he is at an advantage if he receives what he understands to be such direct guidance, something which Calvin would reject. However, there are significant points at which there is contact between each disciple's experiences. Each discovers God's providence for themselves, provisionally earlier for the Pentecostal, but made real for each at the same time when it is received. Each decides and takes action in faith at the time action is decided (albeit effected entirely by the Spirit for Calvin's disciple)—even the Pentecostal who has received particular guidance must rely on his faith that it is indeed from God in order to proceed in accord with it.

Summary

There are therefore distinct differences between the respective theologies of providence or guidance. It is not possible to put them alongside each other and draw easy bridges between them. However, this does not mean that there are not affinities between them which should encourage Pentecostals to learn from Calvin. First, both theologies assert God's sovereignty and, therefore, control over the destination of history. For Calvin, this is absolute in that God governs everything, while for Pentecostals there is the human ability to determine some actions. Nevertheless, no human action can frustrate the ultimate

---

98. Ibid., 79, 81.

99. Parker, *Calvin*, 46, notes there is no such thing as chance for Calvin. See also Zachman, *Image and Word*, 85.

destination of history, so both approaches share this core ideal. History is moving to God's conclusion and no other, both would say.

Second, while the extent of God's determination of historical occurrences differs between the two, the journey for the respective disciples is one of discovery. Each must work at discovering God's providence for them, each must work at discovering what godly activities God has in store for them. While Calvin's disciple is discovering what has already been decided, it nevertheless appears to be real work by the human, relying on the faith she has, that is required; God's prior decree does not lessen her experience of it as involving work. The Pentecostal seeks to discover God's provision in a similar manner, but also through direct apprehension of the Spirit's guidance or application of what he has previously learnt from the Spirit. Having discovered it, he must confirm it by acting on what his faith tells him is real guidance. His is real work also, ontologically so and also experienced as his work, and is also a discovery by faith. For each, God's providence is discovered through their work in faith, based on a confidence that God indeed will provide for them.

Third, the route to God's providence is the same for each, considered in a broad sense. Calvin teaches of a mystical union within the believer through which the aim of the believer, and God's purpose for her, is participation in God through sharing God's trinitarian life by God's grace thus living a godly life. Spirit-enabled, the believer "allows" God into the world as her sharing of his life means his intent for her is lived out by her in the world. Thus, God's purpose that the believer serve Godself, established in the eternal decree of predestination, can be lived out by the believer. Pentecostals acknowledge the union, usually referring to it as a relationship, through which they can know God and be empowered to live a godly life. However, this carries the seed of an understanding where God is helping them, rather than one where service of God is paramount. Spirit release, in its full content, can be a powerful antidote to this understanding as it carries the full majesty of God to the believer and releases the Spirit within him. The impact of the experience and its ongoing manifestation is such that it is calculated to produce a core understanding within the believer that this puny believer exists to serve God and the idea of the reverse is ludicrous. That is, there should be the conviction that the believer is at the disposal of God. Calvin's view of the union and participation in God lends itself well to further informing the Pentecostal. Having been encountered by the fullness of the triune God in Spirit release and had his very being invaded by the Spirit, the idea of participating in God is no longer strange to him as he may feel that he has already been enveloped by God. If he can grasp that this is God's purpose, then he can only acknowledge that God in no way exists for his benefit; he can only place himself at God's disposal.

This understanding further serves to correct any tendency to think that God serves human ends in any way.

Despite the differences, then, there are affinities between Calvin and Pentecostals concerning personal providence and guidance. More, Pentecostals can learn a great deal from Calvin's notion of God's purpose for the elect being participation in the triune life. This second point leads on to consideration of a major doctrine, where the proposal of a Pentecostal scholar concerning justification in the context of Spirit baptism will be explored in conversation with Calvin.

5

Justification

The existence of the union, or relationship, between God and the human and the potential it offers to the believer for participation in the triune communion at the heart of God's being[1] points to another fruitful area for conversation between Calvin and Pentecostals. This is the doctrine of justification, which Calvin certainly understands to be intimately connected to the mystical union he posits.

Calvin

Calvin's position was set out in chapter one, so for the present a brief reminder is all that is necessary. Justification is to be reckoned righteous in the sight of God and treated as such. Hence the estrangement due to sin has disappeared and God's dealings with the justified sinner for the future are not conditioned by that estrangement, but rather by a righteousness which is imputed to humans. The justified human enjoys a completely new status. The righteousness now accorded the human has its origin in Christ and it can be imputed because the believer is in Christ. That is, it can only be received once the "mystical union" in which the believer is "engrafted into [Christ's] body" and "Christ is made ours"[2] is formed. This union results in a new creation, in which the dual possibilities and actualities of participation in God and sin coexist. All this is the work of God, perfectly in accord with God's decree of election, and so occurs in God's time. This work occurs through faith, a gift of God to the believer, but it is not faith which justifies, but Christ. Faith is necessary but is only the way in which the benefits of

---

1. This participation does not mean that the believer becomes part of God, or shares in God's perfections, or intra-hypostatic relations. Rather, it is an intimate communing with God with a degree of intimacy and openness to the other which means it is correct to speak of the believer being "in" God. See 2 Peter 1:4.

2. III.11.10.

Christ are conveyed to the believer though the union, never the cause of, or even a contributor to, justification.

This close association between the union and justification Alistair McGrath describes as the "concept of *incorporation* [being] central to Calvin's understanding of justification," Christ justifying "within the context of the intimate personal relationship of Christ and the believer."[3] Despite this intimacy, McGrath also notes the "strongly forensic" nature of justification for Calvin—it is not that the human is made righteous by justification, but that she is accepted as righteous on account of the righteousness of Christ, something entirely external to her.[4]

There are two points worthy of note here as they bear on the later discussion. The first is that in this conception, justification is christological[5]—God declares the believer righteous and makes him so by the imputation of the righteousness of Christ, received *via* the union by faith. The believer is in union with Christ; within that union, and nowhere else, it is Christ *by* whom the believer understands that the declaration has been made for him; and it is Christ *from* whom the believer perceives the righteousness he receives originates, as it truly does. Justification is thoroughly christological.

The second is that sanctification commences concurrently with justification. Whereas justification is a once and for all declaration, sanctification both occurs and commences with justification. There is an element of sanctification which occurs simultaneously with justification, and a further element which continues beyond this point as a process or development within the life of the believer.[6] This initial element occurs coincident with justification and is inextricably linked with it, but is always distinct from it. It is not conflated with justification in any way.

The place of justification for Calvin can now be illustrated in an *ordo salutis*:

Election

Union

Justification /Sanctification

Glorification[7]

---

3. McGrath, *Iustitia Dei*, 255 (emphasis his). This relationship is within the church as the believer is engrafted into the fellowship of Christ, but this does not detract from either its personal nature or its intimacy.

4. Ibid., 254.

5. Ibid., 255, makes this point.

6. I have so far used the term "regeneration" when discussing Calvin. As Pentecostals tend to use "regeneration" for the first element and "sanctification" for the second, I will use "sanctification" hereafter for Calvin's accounts to avoid confusion.

7. After McGrath, *Iustitia Dei*, 255.

Pentecostal Accounts

Pentecostal accounts of justification are not always extensive, but J Rodman Williams does discuss it at some length.[8] Following him, with comment from other sources to highlight any differences, justification is to be declared righteous by God,[9] an action which has two parts: one is the non-imputation of sin and the other is the imputation of righteousness. The former means that the believer's sins are not accounted to her, they are forgiven; the latter is the righteousness of Christ being accounted to the believer where Christ has become righteousness for her. It is not an absence of unrighteousness, but God instead sees the perfect righteousness of Christ in her—"*it is as if [she] had never sinned.*" This is not an infusion of righteousness, but instead an accounting of what is intrinsically external to her (the righteousness of Christ) which changes her status.[10] Duffield and Van Cleave describe justification as involving "Pardon or remission of sins," by which all guilt and punishment those sins may have attracted is removed; the "Restoration of God's favor," in which the believer is received into God's favor as if he had never sinned; and the "Imputation of Christ's righteousness," where a positive righteousness is supplied in order that fellowship with God is possible.[11] The receipt into God's favor is an additional category which they see creating for the believer the condition where Christ's righteousness can be imputed to her, whereas this is assumed in Williams. Something substantive has occurred within and for the believer which has a real impact on how God deals with her and is also something which the believer can perceive in herself. There has been a "profound alteration of the human situation," and how substantive this is can be seen in that it is brought about by God at great divine cost: the *only* sinless human was made *sin* for us and died but was raised again, a costly sacrifice of God's Son, fully human and fully divine.[12] Daniel B. Pecota has a very similar account, although the union, expressed as regeneration and adoption, occurs simultaneously with justification for him (as also for Duffield and Van Cleave). He also specifically notes that the Biblical terms suggest a forensic setting for justification.[13]

Justification occurs not by any work, but is a gift of grace through faith, which is its instrument,[14] and also the "means of our being *united*

---

8. Williams, *Renewal Theology*, 2:61–81.
9. Ibid., 2:63.
10. Ibid., 2:63–68 (emphasis his).
11 Duffield and Van Cleave, *Foundations of Pentecostal Theology*, 226–28.
12. Williams, *Renewal Theology*, 2:68–70 (emphasis his).
13. Pecota, "The Saving Work of Christ," 364–66.
14. Williams, *Renewal Theology*, 2:72.

with Christ,"[15] and this is a union which is in existence prior to justification. This is so because as the declaration of righteousness is for those who have faith (as faith must exist to be the channel for the substance of the declaration), it is a declaration reflecting what is already true—that the believer is united with Christ in a mutual indwelling.[16] Indeed, the climax of faith is union with Christ, where trust is not only directed to Christ as the object of faith, but "is also—and most profoundly—the reality of being united with Him. The climax of believing in Christ is being in Him." This is "a unity of relationship" where the believer does not lose identity but her life "finds its center in Him." "It is a vital union in which the believer is constantly being invigorated and renewed by the life of Christ."[17] It is vital also for Duffield and Van Cleave, although their discussion focuses on new birth, understood as becoming a child of God, and adoption, being constituted an adult offspring by God in relationship with Godself. Together, these constitute a description of the establishment and ontology of an intimate union between the believer and God.[18]

In the same manner as Calvin, this understanding of the union provides a mechanism for Christ to act in the believer, or towards the believer, without the necessity of direct activity by the Spirit. That is, in the context of the present discussion, Christ acts to justify the individual directly where the Spirit is simply the means through which Christ dwells within the believer. Christ is occupying a place within the believer, from where he can act on him, which is made available to him by the Spirit. However, the Spirit need not be involved to a greater extent than that in any action Christ may choose to take with the believer. Thus, it is open to Christ to justify the believer with no direct involvement by the Spirit, who can, however, be said to be facilitating the activity of Christ. Justification is thus christological—indeed in Williams' entire discussion on justification, there is only one reference to the Holy Spirit, and that to specifically exclude an activity of the Spirit from the act of justification.[19]

Williams also discusses regeneration and, incorporated in it, repentance. Regeneration means a spiritual rebirth which results in a *new being* and is *imperative* as without it, humans are dead in sin.[20] Regeneration is primarily the work of the Holy Spirit and occurs within the individual by

---

15. Ibid., 2:73 (emphasis his).
16. Ibid., 2:74.
17. Ibid., 2:29–31.
18. Duffield and Van Cleave, *Foundations of Pentecostal Theology*, 236–40.
19. Williams, *Renewal Theology*, 1:77.
20. Ibid., 1:35–36 (emphasis his).

the action of the Spirit. The Word certainly plays a role, but it is enlivened by the Spirit in a way which produces regeneration in the individual.[21] Regeneration occurs at the moment of repentance, where the individual turns from "the old to the new, from darkness to light."[22] It is a movement produced by an act of the will, "a movement of the whole self away from sin to God" and a movement rewarded by God who *will* receive the repentant individual.[23] This seems to involve human effort, but repentance is actually "a gift from God" and is only human effort to the extent that God enables it.[24] In regeneration, the Spirit becomes the "resident factor" in the believer's life so that the "believer operates out of [this] new center," in fact the result is a new creature (sic) where at the "deepest level of human existence there is a decisive change" which consists of a cleansing of the heart, an inscribing of God's law and a unification of the heart, by which is meant a singleness of purpose towards God.[25] In sum, repentance (and hence regeneration) brings a new nature in which the "character of God becomes operative in the new man (sic)."[26]

Regeneration must also be understood in the context of the union between the believer and Christ, which Williams has already described. His references to a new nature and a new creature imply that the believer in the union is changed because of the existence of the union. Through the union the Spirit acts to make real changes to the believer. Just as Christ can justify through the union, the Spirit can regenerate, and these two distinct divine acts must occur simultaneously.

Sanctification is understood as being made holy and "has to do with holiness of life."[27] This has to do with an internal and external cleansing and purification as the believer seeks *moral perfection*[28] and is a *continuing process* of *progressive transformation* toward a goal of perfect sanctification which is never attained completely in this life.[29] This is a clear focus on the ongoing nature of sanctification, but sanctification "*already* belongs to those who are the people of God,"[30] so it has an aspect which is present at the

21. Ibid., 1:37–40.
22. Ibid., 1:44.
23. Ibid., 1:44–45 (emphasis his).
24. Ibid., 1:49.
25. Ibid., 1:49–51.
26. Ibid., 1:54–55.
27. Ibid., 1:83.
28. Ibid., 1:84–85.
29. Ibid., 1:88, 89, 90–92 (emphasis his).
30. Ibid., 1:86.

time of justification, as the people of God are surely those who are united to Christ. Thus, it is distinct from justification but cannot be separated from it; those who are justified are those to whom sanctification already belongs, the one does not exist without the other.

There is a great deal of common ground between these Pentecostal sources on justification and the other processes which surround it, with only minor differences and this extends to the *ordo salutis* as each conceives it. For instance, Duffield and Van Cleave and Pecota (with Jenney[31]) include election in their order based on foreknowledge in the Arminian sense, whereas for Williams it is a foreknowing in which God already knows the individual in a kind of proto-union with the yet-to-be created individual.

Pecota usefully sets out a Reformed *ordo salutis* under the headings he uses and contrasts it with that he adopts.[32] This is set out below in comparison with Calvin's as given by Alistair McGrath.[33]

Calvin (after McGrath)	Reformed (after Pecota)	Pecota
		Foreknowledge
Election	Election	Election
	Predestination	Predestination
	Foreknowledge	Calling
Union	Calling	Repentance
	Regeneration	Faith
	Repentance	
	Faith	
Justification	Justification	Regeneration
Sanctification		Justification
		Adoption
	Adoption	Sanctification
	Sanctification	
Glorification	Glorification	Glorification

31. Jenney, "The Holy Spirit and Sanctification," 397–421.

32. Pecota, "The Saving Work of Christ," 355.

33. After McGrath, *Iustitia Dei*, 255, and Pecota, "The Saving Work of Christ," 355, who calls his the Wesleyan approach, so it is Arminian in character.

What is clear here is that if the Arminian tendencies of Pentecostal thought are put aside, then there is substantial agreement with Calvin in the *ordo salutis* and in justification itself. As the discussion above shows, justification in these accounts is a christological occurrence, so there is a substantial identification between them and Calvin and these accounts. This is to be expected, given the fact that Pentecostals have largely borrowed evangelical theology, with its debt to Calvin, in constructing their own, aside from their accounts of being filled with the Spirit and the gifts of the Spirit.

Context: Spirit Baptism and Spirit Release

It is these latter accounts which contain the Pentecostal distinctive: a claim to some direct experience of the Holy Spirit in an occurrence with a variety of labels, but which I have elected to call Spirit release in this work. To look for affinities between Pentecostals, possessed of this distinctive, and Calvin which are more than agreements based on borrowing, requires that justification be examined in the context of Spirit release. Does Spirit baptism, understood as receipt of the Spirit at Christian initiation and an encounter in Spirit release, speak to justification in any way, and if so how? The discussion thus far forms an important preparatory ground for answering this question, as the conclusion may lead to developments or departures from what has been a conventional position in Pentecostalism.

Before heading into that discussion, a brief word on Spirit release is required as there are differences within Pentecostalism about what it comprises. The position reached in chapter two is that adopted here: that Spirit baptism occurs at Christian initiation and that the later experience or encounter Pentecostals testify to is best understood as a release of the already indwelling Spirit. However, there are not two distinct events here, rather the release of the Spirit is a fulfilment of Spirit baptism, so that it is correct to understand Spirit baptism as encompassing both conversion and the release of the Spirit.[34] The coming of the Spirit to indwell the believer is properly a baptism, and the indwelling is necessarily prior to the release: what is not resident cannot be released. However, the event of release is something new to the believer and so pervasive within his being that it can also be called a "baptism". Hence, Spirit baptism occurs at initiation or conversion, but reaches its fullness at release. It is not that there are two separate parts, as that would mean two baptisms and undermine the efficacy of the initial indwelling of the Spirit. Rather, there is continuity

---

34. Classically, release occurred later in time than conversion, but both aspects of the event can coincide in time, although the release is always subsequent to initiation.

between the two events so that once both have occurred Spirit baptism forms a whole, or can be said to be complete.

With this understanding, it is also important to acknowledge that when Spirit release occurs, the Spirit is doing something. Spirit release is an event which comprises the activity of the Spirit with and within the believer. Without limiting any other potential activity of the Spirit, most obviously in the life of the believer following conversion, Spirit release is identical to the Spirit doing something, the Spirit being active in the believer. The Spirit is not isolated in this activity, as Spirit release in its fullness includes the illumination of the triune God with a deep testimony to the reality of God as Father, Son and Spirit and the roles of each. However, the Spirit's activity is not limited to this illumination; there is considerably more direct work with the believer.

Hence, to consider anything in the context of Spirit release is to consider it in the context of the Spirit *doing something*. As Spirit baptism occurs at conversion, an event which includes justification, then justification has something to do with Spirit baptism. Thus, to discuss justification in the context of Spirit baptism is to discuss what role the Spirit may play in justification and so consider whether humans can be said to be justified in the Spirit in any sense. This is just the issue which Frank Macchia has been grappling with in recent work, and it is to that that I now turn.

Justified in the Spirit—A Pentecostal Proposal

Both Macchia and Amos Yong have proposed a pneumatological soteriology which I briefly considered in chapter two. Yong, adopting the view that Spirit baptism is initial conversion, shared by Macchia, offered six points identifying how the activity of Christ and the Spirit are linked in the totality of salvation through Spirit baptism. Point three is:

> Spirit baptism connects Jesus being raised "for our justification" (Rom 4:25) with his being raised by the Spirit (Rom 8:11), so our justification is pneumatological as well as christological.[35]

Here, justification is specifically linked with the resurrection at Rom 4:25, whereas the discussion has so far identified it as christological and so linked it to the cross. The resurrection is an event of the Spirit so the interplay of Rom 4:25 and 8:11 suggests a pneumatological influence on justification at the very least. It is Macchia who has given substantial attention to developing a theology of justification in the Spirit in two works, *Baptized*

---

35. Yong, *Spirit Poured Out*, 102.

in the Spirit: A Global Pentecostal Theology and *Justified in the Spirit: Creation, Redemption, and the Triune God*. In the former[36] he notes that he first became aware of the connection between justification and Spirit baptism through a paper written by D. Lyle Dabney,[37] and it is with that paper that this exploration of justification in the Spirit begins.[38]

Dabney begins with 1 Timothy 3:16, which says of Jesus:

> He appeared in a body,
>   was vindicated by the Spirit,
> was seen by angels,
>   was preached among the nations,
> was believed on in the world,
>   was taken up in glory (NIV).

The verb translated here as "was vindicated" is *dikaioo* which Dabney translates with its usual New Testament meaning as "was justified." He suggests it is generally agreed that "vindicated" is a reference to the resurrection and that most "recent writers" interpret it as meaning the Spirit is the agent of resurrection, hence the NIV translation (also shared by the RSV, NRSV, NASB, NEB). He implies that this way of interpreting the verse arises out of the forensic interpretation of justification deeply rooted within Protestantism which assigns justification to Christ, not the Spirit.[39] This interpretation might hold but for a relationship between resurrection and justification articulated by Paul in Romans, "the very heart of the forensic interpretation of the Apostle's soteriology."[40] This is, of course, Rom 4:25: "[Jesus] was handed over to death for our trespasses and was raised for our justification." Here, the minimum that can be said is that the resurrection has soteriological significance,[41] but perhaps it goes so far as to explicitly link the resurrection to justification. When coupled with Dabney's assertion that "according to the witness of the New Testament . . . it is by the Holy Spirit that God raised Jesus Christ from the dead"[42] (Rom 8:11 above), then the Spirit is powerfully linked to justification.

36. Macchia, *Baptized in the Spirit*, 130.
37. Dabney, "Justified by the Spirit," 46–68.
38. See also Kärkkäinen, *A Constructive Christian Theology*, 1:355. He notes there that the Protestant doctrine of justification, as forensic declaration, lacks "pneumatological empowerment" and neglects the resurrection. He also asserts Romans 4:25 is about justification as well as vindication.
39. Dabney, "Justified by the Spirit," 47.
40. Ibid.
41. Ibid.
42. Ibid., 49.

For Dabney, Paul sees the "resurrection of Jesus Christ as nothing less than the model of our own redemption," citing a parallel drawn between Adam and Jesus Christ as the second Adam (1 Cor 15:45) by Neill Hamilton where in the same way as God breathed into Adam and gave him life (so that life and breath became synonymous), the Father breathed the Spirit into the dead Son to give him life so that "the Spirit and the life of the resurrected Christ became synonymous."[43] Certainly, Paul sees a model of our own eschatological redemption in the resurrection of Jesus Christ[44] and regards receipt of the Spirit not only as a deposit now guaranteeing that future redemption but also that the "deposit" brings new life by the Spirit now (Gal 5:25).[45] The Spirit's vital role in the resurrection means that the Spirit is central to the substance of God's salvation.[46]

This close association of the Spirit in Scripture with resurrection gives a very different meaning to justification than that of a forensic declaration. The resurrection, the future redemption and, explicitly, new life all speak of life, a change of status from death, but this is not merely a change of position as the convicted criminal experiences if pardoned, or an individual is promoted to a new job. Instead it is a life which is active and participatory. If Dabney is right that, for Paul, "resurrection by God's Spirit is virtually synonymous with justification,"[47] then justification is "an eschatological event made manifest in the resurrection of Jesus Christ" and is an act of "gracious inclusion" in the life of the Spirit who incorporates us into the life and death and resurrection of Jesus Christ."[48] This inclusion is certainly a change of status, but being incorporated into the life of the risen Lord Jesus Christ speaks of a life which is being lived, it is dynamic, active, productive, and maturing. In short, it is a real life in contrast to the counterfeit which existed prior to the Spirit coming which, despite appearances, was actually death. This inclusion occurs here and now, so that the present experience of the justified human is of being included in the "life of God in the world,"[49] and to be justified by the Spirit is to show the glory of the new creation amidst the wreck of the old.[50]

---

43. Hamilton, *The Holy Spirit and Eschatology in Paul*, cited by Dabney, "Justified by the Spirit," 50.
44. Dabney, "Justified by the Spirit," 50.
45. Ibid., 51.
46. Ibid.
47. Ibid.
48. Ibid., 53.
49. Ibid., 58.
50. Ibid., 62.

If all this points to the Spirit justifying humans, it does not exclude Christ. Recognizing the role of the Spirit in the New Testament means that it is not only the cross but the "entire life, death and resurrection of Jesus Christ that is of import to God's redemption of God's creation."[51] Jesus is not excluded from justification. Rather, he is explicitly and substantially involved, including being the one who imparts the Spirit.

This ministry of Christ is announced in all four Gospels in John the Baptist's assertion that he baptized with water but that Jesus Christ would baptize with the Spirit. Jesus himself is baptized by John and receives the Spirit, whereupon he is able to embark on his ministry. This baptism marks, in one sense, the start of God's saving work for humanity and his creation and now the resurrected Christ can draw humans into that work by in turn baptizing them with the Spirit. The receipt of the Spirit "roots us in Christ," for Paul,[52] so there is no independence of the Spirit in this account of justification in the Spirit. Certainly, the Spirit is active, but only in accord with Christ who gives the Spirit: justification is both pneumatological and christological.

Macchia's Proposal

Macchia builds on Dabney's essay "to more fully develop justification from a pneumatological perspective,"[53] which he does most extensively in his later work. It is not my intent to give a full outline of his case; my focus will be on the case he makes for a scriptural basis to justification in the Spirit with reference to other aspects as necessary.

He takes a similar approach to Dabney, with a variously expressed definition of justification. "To be justified is to participate in the fullness of pneumatic existence, which means the risen and glorified Christ as well as the communion of love enjoyed among Father, Son and Spirit."[54] The pneumatic influence means that justification in the Spirit is "Through the indwelling of the Spirit and the new birth, sinners are taken up into the righteous favor of God that is inaugurated especially in Christ's death and resurrection."[55] It is "a participatory reality in which the spirit dwells in us and we dwell in God,"[56] so that "receiving the Spirit and being justified are equivalent realities in Scripture so that one could rightly regard justified

---

51. Ibid., 54.
52. Ibid., 54–57.
53. Macchia, *Baptized in the Spirit*, 130.
54. Macchia, *Justified in the Spirit*, 13–14.
55. Ibid., 187.
56. Ibid., 209.

existence as pneumatic existence."[57] He is suggesting that justification results in, and so can be equated to, being taken up to participate in the life of God and if this is so then the Spirit must be involved. This is so because justification, so understood, goes beyond a simple declaration of righteousness to something linking with and involving the creature in such a way that she is taken up into communion with God, and this taking up or communion is certainly a pneumatic action. Thus, justification is pneumatological and it is legitimate to talk of being justified in the Spirit.

This is a departure from the traditional Roman Catholic and Protestant views.[58] Macchia anchors the former to Augustine and Aquinas while observing a significant pneumatological influence since Trent. Augustine's position on justification was anthropological in that the righteousness that justified humans have is a righteousness with which God has endowed them. He did indulge in flirtation with ideas of a pneumatological justification, but ultimately insisted that justification was righteousness which humans acquired.[59] By the time of Aquinas, grace had become distinguished from the Spirit,[60] so his doctrine ascribes justification to grace sure enough, but to habitual grace, a grace or ability infused in the human which enables her to cooperate with God in her justification.[61] Since Trent, Roman Catholic theology concerning justification has moved back toward the Spirit, acknowledging that grace can only be present *via* the indwelling Spirit, but the distinction between the two remains.[62] Thus, while the move holds the potential for a pneumatological expression of justification, this has not occurred.

Protestant views on justification had their genesis with Martin Luther, who grounded justification in Christ—it was his righteousness, alien to humans and not reliant on their cooperation, which justified, despite humans being sinners. This enabled the Spirit to be excluded.[63] This is, of course, Calvin's position set out in some detail previously, although Macchia thinks that Calvin involves the Spirit in justification through the role of forming the union between the believer and Christ through which justification

---

57. Ibid., 214.

58. Ibid., 15–74, gives an extensive summary of what is meant by this comment, which is in turn summarized by what follows here.

59. Ibid., 16–18.

60. Ibid., 18.

61. Ibid., 19.

62. Ibid., 22–24.

63. Ibid., 46.

occurs.⁶⁴ It is this link which Macchia argues imposes a tension upon the forensic view of justification which has encouraged Protestant exploration of a role for the Spirit in justification,⁶⁵ an exploration which has not yet come to fruition.

The difference between the two views is as Macchia expresses it: both ground salvation in grace, but Roman Catholic theology bases justification on *imparted* righteousness while in Protestant doctrine it is based on *imputed* righteousness.⁶⁶ The former means something given to the believer, infused within his being, the latter something accounted to the believer. What they have in common is that the way they have been expressed in both traditions has left the Spirit behind, and it is Macchia's concern to apply a corrective to that as he sees the Spirit being involved in all of Christian life so that "there can be no justification apart from the fullness of life in the Spirit."⁶⁷ It is not sufficient for any trinitarian understanding of salvation to assign roles to the hypostases in isolation from their communion as the forensic declaration does for justification. He thinks also that the Protestant declaration's neglect of the Spirit leaves a gap between the divine declaration and what actually occurs for the believer. Without taking into account the role of the Spirit in his indwelling in the believer through the Christ event and his goal of the believer's participation in God, Macchia considers that the "necessary link between justification as a divine judgement and as a creaturely reality [remains] unclear, explainable only by the questionable biblical notion of 'imputation.'"⁶⁸ That is, the "how" of imputation is not addressed.

Justification in the Spirit in Scripture

All this would reduce to speculation if there were no support from Scripture for a role for the Spirit in justification. Some of the foregoing suggests there is support and both Dabney and Macchia are concerned to examine Scripture to ensure that a basis for justification by the Spirit can be found there. Indeed, it was from Dabney that Macchia learnt of the notion.⁶⁹ Their explorations are grounded in Scripture, albeit a particular reading, so an examination of what they claim to find there is critical.

64. Ibid., 61.
65. Ibid., 73.
66. Ibid., 40 (emphasis his).
67. Ibid., 3–4.
68. Ibid., 47.
69. Macchia, *Baptized in the Spirit*, 130.

I have already touched on Dabney's exploration of the New Testament but will mention here what he sees in the Pauline letters. There he finds that Paul understands becoming a Christian as receiving "the Spirit of God in reconciliation and even 'justification,'" making reference to Rom 8:1–2; 3:2; and 1 Cor 12:13.[70] It is the Spirit who is the Spirit of Christ (Rom 8:9) who roots believers in Christ as they receive him, opening up their true identity. Hence Paul "frequently describes Christian initiation as an event in which our lives are now incorporated into the death and resurrection of Jesus Christ" (eg Rom 6:3–4).[71]

Macchia begins with the Old Testament and first asks what the substance of justification is as an Old Testament concept.[72] His response is to say first that justification is "righteousness from God,"[73] although he is quick to note that justification is not the only way to look at righteousness. Neither is it a part of righteousness, it is a way of looking at righteousness in its entirety. It is his contention that this 'justifying righteousness' is "God's *covenant faithfulness* towards God's people and even toward the larger creation"[74] and that God promises to fulfil this faithfulness by giving the Spirit, "for creation was made to bear the divine Spirit (Gen 1:2; 2:7; 2 Cor 5:4–8)."[75] Adopting the concept that, biblically, righteousness is activity that is faithful to the covenant,[76] he infers that "the forensic and the ethical are inseparable in the Old Testament"[77] by which he seems to mean that as the ethical refers to action which maintains covenant faithfulness and such activity *is* righteousness, then it rightly belongs with any forensic concept of righteousness in a way which is more than being alongside but less than sharing the same identity. Importantly, this activity belongs to both sides of the covenant: God's faithfulness towards humans and their faithful responses.[78] But righteousness is heavily weighted towards activity, as only about eighteen percent of "the uses of the term for 'righteousness' in the Old Testament are legal or forensic" so that righteousness has mainly

---

70. Dabney, "Justified by the Spirit," 57.

71. Ibid.

72. Macchia, *Justified in the Spirit*, 103.

73. Sanders' term which Macchia quotes approvingly. Sanders, *Paul the Law, and the Jewish People*, cited in Macchia, *Justified in the Spirit*, 103.

74. Macchia, *Justified in the Spirit*, 105. He cites this view as a "prominent alternative today" (emphasis his).

75. Ibid., 104.

76. Which he takes from Ziesler, *The Meaning of Righteousness in Paul: A Linguistic and Theological Enquiry*, cited ibid., 105.

77. Ibid.

78. Ibid.

to do with fidelity.[79] He goes on to say that "Righteousness in the Old Testament is a relational and functional concept, stemming from a covenant relationship with Yahweh that is chiefly maintained in the cult."[80] Thus the commandments given in Exodus 20 are "prefaced with election and God's covenant-establishing act of deliverance from Egypt: 'I am the LORD your God, who brought you out of Egypt, out of the land of slavery' (Exod 20:2, NIV)"[81] The relation is established by God who unilaterally declared the covenant and his faithfulness toward it, and from the human perspective, this relationship is maintained by the appropriate faithful response contained within the Law. That is, the people are sustained in righteousness by their observance of the Law, which reflects God's love for them or is a remembrance of that love.[82] Even when righteousness is expressed forensically, it involves "divine self-giving and liberation."[83]

The people of Israel are then in a covenant with God by God's gracious gift and are to live this out in observance of the Law. While there is no cause and effect relationship between observance and righteousness, those in the covenant are counted as righteous by God unless by their non-observance they remove themselves from the covenant.[84] Hence being counted as righteous is a lived righteousness through observance of the Law. While "Israel is ultimately righteous because the nation takes refuge in God and places its trust and hope in the Lord,"[85] that trust and hope is lived out by observance of the Law. This living out is aided by the presence of God among the people, in fact he asserts that the covenant is based on God's presence (Exod 20:1–2),[86] initially in the tabernacle and latterly in the Temple at Jerusalem. The picture he is drawing is that this righteous people are made so through the relation they enjoy with God, which is a lived relation through the Law, enabled by the presence of God among them. The Old Testament thus has a view of righteousness which is expressed as a life lived in the presence of God.

However, the Old Testament does not give an explicit place to the Spirit in this relation. Certainly, the Spirit is active in the Old Testament and

---

79. Ibid., 105–6.
80. Ibid., 106.
81. Ibid., 107.
82. Ibid., 114–15.
83. Ibid., 111.
84. Ibid., 116.
85. Ibid., 111. He gives Pss 5:12; 14:5; 31:18; 36:10; 52:6; 94:15, 21; 118:15; 20 in support of this statement.
86. Ibid., 117.

present in the ministry of Moses, the prophets and judges, but also others including even "the artisans working on the tabernacle" (Exod. 35:35),[87] but these are limited and discrete events. Primarily the gift of the Spirit is a future promise,[88] which has two components to it. One is to involve a pouring out of the Spirit on all so that the Law will become internalized to each person. Hence Jer 31:33: "I will put my law in their minds and write it on their hearts" (NIV) and Ezek 36:27: "I will put my Spirit in you and move you to follow my decrees." (NIV)[89] The other is that the coming Messiah will bring justice as the man of the Spirit, proclaiming the year of the Lord's favor by the empowering of the Spirit (Isa. 11, 42:1, 61:1):[90] the Messiah will deliver Israel and rule by the power of the Spirit, he will be Spirit-anointed.

Macchia suggests that the link between these two components is unclear in the Old Testament. There is a divine indwelling in the Messiah of the sort already seen (e.g. Saul or David) but how this might be linked to the Spirit being poured out on all flesh is not stated. It is not until the New Testament and the introduction of the novel idea that the Son is the Spirit baptizer (in all four Gospels at the baptism of Jesus), that the link is revealed. "Spirit baptism then becomes the link between the vindicated Messiah as the one who bears the Spirit and the Spirit-indwelt and vindicated creation."[91]

Thus, justification, as righteousness, is relational in the Old Testament, lived out as a covenant life with God through a trust and loyalty towards Godself expressed in the observance of the Law. This trust and loyalty is aided, at least, by the presence of God among the people in the tabernacle and the Temple, or indeed spiritually in the absence of the Temple,[92] so that justification is living faithfully within the covenant in the presence of God. This prefigures the new covenant, where the justified believer no longer lives faithfully by observance of the Law, but lives in union with God through the indwelling word and Spirit. This new covenant has come about because the Messiah, the Son, has come as Spirit baptizer and through Spirit baptism is able to pour out the Spirit. This means the promises of the Old Testament concerning the Spirit-empowered Messiah as the bearer of salvation for God's people *and* the Spirit being poured out on all flesh are brought together in the life and ministry of the one Jesus Christ. What Macchia wants his reader to grasp is that the living justification of the Old Testament

87. Ibid., 125.
88. Ibid., 124.
89. Ibid., 117.
90. Ibid., 118.
91. Ibid., 129.
92. Ibid., 125.

prefigures a justification to which the New Testament witnesses as brought about by Christ, yes, but also in the Spirit who brings life.

The New Testament certainly testifies to the activity of the Spirit in creation, but the Spirit's involvement in justification that Macchia wants us to see is not explicit. The only texts which draw the reader directly to the possibility are those noted above (1 Tim 3:16 and Rom 4:25) and 1 Cor 6:11 (discussed below), which are not universally acknowledged as doing so and require some consideration to draw out the involvement of the Spirit. However, they do point to the possibility and Macchia explores this through a discussion of how justification in the Spirit might be heard in the voices of Luke, Paul, John and James in the New Testament.

The coming of the Spirit to indwell believers to draw "them into the righteous favor, witness, and vindication of the Son" is "distinctly Lukan" and this is wrapped up, for him, in the creation of a community of believers for whom these are realities.[93] Macchia calls these "a cluster of justification themes"[94] and refers to Markus Barth showing that "Luke has a justification theology" even though he is sparing in his use of the term.[95] As I have pointed out already, while Luke is writing narratives in his Gospel and Acts so that they contain little in the way of didactic text, he is writing with a theological intent (Luke 1:3–4) so theology can be distilled from the narrative with varying degrees of certainty. Hence, his justification theology needs to be drawn from his narrative.

Macchia thinks a key text is Acts 10, where he sees an explanation of "justification in the Spirit."[96] Peter proclaims to Cornelius' household that God accepts all who fear God and do what is right (10:35), a message which was borne by the Spirit-indwelt Jesus Christ who was executed but resurrected (10:39–40) and is the God-appointed "judge of the living and the dead" (10:42). The implication is that the unjustly condemned Christ has been raised to be the exalted "righteous judge," but this judge is also "first the Savior" who offers his Spirit and favor. Believers are indwelt by the same Spirit, so share this favor "and are taken up into the testimony of the Spirit in history to the vindicated Christ." This is "Luke's understanding of justification in the Spirit . . . By receiving the Spirit, the Christian community is implicitly the rightwised community, the justified community, for *'through him everyone is justified'* [NIV] (Acts 13:39)."[97]

93. Ibid., 189.
94. Ibid.
95. Markus Barth, *Acquittal by Resurrection*, cited ibid., 189–90.
96. Ibid., 190.
97. Ibid., 191 (emphasis his).

What Macchia suggest here is that for Luke, people are "put right" with God by being taken into the new community God elects to form (of which Godself is a part through Christ as its head), and those who enter can look forward to resurrection and vindication in the same way Christ was vindicated. More, this entry includes a sharing of the witness of the Spirit to God's revelation in Christ and a communion with God, a participation in the triune communion which is God. Being taken into the new community includes participation in all this, so the "putting right" includes all these aspects. Putting right, of course, is at the heart of justification, so justification incorporates all these which are the activity of the Spirit who is the agent of incorporation in the community. Hence, believers are justified in the Spirit, confirmed by Acts 13:39 which Macchia emphasizes.

He doesn't discuss this text directly, but his adoption of the translation "through him" (that is, through Christ) suits his position. This is a legitimate translation (so NIV, NASB), but it is also translated "by him" or an equivalent (so NRSV, RSV, KJV). The latter rendering places justification with Christ, so it would mean believers are justified by Christ with no contemplation of any other, the traditional position. But, adopting "through" introduces the need for another. If justification is through Christ, then Christ is involved, certainly, but what is working through Christ? Macchia would reply: "The Holy Spirit." The Greek preposition is *en*, which can be translated "in,"[98] which would give a clumsy rendering, but would emphasize more the work of the Spirit. To say that believers are justified *in* Christ would point emphatically to the Spirit who is the hypostasis who incorporates believers into the divine communion. Whichever rendering is "correct" it is certainly open to the translator to render the text as "through" which points to a pneumatological role in justification.

He notes also that Luke is careful to understand that salvation through Christ and the Spirit is consistent with the Law (citing Acts 24:14 and 26:22) but is clear that righteousness now comes from "the risen Christ and the Spirit (e.g., Acts 20:28; 13:32–39)." This point is emphasized by Cornelius and his household receiving the Spirit even as Peter was preaching, which may indicate that receiving the Spirit is a matter of faith.[99] This reception of the Spirit apart from the Law is a link to Paul's message of justification by faith, he suggests.[100]

---

98. Zodhiates, *The Complete Word Study New Testament*, 899.
99. Macchia, *Justified in the Spirit*, 194.
100. Ibid., 195.

It was just this occurrence for the Gentiles which "convinced Paul that justification is by faith and not law in Galatians (3:5),"[101] and it is from this book that he draws a similar view to that given for Luke: "justification comes or is fulfilled by the gift of the Spirit of life."[102] He suggests that "justification and the gift of the Spirit serve as functional equivalents throughout Galatians,"[103] illustrating this with parallels at 2:16 and 3:2-5; and 3:8 and 3:14. To take the first example, at 2:16 a person is "justified not by the works of the law but through faith in Jesus Christ"; at 3:2 the believers are challenged rhetorically: "Did you receive the Spirit by doing the works of the law or by believing what you heard?"—a question repeated at 3:5. Believing what has been heard is, of course, faith in Jesus Christ, so both justification and the receipt of the Spirit are identified as things which occur by the same mechanism. He suggests that, in respect of justification and the receipt of the Spirit, the occurrence of the one by faith implies the other: they are in some way identifiable with each other.[104] For Macchia this identity is much more than the two being analogous—hence his "functional equivalents" comment. He quotes support for drawing this view from Galatians 3 from Ronald Y. K. Fung who suggests "reception of the Spirit is in some sense equated with justification"; James D. G. Dunn who sees them as two sides of the same coin; and H.W. Heidland who equates justification with reception of the Spirit.[105]

The reason that righteousness does not come by the law is that humans have no power to obey it apart from the Spirit—any obedience requires the Spirit to empower it. For believers, such obedience occurs because the law is taken up in the Spirit, reception of whom is through faith apart from the law. Given that obedience to the law is righteousness, the latter can only be attained as a gift, a gift received in the Spirit.[106] Hence righteousness/justification comes with the gift of the Spirit and justification can be said to be in the Spirit.

He makes a similar case from Galatians 4, where he thinks "Paul's argument . . . is also that believers are children of Abraham by being justified by faith but also *by being born of the Spirit* (Gal 4:6, 29),"[107] and suggesting that

---

101. Ibid., 196.
102. Ibid., 195.
103. Ibid., 196.
104. Ibid.
105. Fung, *The Epistle to the Galatians*, 136; Dunn, *Baptism in the Holy Spirit*, 108; Heidland, "λογίζομαι," *TDNT*, 4:292, cited in Macchia, *Justified in the Spirit*, 196-97.
106. Macchia, *Justified in the Spirit*, 198.
107. Ibid., 200 (emphasis his).

"Paul involves the Spirit in verse 6 at the very essence of justification."[108] The validity, or otherwise, of this view relies on understanding becoming a child of God as intimately reliant on justification, which is not unreasonable in itself. To enter that intimate relationship with God, the human needs to be righteous, and the justified human is certainly that in the eyes of God. Thus, Paul's major point here is having the law is insufficient for people to become children of Abraham: only those "born of the Spirit" are his children, sharing as they do in a "righteousness embraced in faith."[109]

He sees a connection between justification and the Spirit as implied in Rom 1–8, where justification means new life,[110] a new life which is in the Spirit as well as in Christ. Romans 4:25 figures prominently in his discussion but it is by no means the only text brought into his employ: 1:4, 24–26; 5:12–21; 8:18, and 30–38 are all put to work as implying a link between the Spirit and justification. He states that "Justification is implicitly about resurrection, substantially about the Spirit" in this part of Romans so that the conclusion that 4:25 represents is natural to its context. "Since new life through the Spirit is integral to justification, it is quite natural to see the resurrection and impartation of the Spirit from the risen and ascended Christ as the root cause of justification."[111] Thus, "The Spirit is the link for Paul between the justification of the crucified Christ in resurrection and the hope of those who suffer in Christ for final vindication."[112] It is the Spirit who has raised Christ and who turns to believers to resurrect them spiritually to new life here and now and will do so fully and finally in the eschaton. It is the Spirit who raises them to righteousness and thus is integral to their justification.

Before leaving Paul, he visits two baptismal texts, 1 Cor 6:11 and Titus 3:5–7,[113] the former being of more interest than the latter. It reads:

> And this is what some of you used to be. But you were washed, you were sanctified, you were justified in the name of the Lord Jesus Christ and in the Spirit of our God.

To those holding a forensic view, the place of justification and the Spirit here seems odd, but to read justification pneumatologically is to place the work of the Spirit at the center of the three soteriological categories

---

108. Ibid.
109. Ibid.
110. Ibid., 201.
111. Ibid., 204.
112. Ibid., 205.
113. He notes that the latter is Deutero-Pauline, thus acknowledging the likelihood that the apostle Paul is not the author of Titus.

here. This is consistent with the foregoing reading of Paul and with what Macchia calls the "the earlier and broader Christian tradition" of putting the Spirit at the center of soteriological categories.[114] He cites Gordon Fee and James Dunn in support of this; the former saying that each of the three soteriological terms here are "the result of the work of the Spirit in the believer's life." The latter sees a very strong link between the Spirit and justification implying "that 'justification . . . takes place in the Spirit.'"[115] Elsewhere Fee notes that "the three verbs are primarily metaphors of salvation" and that the two prepositional phrases are best understood as modifying all three verbs. He is careful not to press claims for the Spirit too hard, thinking they "refer to what God has done *for* his people *through Christ*, which he has effected *in* them by *the Spirit*" and that "Christ's death was the place in history where such saving activity took place." However, this saving activity can only be appropriated for each believer, is only actualized in each believer, by the Spirit, so the believer is "also saved in these various aspects 'by the Spirit of our God.'" He notes that the Spirit is also linked to justification at 2 Cor 3:8–9 and Gal 5:5.[116]

Macchia's conclusion concerning the Pauline texts he has reviewed is that they "imply that justification in the Spirit is a participatory reality in which the Spirit dwells in us and we dwell in God."[117] He sees the same reality in the Johannine texts, which he briefly touches on,[118] and in James, where it is expressed in his view on faith. For James, justification is certainly through faith, but this is a faith embodied in a changed life—faith is completed by the changed life. So it is not incorrect to say that justification is by faith and works in James, but each carries a different sense.[119] While James is not at all explicit about the role of the Spirit in justification, the embodiment of faith in works is strongly indicative of God's presence and this can be legitimately viewed as the presence of the Spirit.[120]

Through all this discussion, there is a gnawing lack of precision. There is much that points to the activity of the Spirit, and much which is definitive about the Spirit being active. However, there is little which is explicit about a direct role for the Spirit in justification. Clearly justification is intimately

---

114. Ibid., 207.

115. Fee, *The First Epistle to the Corinthians*, 247; Dunn, *Baptism in the Holy Spirit*, 122–23, cited in Macchia, *Justified in the Spirit*, 207–8.

116. Fee, *God's Empowering Presence*, 130–31 (emphasis his).

117. Macchia, *Justified in the Spirit*, 209.

118. Ibid., 209–11.

119. Ibid., 213.

120. Ibid., 214.

related to the union between the believer and Christ and so bears some relation to it in some fashion, but does Macchia's treatment lead to understanding justification as consisting of the union? He does recognize this difficulty, twice pointing to the blurring of distinctions in his proposal. For Luke, "In the Spirit, justification, sanctification, and empowered witness are overlapping and mutually illuminating concepts,"[121] and "regeneration, sanctification, and justification are overlapping metaphors of new life in the Spirit" in relation to 1 Cor 6:11.[122]

Also illustrating this lack of explicit witness, Macchia says that "the cumulative evidence both implicit and explicit strongly suggest that receiving the Spirit and being justified are equivalent realities in Scripture so that one could rightly regard justified existence as pneumatic existence."[123] Further, to use Spirit baptism as a "lens" to view justification shows "how justification objectively viewed is *inseparable* from justification viewed through the lens of its incarnation or embodiment in the life and witness of the people of God,"[124] hence justification does entail a change of status, but this is effected by being taken up into the life of God. This is not a double justification, but the one act of God.[125] Justification consists of this "taking up" which itself embodies the change of status to such an extent that it can be identified with it. It is not wrong to view justification as the change of status, but it is also correct to view it as being taken up into the life of God: each is but a different aspect to the one thing.

Of course, Macchia is not saying that justification is not christological. Indeed, 1 Cor 6:11 certainly points at least as strongly to the Son as the hypostasis active in justification as it does to the Spirit. Equally, Macchia's case does nothing to lessen the force of "the righteousness of God through faith in Jesus Christ for all who believe" (Rom 3:22), or "they are now justified by his grace as a gift, through the redemption that is in Christ Jesus" (Rom 3:24), or "And we have come to believe in Christ Jesus, so that we might be justified by faith in Christ" (Gal 2:16). His case is that justification is trinitarian, so is both christological and pneumatological. When discussing faith, he notes that believers receive the Spirit through Christ in Spirit baptism, thus "faith is spirit-baptized existence; justification is by, in, and toward Christ. This is what it means to be justified by faith."[126] To "participate in

---

121. Ibid., 194.
122. Ibid., 208.
123. Ibid., 214.
124. Ibid., 215 (emphasis his).
125. Ibid., 216.
126. Ibid., 254.

the fullness of pneumatic existence" means "the risen and glorified Christ" as much as it means "the communion of love enjoyed among Father, Son and Spirit."[127] Justification could not occur without the death of Christ, so is inevitably christological, but justification also requires the resurrection, he says, and so requires the Spirit to bring to fruition the possibility that justification opens: sharing the resurrected life of Christ within the divine communion. Thus justification is not limited to that which opens the door to the communion (being declared righteous); it is the communion itself (sharing in God's triune life), it is both door and what lies beyond. It is not that Christ opens the door and the Spirit conducts the believer within, it is that the door and the communion are identified with one another and each is available through Christ and the Spirit.

Other Aspects of Justification in Macchia

While there is an availability, there also needs to be an appropriation, and he starts his discussion on this point by suggesting that there is broad agreement that human fulfilment is found in possessing God, which means possession of the Spirit. Whatever is meant by possession comes about by "a *yielding*," where there is an offering by the creature of itself "in response to the Spirit's embrace."[128] This is the realm of faith, where the gift of Godself interacts with human trust and obedience to comprise faith, as a result of which there is a mutual indwelling and the human "possesses" God in the sense that God in Christ and the Spirit dwell within.[129] It is crucial to his case, therefore, to understand that the Spirit comes through faith.

Scripturally, faith is more than a simple belief. The Old Testament actually has little emphasis on human belief, being more concerned with steadfastness, reliance and loyalty. Its accent is on God's faithfulness, not the "*individual's* response of faith" although the lack of individual focus is affected by the communal nature of the old covenant. In this covenant, it is God who determines who is righteous; the people were to be loyal to him which, of course, involved their obedience.[130] In the New Testament, the word most often used for faith is *pistis*, which means belief with commitment. The Old Testament emphasis outlined above describes commitment, so there is convergence between the two in describing faith as belief and

---

127. Ibid., 13–14.
128. Ibid., 221 (emphasis his).
129. The indwelling of Christ being through the Spirit.
130. Ibid., 222–24 (emphasis his).

commitment.[131] There is a muscular component to faith, it might be said, as faith involves doing something because commitment means the individual must be prepared to be active.

Activity appropriate to faith is that which arises from the believer's participation in God, so "faith means that the creature is . . . a willing participant and respondent by the very power of [the divine] embrace."[132] There is a synergy of a sort at work here. There is a contribution to the activity from the believer as respondent and participant, but there is also a contribution from God who provides the power which enables participation and also contributes to the ability of the believer to respond herself. While there is a human response, this cannot exist without God's empowering. This faith, incorporating commitment and so activity, therefore "responds to the Spirit by the Spirit" and is "the means by which we possess God as God has possessed us in Christ and the embrace of the Spirit."[133] This is summarized as "faith is most deeply *participation* in Christ and his communion of love with the Father through and with the Spirit."[134]

It is the Spirit who enables this faith, this participation, so if justification is understood as participation in God's life, then the Spirit is closely linked to justification. The grace of God, present in Christ and the indwelling Spirit, is the foundational element of justification and incorporation, but faith given by the Spirit is "the creaturely means of incorporation and participation."[135] "Justification is . . . first by 'faith' in the sense that it was accomplished through the faithful act of Jesus as the man of the Spirit in giving his life for the sinner and the outcast. Justification is 'by faith' among us in the sense that the gift of the Spirit creates a correspondence between Christ's covenant faithfulness and ours."[136] It is not that faith is the basis of justification, rather it is the indwelling of the Spirit "that is at the core or substance of justification."[137] The gift by the Spirit of faith to the human enables her to appropriate what Christ has done and thus the Spirit is an agent of justification.

If justification is being drawn into the life of God through a mutual indwelling, then it must be trinitarian, as the life of God is the life of Father,

---

131. Ibid., 227, 228.
132. Ibid., 254.
133. Ibid., 221.
134. Ibid., 230 (emphasis his). Williams, *Renewal Theology*, 2:29–31, who sees the union as the climax of faith, gives him some support.
135. Macchia, *Justified in the Spirit*, 236.
136. Ibid., 240.
137. Ibid., 256.

Son and Spirit in communion. Further, the Spirit is essential to draw together all God is doing in salvation as Father, Son and Spirit,[138] so to maintain that believers are justified in the Spirit is to imply that justification is trinitarian. Hence a trinitarian understanding of justification is imperative if a pneumatological theology of justification is to stand, and Macchia recognizes this in a short penultimate chapter.

One approach is suggested by the work of Robert Jenson who connects the emphasis in justification in each of Paul, the Protestant Reformation and Catholicism (limited here to "the Augustinian heritage") with a different hypostasis within the Godhead. So he sees Paul as emphasizing the justice of God in justification, linked to the Father "who is just in justifying the sinner"; Protestants emphasizing the righteousness of Christ for us from whence justification comes via the cross; and Catholics emphasizing the righteousness produced in believers by the Spirit. Hence, the Father is just in justifying the sinner; the Son fulfils righteousness for all and the Spirit is the source of righteousness produced in believers.[139] This is helpful as it at least speaks into the triune possibilities, but it requires development because as it stands it represents a linear understanding.[140] That is, the just Father looks to the Son on the cross for righteousness who in turn looks to the Spirit to produce righteousness in the believer. More, while the concept is not inimical to justification as participation in the triune communion, it looks to assign functions to each hypostasis rather than focus on the mutual indwelling the communion entails, both *intra* to the hypostases and *extra* to the believer. Nevertheless, it may usefully speak to the character of the contribution made by each hypostasis within the communion, and highlights that each hypostasis does make a contribution.

These contributions are recognized in Macchia's conclusion to the chapter, where he makes four points in respect of a trinitarian theology of justification.

1. Justification has its basis in the triune life of Father, Son and Spirit; in the communion they enjoy, "opened to creation through Christ and the Spirit."
2. Justification is not restricted to the Father's election and his justice satisfied on the cross. It extends to the resurrection life brought by the Spirit.

---

138. Ibid., 295.
139. Jenson, "Justification as a Triune Event," 421–27, cited in ibid., 298.
140. Ibid.

3. Justification is not "legal" in the way humanity in the economy understands it, rather it "is a just relationship that has self-giving and indwelling as its substance."

4. Justification is not only by faith alone but "by faith as fulfilled in love and nourished by hope," reflecting its communal nature inclusive of the witness of the community of faith in the world.[141]

Recalling that the full content of Spirit release in early Pentecostal testimony was an encounter with the fullness of the triune God, so that the believer not only received a conviction of the reality of the Spirit poured out on him, but also a new and deeper knowledge of Christ and the Father, such a trinitarian theology fits naturally within Pentecostal thought. The Pentecostal distinctive is the testimony to this encounter, however experienced, and so to an emphasis on the indwelling Spirit, making justification in the Spirit a natural "fit" with Pentecostal thought. Justification in the Spirit offers a link between the Protestant and Catholic views on justification, although in a much broader fashion than seeing the Spirit as the glue to hold them together.[142] There is the potential for a substantial Pentecostal contribution to draw the views together to form an ecumenical theology of justification.

In all this, Spirit baptism is central. From a trinitarian perspective, the Father sends the Son and bestows the Spirit on him at his own Spirit baptism when water baptized by John so that the Son, in turn, may bestow the same Spirit on humans through their Spirit baptism.[143] Put simply, the Spirit must be received for him to do his work in the believer, and he is received through Spirit baptism. If justification is in the Spirit, then Spirit baptism is the entry point for God to work in the believer. The early church saw the presence of the Spirit as the test of whether an individual was a Christian or not, so Spirit baptism was understood as being at the core of salvation. Thus, Macchia seeks to "restore" Spirit baptism as the "root metaphor of salvation."[144]

Affinities: The Biblical Witness

How is the discussion between Calvin and Macchia to proceed from this point? My task here is to seek affinities between them, not to critique one

---

141. Ibid., 311–12.

142. Ibid., 75, 293.

143. Tanner, *Christ the Key*, 140–206, would agree, although she considers a great deal more than the single progression given above.

144. Macchia, *Justified in the Spirit*, 294.

or the other, *per se*. Such a critique may arise in the discussion and so suggest directions in which the theology of each may be developed, but that is incidental to my purpose. While the above discussion shows that if there is a mainstream Pentecostal position on justification Macchia is not adopting it, that is not his purpose. He is participating in the effort to espouse a global Pentecostal theology and his proposal is in a real sense an initial attempt at a theology of justification in the context of Spirit baptism which is inevitably likely to be subjected to much development in the years ahead. Thus, I have adopted the view that the discussion with Calvin should proceed on the basis that his proposal is a viable Pentecostal theology which may be indicative of the direction Pentecostals should take for the future in order to be true to their distinctives. Thus, it is a legitimate participant in the conversation.

Beginning the discussion with the biblical witness, if the New Testament testifies to justification in the Spirit, the three most striking texts are 1 Tim 3:16; Rom 4:25 and 1 Cor 6:11, as each can be interpreted as being explicit about a connection between the Spirit and justification, as has been set out above. John Calvin would not agree.

At 1 Tim 3:16, he sees the reference to Christ being justified by the Spirit as an identification of the Spirit as divine, that is there was a spiritual power manifested which testifies to the Spirit being God, with "Spirit" being understood in its widest sense—everything in Christ that was superior to humans.[145] So Christ being justified is simply Christ being shown for who he really is. This is different from what Dabney says most recent views are,[146] but it does not link the Spirit to justification in the sense of applying righteousness, although, of course, the righteousness of Christ is one attribute confirmed by the Spirit here.

At Romans 4:25, Calvin acknowledges that the resurrection is necessary for human justification because in it death is overcome. Hence he would agree that Christ was indeed raised for human justification. However, he specifically denies that this means that the phrase refers to newness of life for humans.[147] He states his disagreement with those who see something restorative here as to do so would mean having to examine the first part of the verse in the same way, with its reference to the cross. He thinks such an examination would suggest that grace was given for humanity to take on death.[148]

---

145. Calvin, *The Second Epistle of Paul to the Corinthians, and the Epistles to Timothy, Titus and Philemon*, 233.

146. Dabney, "Justified by the Spirit," 47.

147. Macchia, *Justified in the Spirit*, 65, puzzlingly thinks Calvin hints the opposite.

148. Calvin, *The Epistles of Paul to the Romans and Thessalonians*, 102–3.

Not unexpectedly, then, in 1 Cor 6:11, he thinks that the references to the Lord Jesus and the Spirit do not equally qualify the verbs washed, sanctified and justified. For him, it is not that the Lord Jesus and the Spirit are acting similarly in justification, rather the references qualify the verbs differently. Thus, he reads the verse to say that the Lord Jesus justifies, but this is effective only for those who have access to the blessing by the activity of the Spirit.[149] With this third interpretation, Calvin has effectively barred the door to interpreting the New Testament as teaching justification in the Spirit. Affinities, if they exist, cannot be sought in the reading of Scripture. They must be sought theologically in asking questions around the trinitarian nature of justification, or how each camp sees the ontology of the union between Christ and the believer.

The Union and Justification

When Macchia's proposal is placed alongside the other Pentecostal sources I have examined, it is clear that what he offers as justification differs from their offerings. This is not simply a matter of a change of terminology, as if matters can be materially changed by a matter of redefinition. Macchia's proposal claims to find justification described in the New Testament as being taken up to share the life of God, to participate in the triune communion, and not simply a divine declaration of righteousness. Hence to be honest to itself it needs to deal with it as such. Neither is it that the other views repudiate the reality of Christian salvation comprising, in part, this sharing in God, they simply assign that to regeneration and adoption within the *ordo salutis*. In a sense, what Macchia does is collapse regeneration, justification and adoption into a single stage called justification on the ground that this is true to the early church understanding and its witness in the New Testament.[150]

He is aware of this and makes some effort to gather support for the move. He thinks that the idea that justification is regenerative can be implied from Luther and cites Tuomo Mannermaa approvingly on the subject.[151] He suggests that "key Reformers made justification a regenerative

---

149. Calvin, *The First Epistle of Paul to the Corinthians*, 127.

150. Studebaker, "Pentecostal Soteriology and Pneumatology," 267, makes a similar point in respect of sanctification and justification in reference to Macchia, "Justification and the Spirit."

151. Macchia, *Justified in the Spirit*, 63; Mannermaa, *Christ Present in Faith*, cited in Macchia, *Justified in the Spirit*, 63. He has support on this from Kärkkäinen, "Deification View," 222–23.

and (at least implicitly) pneumatological doctrine," enlisting Philip Melancthon and Martin Bucer in support and noting that justification overlaps with "regeneration, sonship, communion with God," thus bringing adoption into view as well.[152] Casting the net wider, he finds regeneration as "the dominant soteriological category" in pietism,[153] and support also from John Wesley.[154] More recently, John Henry Newman, Emil Brunner and Jurgen Moltmann are all mentioned as theologians seeking to add a regenerative aspect, at least, to justification.[155] If this is correct, as all parties to this conversation agree that regeneration and adoption are works of the Spirit primarily, bringing them within the definition of justification also brings the Spirit to bear in justification.

In proposing this change, Macchia's argument is that viewing justification in the context of Spirit baptism is true to Pentecostalism's distinctive, and that doing so demands the introduction of a pneumatological account of justification. He has introduced such an account by broadening justification so it becomes the participation in God that is represented by regeneration, justification and adoption in other Pentecostal accounts, and union, justification and sanctification (in part) in Calvin. Note also that Calvin uses regeneration and sanctification synonymously[156] and doesn't make the distinction between regeneration and sanctification that Pentecostal scholars do. Much of regeneration as he describes it in Book III of *Institutes*, for example, Pentecostal scholars would term sanctification. The two parts to sanctification for Calvin, as I have used the term here, the instantaneous change within the believer coincident with justification and the ongoing process through later life, Pentecostals would call regeneration and sanctification respectively. There is fruit in comparing these two positions (Macchia and Calvin) in some detail.

For Calvin, the part of the *ordo salutis* we are considering begins with the establishment of a union between the believer and Christ. This is the work of the Spirit and occurs at the instance of the believer's salvation being actualized in his life within the church. The intimacy of the union cannot be overstated, it is a genuinely interpenetrating union where Christ truly comes to dwell in the believer and she in turn dwells in Christ. The testimony of the New Testament, where believers are said to be "in Christ" at about ten times

---

152. Macchia, *Justified in the Spirit*, 63–67.
153. Ibid., 67.
154. Ibid., 68–69.
155. Ibid., 69–71.
156. See n. 136, chapter 1.

the rate that Christ is said to be in them in any fashion,[157] heavily emphasizes the change for the believer in the access to God that is created by the union. This contrasts with the change for Christ in that he now has access to the believer. This is entirely appropriate as the purpose of the union and what God uses it for is not to create humans with the power of God residing within (true as that is in one sense), but to create the opportunity for humans to participate with God in God's purposes.

The union is created by the Spirit and maintained by the Spirit. Thus, the Spirit also dwells within the believer and Christ dwells within through the Spirit. So, in the union, Christ and the Spirit can be said to dwell within the believer, but there is a different character to each indwelling: Christ dwells through the Spirit, the Spirit dwells "directly," so to speak. It is similar from God's perspective: the believer truly dwells in Christ but does so through the Spirit. As the work of the Spirit is secret, the believer cannot perceive the Spirit directly and she is not said to dwell in the Spirit, however she can live in the Spirit (e.g., Rom 8). This living in the Spirit must mean she is taken into Christ and the Spirit.

What the union does for justification is to give access. In broad terms this access allows Christ to bestow all his benefits on the believer, and access is given to the believer for him to enjoy participation with God. This access is created by the Spirit. In respect of justification in Calvin's conception, with the union established, Christ now is able to justify the human by an imputation of his righteousness to her and so enable her to be treated as righteous by God, the effective forensic declaration of righteousness by God. This imputation and declaration causes a change in status for the believer, from condemned sinner to righteous new creation destined for life. It is easy to characterize this justification as a cold, distant declaration, particularly as what is effective for the believer is all external to her, but it cannot be this as it effects a real, ontological change within the believer. Justification in these terms is forensic, but it is also efficacious in the believer so cannot be solely distant. This is emphasized by the fact that it occurs within the most intimate union between Christ and the believer, one of mutual indwelling. It is not that Christ declaims from a distance and some change for the believer is recorded; it is that Christ declares and imputes from within and a change is wrought within the human. After all, if the forensic human analogy is examined, the declaration of a judge to a defendant in the dock does have some distance, but the change of status from accused to acquitted, for example, is genuinely experienced by the defendant, even if the environment is intimidating.

157. See n. 121, chapter 2.

This analysis is suggestive of the creation of the union and justification as separate occurrences with some relation in that the union is a necessary prelude to justification and enables it. I suggest that the relation is more than that between container and contents because it is the indwelling Christ who not only constitutes the union but is also the justifier. Calvin, in fact, goes further than this in linking justification and the union.

In exploring this, it must first be remembered that there is no delay between the establishment of the union and justification for Calvin. While the above description contains within it the possibility that the union could be established then lie fallow, so to speak, for some time before Christ deigned to use it to justify the believer, this is not the case for Calvin. It is proper to place the union prior to justification in an *ordo salutis*, but this is only because the matter of the union is differentiated from the substance of justification and the union is logically prior to justification. For Calvin, justification is coincident upon the establishment of the union.

A link between justification and the union is hinted at when he defines justification as "the acceptance with which God receives us into his favor as righteous men . . . it consists in the remission of sins and the imputation of Christ's righteousness."[158] Here there is the classic imputation of righteousness and declaration expressed as remission of sins, but there is also a receiving into God's favor which implies more and which surely is related to the establishment of the union. Later, in a chapter headed "The Beginning of Justification and its Continual Progress,"[159] Calvin writes that despite the redeeming work of Christ, humans "are both the heirs of darkness and death and the enemies of God," that is not justified, until they "are engrafted into his fellowship by the calling of the Father,"[160] when they are obviously justified. Here there is an identification of being engrafted into the fellowship of Christ with justification; in some sense at least, the union is not only logically prior to justification, but is justifying.

He expands on this a little by saying that humans "are mortal and open enemies of God [cf Rom 5:10; Col 1:21] until we are justified and received into friendship,"[161] here reversing the order of union and justification. To be received into friendship is surely also to be understood as incorporating the establishment of the union, so to place this alongside justification is explicit in identifying that justification and the establishment of the union are coincident and infers that the union is somehow justifying. He concludes

---

158. III.11.2.
159. III.14.
160. III.14.6.
161. Ibid.

the section by asserting what he understands to be fact: "the beginning of our salvation is a sort of resurrection from death into life, because when it has been granted to us to believe in Christ for his sake [Phil 1:29], then at last we begin to pass over from death into life."[162] Some care needs to be taken here, as the second part of this sentence refers to sanctification including its ongoing component. Further, the earlier reference to being engrafted into Christ's fellowship is immediately followed by a comment that the Spirit works sanctification in believers which cleanses them from what makes them enemies of God. Justification must not be confused with sanctification, but it is certainly present with sanctification here; it is appropriate to see justification as the beginning of salvation as much as the union or sanctification, so justification is identified as a sort of resurrection to life. That life, of course, is in union with Christ and is the life found in Christ, the very life of God.

Accordingly, there is a hint of identification of the union with justification here, but they are not the same thing for Calvin. I have said previously that the establishment of the union is part of the happening which is justification;[163] it is also legitimate to say that justification is part of the happening that is the establishment of the union, although it does not have the same force. It is more natural to say that the predestined time for conversion of the believer has arrived, so he must now be justified (which necessitates the establishment of a union with him), than to say that he must now be brought into union within which he can be justified. Thus, it is true to say that the union is justifying in some sense, although it is important not to push this too far in understanding Calvin's thought.

Nevertheless, in the relation between the union and justification, we have coincidence, perhaps part identification and a sort of co-dependency where one requires the other. Justification requires the union and the union always results in justification, there is never an instance of one occurring without the other. The justified believer is the one in union with Christ, and the one in union with Christ is justified.

Here we have what Macchia calls justification: being taken into God through a mutual indwelling where the righteousness of the believer is established. In practical terms the outcome is the same for both: the believer is in fellowship with God and is accounted and made righteous by God in that fellowship. There is a very close affinity between Calvin's construction of the relation and Macchia's when described in terms of the outcome. Where

---

162. Ibid. Note how this comment points to sanctification by the assumption of the believer's humanity into Christ's perfect humanity.

163. See chapter 1.

the difference lies is in the process; For Calvin there are two distinct occurrences, each wrought by a different hypostasis, the union wrought by the Spirit and justification accomplished by Christ. For Macchia there is but one occurrence—being taken into God where the believer is counted as righteous by the synergistic activity of Christ and the Spirit. For Calvin, as he separates the occurrences and the functions of the hypostases, cannot say that the Spirit justifies. Macchia in understanding but one occurrence can say that the human is justified in the Spirit.

This is not to say that the work of the Spirit and Christ in the union and justification cannot be linked for Calvin. They are of course linked because they are hypostases within the one triune God and they work cooperatively in union and justification, but, as far as I am aware, he does not specifically link them so that the Spirit can be said to be contributing to justification in the sense that Macchia means. Macchia does argue that faith can be understood as participation in Christ by the Spirit.[164] From this can be drawn the inference that faith, which is given by the Spirit, enables participation in Christ through the Spirit and if justification is understood as this participation then there is a direct link between the Spirit and justification. Thus, it is legitimate to say that justification is in the Spirit.

Calvin would not disagree with much of this logic. For him, faith is even more a gift of the Spirit than for Macchia as there is no suggestion of a human component to it, and justification is through faith. That is, faith is not the cause of justification, but humans are justified by the grace of God received through faith, a reception which occurs within the union between Christ and the believer. Faith is necessary for justification, and faith is given by the Spirit, therefore the work of the Spirit is necessary for justification. In similar fashion, the union is the work of the Spirit and the union is necessary for justification and the same conclusion concerning the work of the Spirit is reached. There is clearly a link between the Spirit and justification, but Calvin will not take the next step and say humans are justified in the Spirit, even if synergistically with Christ. From his perspective, he has very good scriptural reasons for this.

Nevertheless, one might tentatively suggest that this means there is a contribution from the Spirit towards justification in Calvin, albeit indirect and resting in his cooperative activity with Christ. It is a contribution because his gift of faith and establishment of the union are necessary for justification to occur. Whilst it is Christ who justifies, he does so through mechanisms provided by the Spirit and if those are not provided then justification cannot occur. There is then some affinity here with Macchia in the

164. Macchia, *Justified in the Spirit*, 237–41.

recognition of a contribution from the Spirit, but it falls short of the strong affinity present in the shared outcome for the justified human.

Affinities: The Union and Sanctification

Before leaving this part of the discussion, some comment is required on regeneration/sanctification. Calvin uses the terms interchangeably and Pentecostals separate regeneration from sanctification, in a way that Calvin does not, and Macchia follows this in his use of the terms. Regeneration is the new birth brought by the indwelling Spirit which occurs at Christian initiation,[165] whereas sanctification is a "cleansing or a separation from sin" and "a consecration unto God in preparation for a holy task" and is an aspect of the life of discipleship which "involves a transformation by the Spirit of God into the very image of Christ."[166] Regeneration occurs as an event within the moment of Christian initiation, sanctification is an ongoing event in the believer's life from the moment of initiation. Thus, regeneration can be said to be the beginning of sanctification,[167] and within Macchia's proposal represents one metaphor of the Spirit's work which overlaps with the metaphor representing justification. He notes the contrast this is to "conceptually distinct categories only logically connected"[168] which represents Calvin's view on the two aspects of sanctification, using that term to denote regeneration and sanctification on the Pentecostal side.

For Calvin, sanctification is an event where the believer turns to God, putting off his "former mind" and putting on a new, which represents a putting off of the old nature and seeking a transformation within to take on a new nature.[169] Note the language which roots this activity in the believer and speaks of activity by him. This is not to be understood as a work by the believer, as sanctification is a gift of God which is entirely achieved by God's activity in the Spirit through faith.[170] However, because of the secrecy of the Spirit, it certainly appears to the believer as his own work, both the turning to God which results in initial sanctification, the putting on of the new mind, and the ongoing effort in piety through which the transformation that is ongoing sanctification occurs. The sanctifying activity is directed to

---

165. Ibid., 67.
166. Macchia, *Baptized in the Spirit*, 83. Note the parallel between the positive and negative aspects and Calvin's mortification and vivification.
167. Macchia, *Justified in the Spirit*, 69, 87.
168. Ibid., 64.
169. III.3.5, 6.
170. III.3.21.

God and can only be effective through the union between the believer and Christ—this applies to both God's enabling and the believer's responsive activity. What must be understood is that the substantive activity, effected by the Spirit, occurs in the believer. This contrasts with the establishment of the union itself and justification, where the substantive activity originates in God and is directed to the believer. Thus, while the union is justifying in some sense, it is not sanctifying, either in its initial or ongoing sense. Hence there is no ground for any overlap between justification and sanctification in Calvin, even if the union is added to the mix. Initial sanctification and justification certainly occur simultaneously, but they are separate and must remain separate.[171] While Macchia and Calvin agree on the content of sanctification in Calvin's terms and that it is the work of the Spirit, that close affinity does not extend into the province of justification as Macchia proposes it where an overlap with sanctification is natural. Such an overlap is not possible in Calvin's conception.

Affinities: A Trinitarian View of Justification

Macchia's proposal lends itself to the development of a trinitarian view of justification; strongly rooted in the triune life of Father, Son and Spirit, justification as participation in that communion is inevitably trinitarian. The way in, so to speak, is provided by Christ and the Spirit through their roles on the cross and resurrection, but the substance of justification, for him, is participation in the life of God. While individual roles can be discerned for each hypostasis, the distinction between each is blurred somewhat, particularly highlighted in the synergism between the Son and the Spirit in providing the way in. With justification not ascribed to either but to both, while the contribution made by each can be discussed, the operation of justification is a joint one. Equally, participation in God's life is participation in the communion which consists of the relations between the hypostases; so as much as the believer might be said to be in Christ, to be so is also to place her within the communion enjoyed by Father, Son and Spirit. However, this blurring, or overlap between hypostases, is not to be understood as weakening the account of justification. What Macchia is wanting to say is that his account

---

171. It could be argued that the relation between initial sanctification and the union provides an overlap, but at best this is slight as sanctification is both initial and ongoing, the latter looming larger over a believer's life. Hence it is legitimate to say there is no overlap. Billings, *Participation and the Gift*, 108, confirms the distinction between justification and sanctification for Calvin, but makes the important observation that "the images of union, participation, adoption, and engrafting can move quite flexibly to hold together [justification and sanctification]" in Calvin's thought.

strengthens the doctrine of justification, which is no longer (potentially at least) a distant declaration concerning the believer, but now consists of the establishment of very strong, intimate links between the believer and God. What may have left the believer isolated previously, now explicitly brings her within the fold. He contrasts this to seeing justification as limited to the Father's election and the satisfaction of his justice on the cross, which he understands as excluding the Spirit so implies it is not trinitarian.

This more limited view is, of course, Calvin's position. However, the inter-relation between union and justification for him ensures that God is not distant but is intimately involved with the believer, perhaps in contrast to other Reformed views. However, it is not necessary for Calvin to appeal to that inter-relation for his doctrine to be trinitarian: justification is trinitarian. Remember again his discussion of justification and sanctification in *Institutes*, where he says "however we may have been redeemed by Christ, until we are engrafted into his fellowship by the calling of the Father, we are both the heirs of darkness and death and the enemies of God."[172] Here all three hypostases are present: believers are redeemed by Christ; called by the Father they are engrafted into Christ's fellowship so his work may be effective; and that engrafting is done by the Spirit. Less directly, the beginning of salvation is "a sort of resurrection" to life,[173] a resurrection patterned on that of Christ who was raised by the Spirit and sent by the Father. Justification is certainly part of the beginning of salvation, so the trinitarian nature of divine activity within it is implied here, although there is not the same direct link between the Spirit and justification that Macchia proposes.

While the activity of each hypostasis is present, there is a very strong distinction between them as to their roles in salvation, which reduces to particular roles in particular aspects of salvation. Thus, believers are justified by grace through Christ so justification is his role. While this occurs as a result of the call of the Father, and happens through the union wrought by the Spirit, it is Christ who is efficacious in the act of justification. Justification is trinitarian in that each hypostasis has a role, but as those of the Father and the Spirit enable and promote the activity of Christ, they are not constitutive of the activity of justification itself. Thus, justification is entirely christological for Calvin, as it is Christ who acts to justify; the ontological change is wrought by him, and him alone, although he can only act in this way because he is the Father's Son. Christ is not acting in isolation in doing so, he acts from within a context which includes the contribution of the Father and the Spirit, a context which enables him to act constitutively, but

172. III.14.6.
173. Ibid.

the contribution of the other hypostases is limited to creating that context. This is the operation of the logically connected but conceptually distinct categories referred to by Macchia.[174]

It is not unreasonable to characterize Calvin as having a "looser" view of the Trinity in this doctrine than Macchia. It is, of course, inappropriate to view the Trinity as in any way "loose," but Calvin places distance between the hypostases by allocating distinct functions in a way that Macchia does not. By the blurring or overlap in his conception, Macchia maintains a close relation where each hypostasis has a constitutive role in justification, explicitly for the Son and the Spirit, implicitly for the Father. Nevertheless, each conception is distinctly trinitarian, and an affinity exists between them to that extent.

Summary

Thus, there are affinities between Calvin's entirely christological doctrine of justification and Macchia's justification in the Spirit, surprising as that may seem. Macchia is not simply expanding the definition of justification to include union and initial sanctification, but sees justification scripturally conceived as being in the Spirit and in Christ. Calvin would not accept that this basis exists, but there is a close identification between Macchia's content of justification as participation in God's life and Calvin's engrafting into Christ's fellowship which results from union, justification and initial sanctification. To put it concisely, the result is essentially the same for each.

There is an affinity between each in the trinitarian nature of each doctrine, but the affinity is seen most strongly, and specifically, when considering justification and union for Calvin alongside Macchia's conception. In Macchia there is an explicit connection between the two as justification consists of a righteousness which is contained within the taking up into God's life, a righteousness which exists through the death and resurrection of Christ and which is applied by the Spirit (who raised Jesus) to the believer in the taking up. In Calvin, there is a link which is never addressed specifically, but which exists just as much, for example, as the link between human sin and human responsibility for it. In that case, Calvin's doctrine of election means that the reprobate are always destined to sin, and so to be condemned: they can do nothing about it. However, they are condemned because they are held responsible for their sin. There is some link, the character of which is not available to humans, between human responsibility and sin here which ensures that God is righteous in holding

---

174. Macchia, *Justified in the Spirit*, 64.

them responsible. In the same way, there is a link between the union and justification which is not available to humans but which is real.

This affinity is so strong that if Macchia's reading of the New Testament witness is accepted, then it acts to establish that link between union and justification. It may well be able to be shown that the adoption of such a reading means that Macchia's proposal is a natural extension from Calvin's thought on justification and union. That possibility is discussed in the next chapter, but the potential does appear to exist. If it were to be realized, then Pentecostal theology on justification in the context of Spirit baptism (incorporating the Spirit coming at conversion and a subsequent Spirit release) would become strongly founded on Calvin's work. Of course, the only obstacle to this is the issue of what reading of Scripture is appropriate, which is not an insignificant obstacle! Nevertheless, the existence of the affinity between Calvin and the Pentecostal viewpoint as represented by Macchia is so marked that it is not inappropriate for Pentecostals to view Calvin as a significant forerunner to the development of a theology of justification in the context of Spirit baptism.

6

From Calvin to Pentecostals

The colloquial view of John Calvin does not suggest any easy affinity with Pentecostals. This is reflected well in comments on the New Zealand city of Dunedin and its early history[1] which paint a dour and unlovely place, "a city rooted in the stern teachings of John Calvin as interpreted by the Scottish Presbyterian church."[2] This drew upon another commentator: "Scottish Calvinists were indeed an important influence in early Dunedin. The MacTaliban, as one wit's called them, held sway over the Scottish spirit for centuries. John Calvin's Reformation regime in Geneva was no barrel of laughs either."[3] The view these comments represent paints Calvin as a cold and judgmental figure who represents a God primarily interested in punishing sinners, a vision which so greatly troubled the young Martin Luther.[4] This is reflected in the suggestion of J. I. Packer that it is widely held that the main point of Calvin's theology is "that most people are irretrievably damned."[5] However, there is no question that such views are mistaken—Packer says: "The amount of misrepresentation to which Calvin's theology has been subjected is enough to prove his doctrine of total depravity several

---

1. Dunedin was intended to be a Free Church of Scotland colony and the first settler ship was organized by Rev. Thomas Burns and others of that church, arriving in 1848. Davidson, *Christianity in Aotearoa*, 34.

2. Chapman, "Sunday Morning."

3. Brittenden, "Wayne Brittenden's Counterpoint."

4. See *D. Martin Luthers Werke: Krtische Gesamtausgabe*: "I had certainly been overcome with a great desire to understand St Paul in his letter to the Romans, but what had hindered me thus far was not any 'coldness of the blood' so much as that one phrase in the first chapter: 'the righteousness of God is revealed in it.' For I hated that phrase 'the righteousness of God', which according to the use and custom of all the doctors, I had been taught to understand philosophically, in the sense of the formal or active (as they termed it) righteousness by which God is righteous, and punishes unrighteous sinners" (in McGrath, *Iustitia Dei*, 218–19).

5. Packer, *Evangelical Influences*, 19.

times over."[6] Any dispassionate reading of *Institutes* reveals an author with an intense pastoral concern for his readers, where those who are saved are so by the grace of God and are brought into an intimate union with Christ through the Spirit so as to be able to participate in the life of God. Certainly, his doctrine of predestination raises uncomfortable questions, dark as it is,[7] but Calvin himself says that justification by faith is the "main hinge on which religion turns"[8] and nowhere suggests that predestination is the foundation of his theology.

In the face of what the colloquial view may say, there is in fact a strong parallel between Calvin's account of the union between the believer and Christ and Pentecostal understandings. Where Calvin sees an intimate personal union established in the church in which God is directing all that occurs within the believer's life (although in a way which leaves responsibility for the ungodly with the believer) and where the believer can look to God for providential care, Pentecostals see a God who is concerned to provide for the believer in every way and who invites the believer to seek divine assistance even down to the minutiae of life. For the Pentecostal believer, there is no issue too trivial for God, so he sees a godly concern for him which is identical to the providential care Calvin expresses.

This being the case, it is not surprising that I have found distinct affinities in the account of the union and pneumatology between the two theological systems.[9] While there is a disjunction in the view of the secrecy or otherwise of the Spirit, there is substantial affinity in the transformation wrought by the Spirit in the believer and significant common ground in the assurance of faith for each believer. There is also a strong affinity between the respective views on providence: God is strongly and widely providential towards each believer, but there is a difference in how it is approached. For Calvin, providence consists of God's complete provision for each believer which is already in place, ready to be discovered by the believer as he pursues the spiritual disciplines of the Christian life. For the Pentecostals, providence consists of this in part, but there is also substantial guidance to be sought which is contingent on the believer's decisions and actions. The difference between the views is rooted in the degree of synergism the

---

6. Ibid.

7. "How can the doctrine of election be anything but 'dark' and obscure if in its very first tenet which determines all the rest, it can speak only of a *decretum absolutum?*" (Barth, *CD* II/2, 104).

8. III.11.1.

9. In respect of Pentecostal theology, I mean the particular threads I have followed in Pentecostal theology here. There is, of course, no Pentecostal theological system as yet of the type which certainly exists for Calvin's followers.

Pentecostal would assert, a synergism absent in Calvin, but providence is experienced identically from the point of view of the believer—each needs to discover it, albeit in somewhat different ways. That is, the journey of finding God's providence appears of the same character to each believer, the "disciple" of Calvin and the Pentecostal.

Similar affinities exist in the accounts of justification I have considered. Macchia's conception of justification as in Christ and in the Spirit by which believers participate in God's life is exactly parallel to Calvin's engrafting into fellowship with Christ which results from union, justification and initial sanctification. While Macchia is not simply redefining justification as being these three, Calvin's thought implies a link between union and justification as the former is a necessary prior event following which justification is possible. The nature of this link is not available to humans, but in it there is some common ground with Macchia beyond the simple parallel.

What all this suggests is that there is fertile ground for exploring how these affinities may lead to more explicit links between Calvin and Pentecostals in the context of Spirit release. I will first consider Spirit release itself, beginning with the question of whether it is a suitable term for the happenings in Acts most often termed the baptism of the Spirit.

Spirit Release as a Suitable Metaphor

What I am seeking to establish here is whether the description of the occurrences in Acts as Spirit release rather than Spirit baptism, or some other term, is a legitimate way to understand them in Pentecostal thought. I have already highlighted the advantage of being able to understand them as release,[10] a concept which allows "Spirit baptism" to be applied to the coming of the Spirit at conversion, a more widely accepted view of Spirit baptism which retains the "once only" nature of baptism. It also allows Spirit baptism to be conceived of as encompassing both the coming of the Spirit at conversion and the event of Spirit release without doing damage to maintaining a distinction between the two occurrences as being of different character. Thus, Spirit baptism (or the conversion occurrence) can be conceived of as the Spirit coming to dwell within the believer and Spirit release as some action of the already indwelling Spirit within the believer which produces some change. This concurs with Pentecostal thought which sees two distinct occurrences, but does not accord with the Pentecostal doctrine of subsequence. This is because that doctrine envisages two distinct "comings" of the Spirit—a coming to indwell at conversion,

10. See chapter 2.

and a further coming to fill at "Spirit baptism." Thus, a Spirit baptism at conversion followed by a separate and distinct Spirit release or a Spirit baptism consisting of both events do not confirm subsequence or redeem the doctrine from my critique in chapter two.

Macchia briefly considers the concept of release,[11] noting that the church fathers linked Spirit baptism with charismatic experience, suggesting a view that sacramental grace given at conversion will burst out in charismatic experiences at some point,[12] a view popular among "charismatics in the mainstream churches who preferred to speak of Spirit baptism as a 'release of the Spirit' in the Christian life."[13] He then goes on to say that Pentecostals do not agree on how to relate the two occurrences, but he does regard as a helpful trend "the tendency now among many Pentecostals . . . to accent the gift of the Spirit given in regeneration and to view the Pentecostal experience of Spirit baptism as empowerment for witness as a 'release' of an already-indwelling Spirit."[14] Is this tendency supportable from the testimony of the activity of the Spirit in Acts?

In addressing this, it first needs to be acknowledged that to call the occurrences "Spirit baptism" is true to Luke's terminology. The promise of Jesus at Acts 1:5 that the disciples will soon be baptized with the Holy Spirit is surely fulfilled at Acts 2:4 where we are told they were "filled with the Holy Spirit." Thus being "baptized" and being "filled" with the Spirit are synonymous for Luke. This difference in terminology highlights a feature in Acts which is not helpful in trying to establish precisely what Luke means on the five occasions Pentecostals appeal to in their accounts of Spirit release (Acts 2:4, 8:17, 9:17, 10:44 and 19:6) or exactly what the relation is between Christian initiation and the occurrences of Spirit release: there is no consistency of accounts of the Spirit's activity. This is well summarized by C. K. Barrett, who comments:

> Luke's account of the Christian experience of the Holy Spirit is vivid, and central in his thought, but lacks consistency, thereby raising many questions. It is not easy to answer the question whether, for him, the Spirit, once given, is a permanent possession, or spasmodic. He says nothing that actually suggests that the Spirit was at any point taken away from those who had received it, yet at Acts 4:8 Peter is *filled* with the Holy Spirit.[15]

---

11. Macchia, *Baptized in the Spirit*, 74–77.
12. A view which he ascribes to McDonnell and Montague, ibid., 73.
13. Ibid, 74.
14. Ibid., 77.
15. Barrett, *The Acts of the Apostles*, 1:115 (emphasis his).

The tense of the Greek at 4:8 suggests the filling took place there and then. Later, (4:31), the same thing is said of the whole group.[16]

In his later discussion on Acts 10:44, Barrett lists six verbs associated with the coming of the Spirit used at eight locations (1:5; 1:8; 2:4; 2:38; 8:16, 18; 10:44 and 11:15) in the book.[17] The verbs are respectively rendered in the NRSV as *baptized; come upon; filled; receive; come upon; given* and *fell upon* (twice). The one verb used at 8:16, 10:44 and 11:15 has a meaning which is "not different from that of" the others.[18] Of the five instances to which Pentecostals appeal as occurrences of Spirit release, only at 19:6 is a different verb used (rendered *came upon* in the NRSV).[19] I. Howard Marshall makes a similar point in his discussion on Acts 2:4, suggesting that the word *fill* "is used when people are given an initial endowment of the Spirit to fit them for God's service (9:17; Lk 1:15) and also when they are inspired to make important utterances (4:8, 31; 13:9); related words are used to describe the continuous process of being filled with the Spirit (13:52; Eph 5:18) or the corresponding state of being full (6:3; 5: 7:55; 11:24; Lk 4:1) . . . what is here called a 'filling' is called a 'baptizing' (1:5 and 11:16), a 'pouring out' (2:17f; 10:45), and a 'receiving' (10:47)."[20] He also comments that "no one synonym can do justice [to the range of meaning of baptism] as a Christian technical term for the reception of the Spirit."[21]

For Marshall, this range of meaning includes initial reception of the Spirit, but he also allows for further occurrences after that initial reception.—"a person already filled with the Spirit can receive a fresh filling for a specific task or a continuous filling." However he does make a distinction in the use, going on to note that "The basic act of receiving the Spirit can be described as being baptized or filled, but the verb 'baptize' is not used for subsequent experiences."[22] On this distinction, 1:5; 2:17f; 10:45, 47: and 11:16 refer to initial reception of the Spirit and the other references he mentions to a subsequent filling. If this is the case, then Luke is describing two types of occurrence in his clutch of synonyms. However, there is at least one "crossover" verb in Marshall's lists—on his view "fill" is used of initial reception at 2:4 and then of what can only be a subsequent filling for Peter at 4:8. Barrett doesn't make this distinction in this way, regarding filling

16. Ibid.
17. Ibid., 1:529.
18. Ibid.
19. Zodhiates, *Complete Word Study*, 451.
20. Marshall, *Acts*, 69.
21. Ibid., 58.
22. Ibid., 69.

and baptism as synonymous, but also noting that, for Luke, "the gift of the Spirit is constitutive of the Christian life" and that the Spirit's aid is given on specific occasions. However, he thinks it wrong to "deduce from Acts a clear-cut and consistent doctrine of the Holy Spirit," although it is the Spirit's aid on specific occasions which predominates in Acts.[23] Eckhard J. Schnabel is more definitive about the close relation between "baptize" and "fill". Noting that he prefers to render the verb at 2:4 as "immersion in" or "being washed by," he sees the filling of 2:4, as "fulfilment of Luke 3:16 and Acts 1:5, being synonymous with the term at 1:5." He comments:

> The verb 'fill' ... is a more intense form ... Luke uses the aorist indicative with genitive of divine Spirit to designate 'short outbursts of spiritual power/inspiration, rather than the inception of long-term endowment of the Spirit', a fact that explains why a person might be 'filled with the Holy Spirit' on many occasions while remaining 'full' of the Spirit.[24]

This reading means that Jesus' promise at 1:5 does not refer to initial reception of the Spirit at conversion, but the giving of specific aid through outbursts of spiritual power or inspiration. As those who are filled with the Spirit at 2:4 are believers (see 1:15), they must have already received the Spirit in a different occurrence prior to the Pentecost event. Calvin refers to this first reception of the Spirit as receiving the "grace of regeneration"[25] and that points to a useful way of describing the initial reception as receiving the Spirit for regeneration. As I have already noted, Calvin shares the opinion that Schnabel implies, that the apostles had already been baptized with the Spirit for regeneration before Pentecost.[26]

This, of course, is the Pentecostal view. Williams, for example, says that the Spirit is given to the saved, that salvation is the background against which the Spirit comes; and that prior to Pentecost the Spirit was not absent from the disciples, but that the Spirit had not "come on" them.[27] This amounts to saying that the Spirit dwelt within the disciples but had not yet manifested himself in the way he was to at Pentecost.

There is little Biblical evidence to support one view against the other, but there is one text which argues for the Pentecostal view, John 20:21–23:

---

23. Barrett, 115.
24. Schnabel, *Acts*, 115. He cites Turner, *Power from on High*.
25. Calvin, *The Acts of the Apostles*, 1:27.
26. Ibid.
27. Williams, *Renewal Theology*, 2:187, 196.

> 21 Jesus said to them again, "Peace be with you. As the Father has sent me, so I send you." 22 When he had said this, he breathed on them and said to them, "Receive the Holy Spirit. 23 If you forgive the sins of any, they are forgiven them; if you retain the sins of any, they are retained."

Here, before his ascension, Jesus bestows the Holy Spirit on the disciples. Along with the bestowal comes authority, indicating that it is a real, contemporary happening, not a prefiguring of what is to come in Acts. The great strength of the view that the Spirit is already with the disciples prior to Pentecost is that it resolves any conflict between this text and Acts, even allowing for the different Johannine and Lukan voices. Barrett's apparent view cannot "harmonize Luke's narrative of Pentecost with the Johannine gift of the Spirit." Instead, he suggests that Luke might "find it natural to pick out particular incidents to represent what was in fact a continuous process or state."[28]

It is not unreasonable then to adopt the reading that the occurrences in Acts do not record the initial reception of the Spirit. At 2:4, the disciples had already received the Spirit; at 8:17 the Samaritans had already been baptized in Jesus' name before they received the Spirit; at 9:17 Paul had already received the revelation of Jesus as Lord (Gal 1:12); at 10:44, Cornelius and his household were already devout God-fearers (10:2) and, while there is no indication that they knew the gospel prior to Peter's preaching, the occurrence leaves open the possibility of them receiving the Spirit of regeneration immediately before the Spirit "falling on" them in a separate happening. Only at 19:1–6 is there some doubt, with arguments being made both ways concerning the initial status of the Ephesian believers. It is not necessary for my purposes to make any sort of judgement on their status as both my subjects agree on that question. Pentecostals view them as Christians prior to receiving the Spirit at 19:6,[29] and so does Calvin, on the basis that the reference to the baptism of John refers to the person doing the baptism, not the baptismal content.[30] This happy agreement also extends to Calvin's adoption of this reading (as already noted at 2:4) at 8:17 and 10:44,[31] while at 9:17 he says Ananias laid hands on Paul "partly to set him apart for God, and partly to obtain the gifts

---

28. Barrett, *Acts*, 74. It must be pointed out that Barrett's aim is to present a commentary on Acts, not to resolve this doctrinal point.

29. See for example, Duffield and Van Cleave, *Foundations of Pentecostal Theology*, 310; and Menzies and Horton, *Bible Doctrines*, 126 n. 4.

30. Calvin, *Acts*, 2:148–50.

31. Ibid., 1:235–36, 317.

of the Spirit for him,"[32] thus suggesting the Spirit for regeneration is received by Paul at the same time as coming to confer gifts, but that the occurrences are distinct from one another.

Adopting this reading means that in all five instances a distinction is made between initial reception and a baptism or filling. All the texts describe at least this later filling and in all places the verbs used are synonymous for Luke. Therefore, it can be said with a degree of confidence that he believes he is describing the same occurrence, perhaps in part only in those instances where the Spirit of regeneration is also received. Certainly, within the context of this discussion between Calvin and Pentecostals, that is the case. That is, both Pentecostals and Calvin agree that he is describing a number of occurrences, but they are all of the same character, whereby the Spirit manifests himself in a way *after* he has come for regeneration which has a substantial impact on the individual believer. A result of this manifestation is the release of obvious spiritual gifts in the believers. Because it is the same occurrence, it is perfectly proper to search for a single term to describe all the occurrences. In this, it must be recognized that while the words he uses may be synonymous, there may be some emphasis which Luke is keen to express at some points compared to others, so any word chosen must allow for this variation.

The character of the occurrence itself must be considered. Pentecostals describe Spirit release as being overwhelming, where every part of the believer's being is affected. Williams refers to it as a possession by the Spirit,[33] a "divine visitation in fullness,"[34] where "the whole community or person is inwardly pervaded by the Holy Spirit . . . a totality of penetration with the Holy Spirit whereby . . . all areas of one's being . . . become sensitized to the divine presence and activity."[35] Duffield and Van Cleave call it "a total yielding to the Lord Jesus Christ [which] brings the recipient into a more intimate relationship with Jesus Christ."[36]

I suggest "release" is an appropriate single term to use for these occurrences in Acts. By "release" I mean to describe the occurrence as one where the already indwelling Spirit can affect the believer in new and deeper ways, where he is able to manifest a capacity new to the believer within the believer. This new capacity might be so overwhelming as to cause the believer to feel that she has been "filled," or that the Spirit who dwells within

---

32. Ibid., 1:267.
33. Williams, *Renewal Theology*, 2:198.
34. Ibid., 2:201.
35. Ibid., 2:202–3.
36. Duffield and Van Cleave, *Foundations of Pentecostal Theology*, 321.

her has been released to "occupy" every part of her being. Of course, it must be recognized that any term will have its shortcomings, but if the circumstance before and after the occurrence are considered, "release" is suitable. Beforehand, the Spirit dwells in the believer for regeneration, but there are no visible signs of this grace, to use Calvin's terms. That is, there are no gifts manifested. After, the Spirit is said to have filled every part of a believer and has brought gifts or new capacities which are now seen. It is as if the Spirit has come and spilled out, so to speak, as seen in the gifts which are visible indications of his presence. A metaphor of release is highly appropriate to this occurrence as it evokes images of the indwelling Spirit "expanding" so as to affect all parts of the believer and doing so so energetically that the evidence of the "expansion" is visible externally. Duffield and Van Cleave's "total yielding" evokes release in these terms as it sees the believer offering up the totality of her being to Jesus Christ who is then able to usher the Spirit into areas of her being not fully yielded previously. To express it in terms of the manifestation of new capacities, something new to the believer is introduced within him in such a way that can be overwhelming.

"Release" is also consistent with the synergism present in Pentecostal accounts of salvation, where the believer makes some contribution. This synergism can be seen in the conditions which are attached to Spirit release by Pentecostal writers. Both Williams[37] and Duffield and Van Cleave[38] give lists of conditions (or necessary contexts as Williams prefers), in addition to the necessity of salvation prior, to be satisfied before Spirit release can occur. These include prayer, obedience, repentance, a complete yielding, and expectancy. Each of these imply, and are expressed in terms of, activity by the believer to create the conditions in which Spirit release can occur. In the early years of Pentecostalism they were embodied by the use of tarry meetings, where individuals seeking Spirit release came to pray and examine their consciences so as to identify sins for which repentance could be offered.[39] Under the leading of God, they sought to repent sufficiently so as to create sufficient holiness within themselves so that their internal environment was appropriate for the Spirit to fill. This, of course, contains echoes of the early view that total sanctification was necessary for Spirit release.

This synergistic activity on the part of the believer fits well with the concept of release. It is as if the individual has internal barriers which constrain the indwelling Spirit and by the meeting of all the conditions, these barriers are removed. The Spirit can then operate more freely in, or

---

37. Williams, *Renewal Theology*, 2:272–306.
38. Duffield and Van Cleave, *Foundations of Pentecostal Theology*, 317–20.
39. See Worsfold, "Subsequence," 75–84, for a good description of tarry meetings.

bring new capacities to, the believer—she is released by the removal of the constraints.

However, release as a metaphor does not require human action. It can be conceived of as entirely God's activity within the human. While the human may be involved in the sort of activity I have described, the release which follows need not be conditioned by the activity at all. All it requires is for God to choose to add a new dimension to the indwelling of the Spirit by expanding the Spirit's activity within the human. It might be that God was exercising a voluntary constraint on action within the human and this expansion of activity is achieved by the ending of this constraint. In this case then it has been totally God's action. Thus, release is not a human action in itself—the release is effected by Christ in response to the conditions created within the human, which themselves could be entirely a work of the Spirit. It is not as if the believer calls the Spirit to release at all, it is that the believer seeks to create the conditions within himself which allow Christ to act to release the Spirit, but that the believer has no influence on that act—it is the sovereign choice of Christ. On his part, Christ has promised to release the Spirit in such circumstances, so the believer is entitled to have faith that Christ will act, whilst also not "forcing" Christ to act.

Release also allows for repetition, that is for an initial release to be followed by another, and so on. As noted above, the occurrence in Acts can be repeated (e.g., Peter at 2:4 and 4:8), so the scriptural evidence is clear that Spirit release, having occurred once, can and does occur again. In Peter's case, this is described in both instances as being *filled,* which introduces a conceptual difficulty. If something is filled, unless it is emptied, it remains filled. There is no suggestion that the Spirit deserted Peter between 2:4 and 4:8, so how can a filling occur again? While acknowledging that Scripture uses just this term in these instances, if each is thought of as release the conceptual difficulty is largely resolved. The indwelling Spirit is released at 2:4 and Peter is overwhelmed, with every part of his being affected (so much so that he can be properly described as "filled") and he is divinely equipped to speak in another language and preach a powerful message. However, this release does not exhaust the capacity of the Spirit within him, so on the later occasion there is capacity also able to be released for the purpose then. Again, he experiences this as being filled as this new (to him) capacity of the Spirit overwhelms him, but again this does not exhaust the Spirit and capacity exists for a further future release, and so on.

Spirit release therefore sits easily within Pentecostal thought as an explanation of the occurrences in Acts and the Pentecostal testimony to the Spirit's activity within them in the primal encounter which is distinctive of their witness. The next step is to enquire whether Spirit release, so envisaged, can be conceived as a natural extension from Calvin's thought. This will involve looking at the occurrence itself and how it might impact on other doctrines within his theology.

Spirit Release: Christ Alone for Calvin?

Turning now to whether a link to Calvin for Spirit release can be established, there are two ways in which such a link or links could exist: either the concept of Spirit release is within Calvin's thought,[40] or it can be described as a logical progression or extension from it. On the face of it, the former appeals as highly unlikely in view of the contrast between the secrecy of the Spirit in Calvin and the highly public position occupied in Pentecostal thought, but the possibility that Spirit release as testified to by Pentecostals is actually an encounter with Christ facilitated by the Spirit appeals as having some potential.

To examine this, I return to Hocken who has pointed out that the early Pentecostal accounts of Spirit release show a new and deeper knowledge of God as Father, Son and Spirit. They are not confined to an experience of the Spirit alone. Early testimonies of the occurrence include such comments as:

> I turned to Jesus in my weariness and found in him rest and peace for my soul . . . He found me thirsting for Him . . . now I am drinking of the living waters and find refreshing for my spirit . . . Jesus is so precious to me[41]

> My Jesus is more real to me than ever, the Holy Spirit is more jealous of my life and heart. . . . We are tried and molded and purged and chastened and cleansed by the Holy Ghost, through the blood of Jesus Christ[42]

> That night she came through, she had a vision of Jesus and sang and preached in Chinese.[43]

Each of these comments relates part of the experience of Spirit release for the writer, but each also has a tight focus on Jesus Christ, one who is precious, more real than previously, and actually seen in a vision. Taken on

---

40. By which I mean it could be understood to be present with very little modification. This would occur if the answer to the question "Is Spirit release as understood by Pentecostals part of Calvin's theology?" would be "Yes, but it is expressed in *these* terms."

41. "A Testimony in Tongues," 2.

42. "Ye Are My Witnesses," 4.

43. "In a Divine Trance," 2.

their own terms, at the very least part of Spirit release for these individuals had been a more powerful impression of Jesus Christ in his union with them. The Spirit can be said to have pointed clearly to Jesus as a part of the occurrence, so in some way directing the believers' gaze away from himself and towards Christ. Calvin would be very comfortable with the idea that the Spirit acts in this self-effacing manner, although uncomfortable with the muted role of Scripture in the whole affair. Nevertheless, it can be speculated that it may be possible to find a way in which Spirit release could be aligned with Calvin's thought by conceiving it to be a work of Christ through the secret Spirit. That is, that what is encountered by the believer, and directly apprehended by her, is solely Christ, not the Spirit, although the encounter is brought about through the work of the Spirit.

From Calvin's perspective, this has the benefit of maintaining the secrecy of the Spirit so that the revelation of God remains Jesus Christ. However, his view of the church and close association of Scripture and the Spirit challenge the concept. It is Scripture which shows forth Christ when it is "branded on hearts" by the Spirit, and Scripture "is the instrument by which the Lord dispenses the illumination of his Spirit to believers."[44] While "God is the sole and proper witness of himself,"[45] that witness is provided by Scripture, quickened in the believer's heart by the action of the Spirit as it is read or, primarily, expounded in the church, and the sacraments. Spirit release as Pentecostals describe it gives a direct role beyond this for the Spirit and breaks the tight linkages of the Spirit's work to the church and Scripture. Is there a way of reconciling the two?

It could be argued that there is a consistency between Scripture and the content of Spirit release and that God, as the sole authenticator of himself, is able to use the occurrence to bear witness to himself and work in the believer to his ends. More radically, Walter Hollenweger, in a discussion on dreams and visions, asserts that Scripture is the final authority for Pentecostals so that numinous experiences function as interpretations of Scripture in their theology. This is so, even if Scripture contradicts the experience.[46] Hence, the believer must deny that she encountered God in her experience if its content contradicts Scripture, even if every part of her being wants to insist it really was God she encountered. This position is a stronger view than simple consistency as it rules out any new knowledge of God being furnished through the encounter,[47] something which consistency does not do.

---

44. I.9.3.
45. I.11.1.
46. Hollenweger, *The Pentecostals*, 133.
47. Note that this does not contradict the view I have expressed that Spirit baptism

However, neither consistency nor this subordination is likely sufficient to satisfy Calvin's desire to maintain a close link between Scripture, the Spirit, and his activity in pointing to Christ as God's revelation.

The final blow is administered by the role of the church for Calvin. The union between the believer and Christ is formed in the church—while personal, the union is an engrafting into the church—and it is there that the believer is nourished through the ministry of the church. If it can be said that the believer "encounters" Christ within Calvin's thought, that occurs in the church through the Word preached and the sacraments celebrated. To admit the experience of Spirit release as Pentecostals understand it is to do violence to Calvin's position. The idea of Spirit release being an encounter with Christ and so in some way to be incorporated within his thought founders on these points.

This is confirmed when the idea is examined from the Pentecostal side. While it is true that the full content of Spirit release is trinitarian, there are many accounts which attest to the direct work of the Spirit with Christ being acknowledged as having sent the Spirit. Thus:

> In the meeting at Dunn, N. C., the first of the year, God wonderfully baptized me with the Holy Ghost and spoke with my tongue to the extent that myself and those who surrounded me knew that it was the Blessed Holy Ghost who was talking. Bro. R. B. Jackson, holiness preacher with whom I used to preach, also received the Holy Ghost. Bro. Jackson and myself went off into the white fields of harvest to reap for Jesus. O, how He has poured out His Spirit in saving souls, sanctifying believers, filling hungry hearts with the Holy Ghost. We are now engaged on one of the most wonderful meetings I ever saw. Praise His sweet name forever.[48]

Here, while it is obviously a Christian account of a Christian occurrence, the focus is on the Spirit and what he is doing in believers, manifesting in a way which convinced the writer and those around him that it was indeed the Holy Spirit who was present. This exemplifies the testimony of Pentecostals: while the full content of Spirit release is triune, the occurrence includes a direct encounter and apprehension of the Spirit. Thus, they witness to the occurrence being one of the Spirit being poured out, recognized by the believer to whom the Father and Son are revealed by the same Spirit. To suggest

---

brings a new and deeper knowledge of God. This remains true for the believer in the encounter, but the knowledge is already present in Scripture.

48. "From Other Pentecostal Papers," 3.

that it is only Christ who is directly apprehended would produce a torrent of denials, and against this it is extremely difficult to make way.

There is no prospect of being able to incorporate Spirit release in Calvin's thought by such an identification; both sides of the issue would agree that it is not Christ "writ large" who is apprehended in Spirit release.

Spirit Release in Calvinist[49] Guise

This leaves the second possibility: is there a way in which Spirit release can be conceived as an extension from Calvin's theology? That is, can a theology of Spirit release be developed which can be shown to be a natural extension from Calvin's thought?

I shall start with what Calvin made of Spirit release. In his commentary on Romans, at 8:9, he notes:

> These, however, are not said to be "after the Spirit" because they are filled with God's Spirit (which happens to no one today), but because they have the Spirit dwelling in them.[50]

This is, of course, a cessationist view: that certain manifestations of the Holy Spirit which the first century church experienced ceased at the end of the establishment period, but it is still the same Spirit in the same fullness who has indwelt Christian believers ever since. However, it reveals something more than that; Calvin makes a significant distinction between being "filled" with the Spirit and having the "Spirit dwelling" within and thus must have different "operations" of the Spirit in view. In other words, he understood that the Spirit coming to dwell within a believer is something of a different character than the Spirit filling a believer. In this, he presumably has the occurrences in Acts in mind and, indeed, we find the same thought expressed in his commentary on the book. Acts begins with a promise that the Spirit will come upon believers at 1:5:

> For John baptized with water, but you will be baptized with the
> Holy Spirit not many days from now.

This is undoubtedly a reference to the occurrence recorded at 2:4, where the believers were "filled with the Holy Spirit," so to be filled is to be baptized with the Spirit. Calvin's comments on 1:5 make it clear that he considers Pentecost to be not the only baptism with the Spirit; the believers

---

49. I hesitate to use this term, but everywhere I do it means "of the theology of Calvin," not the later Reformed theology also called Calvinist or Calvinism.

50. Calvin, *Romans and Thessalonians*, 164.

had already received the Spirit and the elect are baptized with the Spirit in this fashion daily. What happened at Pentecost was a spectacular outward sign given to demonstrate the ministry of baptism with the Spirit.[51]

His view is expanded in his discussion on Peter's promise to the hearers of his message at 2:38. There, he comments that the audience has been impressed by what happened to the believers and Peter promises the same to them. What occurs is that Christ sets forth the beginning of his kingdom with miracles as a visible testimony to him being the giver of the Spirit. However, this was given for that time of the beginning. Nevertheless, what Peter said certainly applies to the church beyond the beginning—the contemporary church for Calvin does not see such miracles, but receives the Spirit for a better use, which he outlines as creating belief with the heart so that believers may have life and stand against Satan and the world.[52] He reiterates these points again in his comments on 10:44, where Cornelius' household is speaking in tongues (45). This he identifies as a grace of the Spirit distinct from the grace of regeneration that, nevertheless, shows that Peter's message was received and embraced by the hearers. The gift of tongues, he says, ceased long ago in the church, but the Spirit of understanding and regeneration is still in force and shall always be in force. Even though tongues have ceased, the elect feel in themselves the consent of the external word and the secret power of the Spirit.[53]

This cessationism is paralleled by his view on Scripture as the successor of apostolic teaching. Before the New Testament, the church was served by the Old Testament and apostolic teaching, which had doctrinal authority. Now it is served by the Old Testament and the writings of the apostles which capture their teaching.[54] Where there was no written form, the testimony was the teaching of the apostles, immediate, alive, new, to hand, and authenticated by the visible activity of the Spirit. Now, this excitement of the new revelation who is Jesus Christ has passed, but the testimony in Scripture remains.

So, Calvin does see Spirit release as recorded in Acts as different from the indwelling of the Spirit at conversion. The former he identifies very closely with the gifts of the Spirit, so release is given so that the gifts may manifest themselves. In fact, the release is essentially identified with the gifts, so the distinction can be expressed in those terms—the Spirit comes to dwell in believers to produce faith and regeneration, but his release is to see spiritual

---

51. Calvin, *Acts*, 1:27–28.
52. Ibid., 1:82.
53. Ibid., 1:317–18.
54. IV.8.4, 8.

gifts manifested. There is acceptance of the occurrence of release, but denial that it occurs any longer, so he takes no time to develop his thought on the issue. Hence, there is certainly room within Calvin's theology for Spirit release, but it does face the obstacle of the place of Scripture. That is, just as the release is paralleled by the word to the church comprising the apostles' teaching, its cessation is paralleled by the existence of the apostles' teaching now being in writing (the word as the Old Testament being common to both). To admit Spirit release in Calvin's thought is not simply a matter of pushing a reset button to get the gifts going again; the task must deal with the close relation the work of the Spirit has with Scripture.

There is no question but that Calvin considered the occurrence an entirely valid Christian occurrence, a genuine work of Christ in bestowing the Spirit in a particular way upon believers. As I have already pointed out, Calvin considered that in the early church, the new revelation, Jesus Christ, was given through the Old Testament and the apostles' teaching accompanied by the Spirit being a Spirit of regeneration and a Spirit of gifts. The former is represented by the Spirit coming to dwell in the believer, the latter by the Spirit being released within the believer.[55] However, following that initial period the revelation was given through the Old and New Testaments. Indeed, he views the apostles' teaching as Scripture,[56] prefiguring the written version to come. He means that in the early church, the Spirit came to dwell in the believer for their regeneration, but it was also necessary that the Spirit be released in the believer to demonstrate the truth of the apostles' teaching by the manifestation of gifts. Now, with the New Testament, the truth of the revelation can be attested by the Spirit illuminating the totality of Scripture, available through its preaching in the church, reading it under the guidance of the church, and participating in the sacraments. Therefore, the manifestation of gifts is no longer required to show the truth of Jesus Christ, so it doesn't happen—Spirit release no longer occurs. Indeed, the manifestation of gifts as Pentecostals understand it cannot occur as this would mean Scripture was effectively being added to in his conception.

The Effect of Calvin's Environment

While this was what Calvin thought, it was not universally held within the church. The eastern church, for one, would claim that the manifestation of

---

55. Where the Spirit dwells in believers to produce regeneration (the "Spirit for regeneration") and is released in believers to produce gifts (the "Spirit for gifts").

56. I.7.2.

gifts has been continuous since Pentecost.⁵⁷ It is useful to briefly explore a possible explanation for the difference in view, while noting that my aim here is to explore Spirit release as an extension from Calvin's theology, not to incorporate it within it, so defining the difference is not strictly necessary. However, speculating upon it will give a useful context.

Calvin lived in Christendom, a very different environment from the Roman Empire in which the early church was established and developed. Rather than Christianity being a small minority religion attempting to thrive in a culture dominated by pagan religion, Christianity in his time was essentially universal in western Europe and closely identified with the state. While there was obvious turmoil in the faith, the struggle was concerned with Christian theology and church praxis, not whether God exists.⁵⁸ Calvin had no need to convince his readers that God existed or that Jesus Christ was God's revelation to humanity—that view was effectively universally agreed by his audience, even by the reprobate. There was no need to demonstrate the truth of Christian claims through the Spirit for gifts as Scripture was accepted as revealing that truth.⁵⁹ While it might be unfortunate that such things as divine healing as a spiritual gift had ceased, the elect were destined for life eternal with God, in any event.⁶⁰

The eastern church was in a very different context. Its experience of Christendom (dating its establishment to the fourth century within the Roman Empire) was relatively limited, with significant areas under Islamic sway for the majority of its history. Thus its context was largely closer to the context of the early church, attempting to thrive in the face of a vigorously competing alternative religion with its own scriptures. An appeal to Christian Scripture as the truth about God and God's revelation to humanity simply does not have the authority it has in the West. In such an environment, there is a need for a defense of the faith and perhaps a renewal of evangelism, in which case being able to point to the manifestation of gifts as an indication of the truth of the Christian revelation of Jesus Christ is surely at least a useful adjunct. It is therefore an advantage to the proclamation of the faith to retain the Spirit

---

57. Burgess, "Implications," 25–28.

58. At I.3.1, Calvin says "Men one and all perceive that there is a God and that he is their Maker."

59. This was true for all parts of the church, even though appeal was made to other authorities by some.

60. Sweetman, "The Gifts of the Spirit," 278–79, makes the point that in Calvin's society each person was in his or her niche as ordained by God. Hence, to seek to leave the niche is rebellion against God. The sort of championing of gifts and response to them seen in Pentecostals may well have been seen as rebellion in such a society, so the environment would restrain gifts in that regard.

for gifts in that proclamation and the experience and praxis of the church. Put simply, in the East the context was conducive to the continuation of Spirit release and the resulting gifts; in the West it was not.

Pentecostalism dates its beginnings to the first decade of the twentieth century, but its roots extend back to the Holiness movement of the nineteenth century and the Wesleyanism of the eighteenth century.[61] Thus, its emergence coincides with the so-called Enlightenment and the rise of modernity with its emphasis on reason. While Christendom continued to hold sway in the West, its religious assumptions were severely challenged by the theology (or rejection of it) bred in the climate of reason. Hence, Christianity faced a challenge in which a response based on an appeal to Scripture as revelatory truth was no longer sufficient. Once again, the arsenal for proclamation of the faith required enhancement and the Spirit for gifts was one suitable response.[62] Over the century or more since Pentecostalism's genesis, Christendom has been eclipsed in the West and the context has moved towards a similarity with the first century Roman Empire, with secular attitudes and beliefs replacing the ancient pagan religion. While spiritual gifts may be greeted with skepticism in contemporary western culture, at least they do confront the prevailing assumptions concerning what is true. Beyond the West, Christianity confronts other faiths and pagan beliefs so the ability of Pentecostalism to point to Spirit release functions exactly as I have suggested it has in the historic eastern context.

What this suggests is that Calvin's cessationism is insufficient in the context surrounding the inception and development of Pentecostalism and that the response to that context would require an extension from his thought. Whether that is the case or not, being able to show that such an extension would sit comfortably upon his theology will provide a helpful link and assist the development of Pentecostal theology.

Spirit Release and Union

The issue for Calvin is not whether Spirit release can happen, but when; thus, my consideration cannot do violence to his conceptions, but must work with them. The starting point must be with the indwelling Spirit and thus the union between the believer and Christ—can Spirit release be said to occur while still retaining Calvin's doctrine of the union in all its riches?

---

61. McGee, "Historical Background," 9–14.

62. It was not the only one of course. Schleiermacher's appeal to religious experience in the early nineteenth century was also a response to reason which can be said to be of the same flavor but not the same ilk!

The union is a real one which brings real ontological change to the believer. There is an intimate bond established between Christ and the believer by the Spirit who now dwells within the believer. The union cannot be separated from the church and always occurs *via* the church. Nevertheless, it is a personal union—the branch grafted into the vine remains a branch and the nourishment it receives from Christ comes through the vine, but is for *this* branch.

In this context, through the indwelling Spirit and within the intimacy of the union, Christ also dwells within the believer. The union establishes a new creation in which the believer is changed at the level of her being as she exists as herself, but also as one in union with Christ, intimately linked to the Son of God by the Spirit. This union allows the fullness of God to dwell in her, by the Spirit and in Christ, and allows her to participate in God as she shares in the intra-divine relations through the relation she enjoys with Christ. Through the union, ontological change has been wrought in her as the Spirit and Christ are now part of her being, but she remains. The new creation retains elements of the old as it comprises her and Christ—therefore she still sins, even while in such intimate communion with God. Such sins are her acts, in which she is, of course, closely involved, but the corollary does not apply—godly acts are not her acts, but acts of God in which she certainly participates, so she is involved in them.

In fact, she is involved to the extent that they will seem to her to be her acts, even though they are willed and worked by God. They result because she appears to be applying what she has learnt, but in fact God dwells in her through Christ and uses her in this "higher" operation of the Spirit to achieve the desired act.[63] But in the union she is able to participate in God, so she is able to have the involvement she does—if this participation was not available to her, she would not be involved at all. It would still be a godly act as it is God who initiates it and causes it, but if it does not arise in part out of her participation in him then it is solely God using her. In this case it could be said that she is making herself available for God to use, so perhaps she has a passive involvement, but Calvin's doctrine of election shows that even that making available is God's work, not hers. So, her involvement in any godly act only arises out of her participation in God—it is from there, where the conceiving of the act and its completion is sourced that she can be involved.

This is a union between two parties, Christ with his irresistible grace and close activity in all things being one, and the other the believer with his

---

63. As opposed to the "lower" operation with the reprobate whom God is able to use to achieve his ends, but whose acts in that case cannot be said to be "godly" in the sense I describe above. For the reprobate, direction by God must all be external to them.

involvement. This involvement does not extend to a choice in his salvation and eventual destination but does include his responsibility for his sins. It is this responsibility for sins which means that he is involved, without being synergistically so in respect of his salvation or the work of Christ through the Spirit in him. It is not given to humans to understand how this irresistible grace is reconcilable with responsibility for sins, but the key point here is that the believer is involved in some way, without contradiction of either, and that involvement is connected to decisions he makes.

It is these three points concerning the union that allow for Spirit release in a way which is sympathetic to both Calvin and Pentecostalism—the union is between two separate parties; the human is involved in all that happens; and this involvement extends to godly acts through his participation in God. The appropriate starting point exists,[64] with the Spirit dwelling within the believer in the union, a "place," so to speak, from where influence can be exerted on the believer in whatever way. Spirit release, conceived as making available some capacity of the Spirit not previously manifested in the human, is entirely in accord with some new activity of the Spirit within the union. This making available speaks of something given to another, so requires an "other" to be true to the conception. If there is no "other," then there is no destination for what is made available: there is no receptive party in which the Spirit can extend a capacity new to the other party, no-one in whom the Spirit can be released.

The believer is the other within the union who forms the destination for the Spirit's capacity. Thinking now of release being a removal of constraints to the Spirit's activity within the believer, or a repenting to produce an internal environment of sufficient holiness in which the Spirit can extend new capacity, within Calvin's thought such a removal or repentance can only be a godly act. It cannot be that the believer has removed the constraints by her actions (as in Pentecostal thought), as the ends of such activity make it clear that it is godly activity. It is not that the believer has created this internal environment conducive to the Spirit—God has through the Spirit. However, the believer is involved in such activity and whether it takes the form of a simple request in prayer for the Spirit's release, or a long process of prayer and repentance, it will appear to her as her actions. Thus, her involvement in a way which is not synergistic is necessary to God's activity in extending new capacities of the Spirit to her.

64. For Calvin, this starting point is in, and through the means of, the church by the Spirit. Nevertheless, this is a personal union and the discussion which follows focuses on that. What needs to be borne in mind is that the continual maturing and operation of the union is *via* the church, which simply establishes a context for how Spirit release might be considered in a way sympathetic to Calvin.

As this is a godly act, her involvement is only possible through her participation in God. This is a crucial point. As she participates in God, her involvement is in fact more than a synergistic activity; she is participating in all aspects of the act itself. It is not that she is initiating it, or determining the act, or using the divine nature to assist her; or contributing any effort intrinsic only to her; it is that she has a real participation in an act determined by God through her participation in Godself. Thus, she *is* involved in creating the conditions within her in which new capacities of the Spirit can be manifested in her through this participation. The involvement is not synergistic at all, but it is not incorrect to say that she has removed the constraints within her, or that she has created a sufficient condition of holiness through prayer and repentance, to allow the new manifestation of the Spirit. All this has been effected by the Spirit, allowing her participation in God by which she has participated in the acts themselves.

Hence Spirit release is not at all inimical to the union between the believer and Christ which is so important in Calvin's theology. In fact, Spirit release fits comfortably within the union as he conceives it, in a way which closely parallels Pentecostal thought. Of course, this parallel is not an identification with Pentecostal thought; for example, the synergism of Pentecostal accounts of the release cannot be part of the extension from Calvin's position as to regard it as such would do serious violence to his thought. However, the involvement of the believer in the occurrences of Spirit release in the union is real and sits easily as the calvinist equivalent of the synergism of Pentecostal views on the release.

In this construction, then, God acts in the believer through the union with him in Christ in such a way that capacities of the already indwelling Spirit which are new to the believer are exercised within the believer. This is Spirit release which can bring manifestations of spiritual gifts which are observable externally; exactly what happened at Pentecost and the other four occurrences in Acts. This is Spirit release conceived in calvinist terms, identical with the Pentecostal testimony in its essence.

Further, the nature of the union is unaffected; it still exists as it did previously, and the believer is still the same new creation he became when he was converted, or his election was actualized. Certainly, there has been change to the new creation as there is divine capacity new to the believer manifested within the union, but this has not changed its basic ontology. This new capacity produces a greater manifestation of Christ in the union— the believer becomes more godly in exactly the way Calvin says he should in the ongoing component of regeneration.

Neither is the irresistible nature of God's grace offended by this occurrence. Throughout it all, it is the Spirit who works in the believer and it is

God's intent which will be achieved. While the believer has an involvement, it in no way frustrates what God chooses to do with her in Spirit release.

There is also nothing in this construction which suggests that Spirit release cannot be repeated. The never-ending capacity of God to do something new in the believer through Spirit release is not exhausted by just one occurrence, so the process can be repeated as many times as God desires. Hence the Spirit can be released once in the believer, then released again and again, in a fashion entirely in accord with the witness of Scripture and analogous to the ongoing sanctification of the believer. Certainly, each release is an act of grace, a gift freely given by God, but each release, including the first, is of a different character from the coming of the Spirit at conversion. The new creation comes into being at conversion and is matured through the Spirit's work, including any Spirit release which follows. Spirit release thus conceived is clearly no second work of grace after conversion. Thus, in suggesting this construction a second work is not introduced into Calvin's thought.

Difficulties for a Calvinist Spirit Release

However, this construction is not without its difficulties for Calvin. Two major issues come to mind: the secrecy of the work of the Spirit for Calvin and the relationship of the Spirit and Scripture. The latter also naturally leads to his concern over those who appeal to the unmediated work of the Spirit directly with humans, which cuts the Spirit adrift from Scripture in his view.

Both the secrecy of the Spirit and his relationship to Scripture were discussed above when considering whether Spirit release could be conceived of as an encounter in which Christ alone is apprehended by the believer and the Spirit remains self-effacing. The construction I have just outlined for Spirit release represents, I suggest, a valid Pentecostal account of the event, but within it there is no requirement that the Spirit be apprehended directly by the believer. Thus, it can also be a calvinist construction. The Spirit is certainly released within the believer and some new capacity of God is manifested within her; and this may be seen externally through spiritual gifts; but all that needs be affirmed is that this is the work of God. This is suitable for Calvin for whom one way the presence of the Spirit in the believer is affirmed is by the existence of faith,[65] so that faith is experienced, but the faith-creating Spirit is not apprehended directly. Faith is, in a sense, a surrogate for that direct apprehension. In the same way, spiritual gifts could be surrogates: they are experienced, but do not represent a di-

65. This is affirmed at many places in *Institutes*, see III.2.8; 2.35: IV.14.8.9, etc.

rect apprehension of the Spirit who produces them. There is no necessity that the Spirit be directly encountered in such a way as to be recognizable to the believer in this account.

However, in considering this earlier I concluded that secrecy of the Spirit cannot be maintained within the Pentecostal testimony of Spirit release. To remain true to this witness, the direct apprehension of the Spirit in Spirit release must be maintained. Thus, it is not possible to maintain a calvinist construction of Spirit release which is entirely true to Pentecostal accounts.

The same is largely true of the close relation of Spirit and Scripture which Calvin maintains. Again, I concluded above that Pentecostal views of consistency with Scripture, or even subordination to Scripture, are insufficient to cohere with Calvin's thought. However, in the context of this part of the discussion it is useful to consider how the Spirit for regeneration functions alongside the Spirit for gifts. The Spirit for regeneration comes to the believer, but how is he to know that this has occurred? Certainly, the presence of faith is indicative of the Spirit's presence dwelling within, but the primary means by which the believer knows this is true is through the witness of Scripture. The Spirit illuminates Scripture for the believer, primarily through preaching, to show her that the Holy Spirit indeed dwells in the one who experiences faith. This is also sealed for the believer through the Lord's Supper, where "the visible sign of the invisible grace" shows the presence of the Spirit. However, even here, the truth of this is shown by Scripture under the illumination of the self-same Spirit.

If it is allowed that the Spirit for gifts now comes to the believer through Spirit release, then it can be observed that the validity of these gifts is attested to by Scripture. This is the consistent Pentecostal position: it is not that the Spirit has come and brought something entirely novel. In fact, Pentecostals were concerned to explain what was happening and particularly to assure themselves that this was Christian, that this was God's work. To do so, they turned to Scripture[66] and found in Acts similar occurrences and similar gifts, tongues in particular. That is, they validated their experience by reference to Scripture. Just as Calvin assures his readers that the Spirit for regeneration has come to them because Scripture

---

66. See Wyckoff, "The Baptism in the Holy Spirit," 427, for example. If the experience is authentically Christian, then it will be validated by Scripture. He notes (in a discussion concerning the separability of Spirit release) that Scripture is the authority concerning Spirit release and so is used to validate the experience. Railey and Aker, "Theological Foundations," 51, 59, assert the authority of Scripture in respect of experiences of the Spirit.

shows it to be so, so Pentecostals assure their constituency that the Spirit for gifts has come in the same way.

Accordingly, in this respect, there is a close relation between the Spirit and Scripture in Spirit release. Just as the Spirit for regeneration is validated by Scripture, so Spirit release with gifts following is validated by Scripture. Again, if a solely calvinist construction of Spirit release is sought, it can be said that the truth of the Spirit for regeneration and the Spirit for gifts are both taught by Scripture illuminated by the Spirit. To this extent, Calvin's close linking of the Spirit and Scripture is maintained.

However, as with the secrecy of the Spirit, so with the relation of the Spirit to Scripture. Calvin links the Spirit very closely to Scripture: the Spirit can only speak through Scripture; it is only the words of Scripture which can be the Word of God to the believer and the Spirit seals the promises of the Word on believer's hearts. Accordingly, any other utterance of the Spirit is not admitted to Calvin's thought outside the time of the early church and the apostles' ministry, the most high-profile example being tongues. If glossolalia is understood as the Spirit speaking in an unknown language through the believer, then the direct linkage to Scripture is broken. Similarly, prophetic utterance will break the link.[67] A strict application of Calvin's position would mean that any divine nature claimed for such utterance is to be rejected.

Expanding upon this, Calvin's condemnation of those who exalted "the teaching office of the Spirit" and refused to follow Scripture which they regarded as the "dead and killing letter"[68] is brutal and he regards such as clearly Satanic.[69] It is evident that these, whom he calls Libertines, promote their teaching as sourced in the Spirit of Christ[70] and are making no attempt to ground their views in Scripture. In fact, they view Scripture as a fable,[71] he says, so for Calvin they actively reject Scripture, rather than simply taking little or no account of it. His response is that the apostles of Christ certainly agreed that their source was the Spirit of Christ, but that his influence on them was not to drive them away from Scripture, but

---

67. The evidence of Acts 2 makes clear that tongues can include the speaking of other earthly languages so that their speakers can understand. The possibility that what is being said is Scripture (Old Testament in Acts 2) must be admitted, so this is a special case where tongues could be linked to Scripture in a manner acceptable to Calvin's thought. A similar comment can be made for prophecy.

68. I.9.1

69. Calvin, "On the Authority the Libertines Give Holy Scripture."

70. I.9.1.

71. Calvin, "On the Authority the Libertines Give Holy Scripture."

rather to draw them to it.[72] Imbued by the Spirit, they regarded Scripture with greater reverence.[73]

It is certainly an understatement to say that Calvin mistrusted those who made any claim to receiving anything from the Spirit not contained in Scripture, so one might think that he would view Spirit release askance. Certainly, the Pentecostal claim concerning Spirit release does not have the tight linkage of Spirit and Scripture which Calvin postulates, but neither does it represent the reckless abandonment of Scripture which Calvin condemned in the Libertines. Rather, the Pentecostal position that Scripture has authority over Spirit release, so that whatever occurs within the event or in the operation of spiritual gifts subsequently must be held subordinate to Scripture or consistent with it, gives Scripture the same status as it has within Calvin's thought. It is not the status of Scripture which varies between the two, it is the degree to which the Spirit, in operation in and with believers, is tied to Scripture. Must he be unapprehended by the believer, not perceived directly but revealed only in and through Scripture by a light he provides, or can he be apprehended directly, a glorious vision in complete accord with the scriptural witness concerning him? The latter is very different from the Libertines' position, and while Calvin's view can be inferred as being at the least dubious of Spirit release and its surrounding manifestations because it places the Spirit in a different relation to Scripture from his thought, he would be more kindly disposed towards it in view of the place given to Scripture. However, this is not to say that Pentecostal Spirit release can be aligned with Calvin's theology in respect of the relationship of the Spirit and Scripture; clearly it cannot.

In respect of the secrecy of the Spirit and the Spirit's relation to Scripture then, while a calvinist concept of Spirit release can be conceived as I have outlined, this does not result in a doctrine which is a Pentecostal doctrine. To be a Pentecostal doctrine, some movement from Calvin's position on these two points is necessary. However, this does not leave this discussion bereft at this point, as what I am seeking is an extension from his thought. That is, is there a logical and natural extension of Calvin's thought possible which will establish a strong link between him and Pentecostals in respect of Spirit release? The move required to make the link is to allow the Spirit to be directly apprehended and placed more distantly from Scripture, just as Calvin allows occurred in the early church. It is not inconceivable that

---

72. Parker, *Calvin*, 79, observes that, for Calvin, there is one Christ, one Spirit and one Scripture and that each is consistent with the other and that each is needed. He cites III.3.14 where Calvin says that the Spirit "is not a disturbing apparition," but Christians are to "earnestly seek a knowledge of him from Scripture."

73. I.9.1.

the thought environment of the twentieth and twenty-first centuries would move him to concede that this was once more necessary. It is also worth noting that even the calvinist doctrine of Spirit release I have suggested is a substantial extension from his thought, so it is by no means detrimental to the argument to take the development further to achieve a close identity with Pentecostal thought on Spirit release.

I suggest that what I have briefly outlined is a legitimate extension from Calvin's theology so as to take it towards Pentecostal theology in respect of Spirit release. Taking his union between the believer and Christ and examining the role of the Spirit in it has shown how Spirit release can be conceived in calvinist terms. Discarding the necessity for the secrecy of the Spirit is more *contra* Calvin, as is changing the relation between the Spirit and Scripture. However, Calvin acknowledges both occurred during the early church in the absence of the New Testament. At the very least, tongues and other gifts reveal the Spirit, even if indirectly, and the Spirit directs the apostles' teaching which Calvin views on the same plane as Scripture. Hence, it is not a matter of whether he considered they *could* occur, it is a matter of whether God *wills* that they should continue to occur. Given the different context of Pentecostalism compared to Calvin in sixteenth century Europe and the parallels between Pentecostalism's context and that of the early church, there is ground for an appeal to God giving rise to Spirit release and its accompanying manifestations once again. Taken together, an extension from Calvin's thought can be conceived to produce a doctrine of Spirit release which is well founded in his theology.

Doctrinal Affinities

This study has been concerned to discover whether there is a relation between Calvin's pneumatology and account of the union between the believer and Christ and Pentecostal thought on the subjects and, if so, to show how it might be expressed. After reviewing Calvin's thought, my review of Pentecostal theology, after noting that it was in its infancy, was focused around Spirit release and how it might be employed in contributing to the maturing of a global Pentecostal theology. After all, a person who calls herself a Pentecostal is claiming to be living a post-Spirit release life and one heavily influenced by that release. That is, the Pentecostal life is lived in the context of Spirit release and it is only appropriate that this study be within that context.

The three topics I reviewed are each within this context. The affirmation of faith is heavily reliant upon the Spirit and God's self-authentication through the Spirit for Calvin, something which can only happen through the believer's union with Christ. The Pentecostal looks to the same relation and the initial encounter with the Spirit in Spirit release followed by further encounters of the directly apprehended Spirit for the affirmation of his faith. Calvin affirms a providence of God which the believer discovers through the union and the work of the Spirit; similarly, the Pentecostal affirms the same providence discovered as he relies on what he understands as the direct influence of the Spirit on him and the happenings in his life. When it comes to justification, for Calvin it is entirely christological although it occurs through the union established by the Spirit. Macchia, from the Pentecostal side, suggests that justification is both christological and pneumatological, gathered up in the taking up to participate in God's life, something broader than Calvin's concept of justification, but nevertheless identical to the totality of union, justification, and initial regeneration for Calvin. All three topics are closely concerned with the union between the believer and Christ and the work of the Spirit in and through it.

In considering each, I have looked to discover affinities between Calvin and the Pentecostals. Affinities can be agreement but are not necessarily so. An affinity can be a close identity, so that the core concept is the same, but it is expressed in a differing manner, perhaps by choosing to emphasize some aspects in preference to others. For example, Calvin's doctrine of providence can be said to be "top down"—God has decided what to provide for the elect believer who discovers this provision through Spirit-effected piety—whereas the Pentecostal view, better described as guidance, could be said to be "bottom up." That is, the believer seeks God's guidance and her seeking affects what she receives from God. Through this process she discovers that God makes provision for her. Despite the differences in approach and emphasis, I contend that what each believer has discovered is the same thing: God's provision for them individually. Certainly, the synergistic nature of Pentecostal thought means the Pentecostal believer thinks she has some influence on divine providence (whether she finds a particular provision depends, for her, on whether she seeks guidance on the matter), whereas Calvin's disciple is closely involved, but thinks he has had no influence on the provision. However, the provision itself is the same for each. Thus, while there is no great identity between the two doctrines, there is great affinity as each postulates the discovery of the same thing, a discovery led and enabled by the Spirit.

For each topic, I have identified affinities of this nature. Therefore, looking at only the affinities for the moment, there is a significant alignment between Calvin and Pentecostals in these areas in the context I have used. Such an alignment suggests that there is a helpful relation to be discovered between the two systems,[74] without demonstrating that it exists. Coinciding views on some points do not demonstrate a relationship in which Calvin can be a helpful influence on Pentecostal thought, it is necessary to identify how the relationship might exist and whether, in fact, it does. If a relationship exists, it will be possible to identify bridges between the two systems—logical ways in which they can be related. The example I have just given concerning providence is a good example of a bridge between the two systems. There is common ground between the two doctrines: the providence of God each proposes is identical, so this forms a very real connection. The historical nature of Calvin's theology means that the bridges may offer to Pentecostal expression ways of providing a foundation in the form of Calvin's theology to assist in the development of a global Pentecostal theology.

The Nature of the Affinities

It remains in this part of the discussion to investigate the nature of the affinities identified in chapters three to five and see whether a relation can be hypothesized. They are summarized below.

Assurance of Faith

- There is assurance of faith through the transformation wrought by the coming of the Spirit in both Calvin and Pentecostal thought.
- There is some element of human appraisal of faith in both systems, muted for Calvin but clearly synergistically for Pentecostals.
- In both systems there is reliance on the self-authentication of God in assuring the believer that her faith is genuine and that the object of her faith is, indeed, God.

Providence and Guidance

In addition to God's providence being identical as outlined briefly above, three other points can be made.

- Both systems emphasize the sovereignty of God. This is in different terms, however. Calvin proposes an absolute sovereignty where all that occurs is under God's direct provision (although this is not to mean

---

74. By relation, I mean that one system can look to the other within the affinities and incorporate an identified affinity within the development of its own views.

that he solely determines all that occurs). Pentecostals adopt an Arminian position, where individual actions are affected by human decisions, although with the concurrence of God. However, none of these actions frustrate God's over-arching purposes for his creation in any way.

- Providence is to be discovered. The Calvinist believer discovers what God has already determined to provide as it occurs, the Pentecostal discovers that same providence by actively seeking it, almost bit by bit.
- Each believer, whether Pentecostal or Calvinist, makes this discovery in the same way. It is a journey facilitated by looking to God and working to be a more godly person as time passes, although for Calvin this is entirely worked by the Spirit, whose secrecy means the believer experiences it as their work.

Justification

Macchia's proposition sees justification as being a unity in which the believer is taken up into God's life. This is equivalent to three separate actions for Calvin: union, justification, and initial regeneration. Macchia is not merely redefining justification but is proposing a direct role for the Spirit in justification based on his reading of the New Testament. As Calvin adopts a different reading, Macchia's proposal does not align well with Calvin's view, but there are nevertheless affinities to be seen.

- The union is separate from justification for Calvin but occurs immediately prior to justification and is necessary for justification. The union is established by the Spirit, so there is an indirect link between the Spirit and justification. Justification is not possible without the union, so while it is Christ who justifies, the activity of the Spirit is necessary for justification to occur.
- Similarly, for Calvin, justification is through faith which is in turn a gift of the Spirit to the believer. Again, the activity of the Spirit is necessary to justification.
- Justification is trinitarian for both Macchia and Calvin. It is more directly so for Macchia as he postulates the direct activity of Christ and the Spirit in justification synergistically, where their roles are not clearly distinct. Calvin assigns distinct roles to each hypostasis and gives a direct role only to Christ.[75]

75. I have said previously that justification is entirely christological for Calvin. These three points highlight an involvement of the Spirit, but it is still true to say that justification is entirely christological for him as the Spirit is sent by Christ.

Within these affinities there can be discerned at least two kinds of linkages between the two systems of thought. The first is where there is common ground, some aspect in which each conceives of something which is identical and so common to both. Under *Assurance of Faith* this is seen in the role of the Spirit in transforming believers and a reliance on the self-authentication of God. For *Providence and Guidance* it is God's provision for each believer; the journey of discovery for each believer concerning God's providence; and the fact that it is experienced in the same way for believers in each system.

The second is where there is no real common ground, but there are very close conceptions. These are, of course the remaining affinities listed above, but there are differing characters of similarity. Hence, under *Assurance of Faith* there is human appraisal in each system, but it differs in degree between them: it is substantively the believer's appraisal for Pentecostals, but of a very muted nature for Calvin and always struggling with his doctrine of election. Under *Providence and Guidance*, the sovereignty of God is asserted by both systems, but is of a significantly different nature in each. For *Justification*, the existence of the union and faith mean that for Calvin the Spirit's activity is necessary for justification, but without direct involvement, so the affinity is in the nature of an association. Similarly, characterizing each system's view of justification as trinitarian is correct, but Calvin assigns distinct roles to Christ and the Spirit in a way that Macchia does not, so here the difference is one of roles assigned to the hypostases within the Godhead.

I suggested above that the sort of common ground I have described under the first category can form a bridge between Calvin and Pentecostals—here there are things in respect of the relationship between the believer and Christ and pneumatology on which they can agree. Of course, there are many things on which they can agree on account of Pentecostals' borrowing of evangelical theology, but these two subjects—the union and pneumatology—are at the heart of Pentecostal thought and they are brought together in Spirit release. There, the Pentecostal believer encounters the triune God in a new and deeper way through the directly apprehended work of the Spirit and sees that encounter enriched by the operation of spiritual gifts. After Spirit release, the Pentecostal has a new sense of intimacy with God in the union she enjoys with Godself which leads her to seek God more and more as an active agent in her life.

As she seeks to explain what has occurred she can look to these bridges and see another context which reaches out to give shape to the thing she has experienced, a context which does not include Spirit release. It is not that Spirit release has left her isolated from Christian thought, it is that it has brought a different perspective to what already exists in Christian thought represented, in this case, by Calvin. Spirit release brings her to a place where she can agree with Calvin on a common ground and then work out, from there, a theology which makes sense of her experience.

I have already shown that Spirit release can be couched in calvinist terms, so the event itself is not isolated from his thought. There is no need for Pentecostal thought to deny its fresh expression to align with Calvin, but it can easily say that from this common ground it chooses to understand its experience in *this* manner. In doing so it is extending from Calvin's position to give shape to its testimony concerning Spirit baptism.

The same applies to the bridges I have identified under the topics above. For example, Calvin relies on the self-authentication of God in addressing the assurance of faith for the believer. The Spirit is involved in this, and uses the means employed through the church, preaching the Word and the sacraments, to give assurance. The Spirit illuminates them to the believer and thus demonstrates the truth of them. At a more elemental level, the very existence of any faith at all is a gift of the Spirit, so is a form of God's self-authentication to the believer. The Pentecostal also appeals to God's self-authentication to assure himself that it is God he encountered in Spirit baptism and it is God who continues to ensure that the believer knows it is God in whom he places his faith. In this, he is greatly assisted by Scripture which he regards as authoritative beyond his experience and he must see his experience reflected there to give it validity. He can comfortably borrow from Calvin the assurance that the Spirit will illuminate Scripture for him, so if he sees his experience validated there according to a defendable Pentecostal reading of Scripture, then he can have confidence that he did indeed encounter God in Spirit release and that it is indeed God who operates in spiritual gifts and other experiences of Spirit release. Once again, a legitimate Pentecostal theology can be developed from a common position with Calvin which simply takes *this* view of Scripture and experience and so differs from Calvin.

I do not propose to rehearse this approach for each of the affinities I have identified which rest on common ground as these two samples amply demonstrate what is available in the bridges or touch points. But those affinities which are based on similarities do need further consideration. Take the first I highlighted, the human appraisal involved in the assurance of faith in each system. For Calvin this has to be teased out, which results in some implication that there is an essential human response of sorts to confirm faith and an introspective judgement of conscience on the part of the believer, both of which contribute to assurance of faith. This is different to the Pentecostal account in which the believer, occupying a different thought world in which the concept of objective observation being able to be utilized to show the truth or otherwise of a thing holds sway, can own his faith and use his own judgement of what occurs and so overtly use his capabilities to gain assurance of his faith. While here the Pentecostal cannot point to agreement, he can say that there is a seed of his view within Calvin. There is no touch point, but there is a starting point.

There are real differences between the views on the sovereignty of God, which mirror the differences between Calvin and the Arminian position. It is difficult to conceive of Calvin ever being other than dismissive of the Arminian position, as the idea that individual humans (even with the concurrence of God) can affect the detailed progress of history cannot be reconciled with his detailed view. However, they do share the core ideal that the ultimate purposes of God cannot be frustrated, and here the Pentecostal can agree with Calvin. Her experience of Spirit release has given her a new appreciation of the magnitude of God and God's concern for her. While this contains within it the risk that she will begin to see God as there to assist her in achieving her own objectives, it equally, if not more so, contains the opportunity to understand that God overwhelms her and is to be served; so she should subordinate her desires to his. If this opportunity is taken up, then she understands she must dedicate herself to God's purposes and she can wholeheartedly agree with Calvin on those and commit herself to assisting them by placing herself at the disposal of God. Calvin's view of God's purposes will assist her in placing herself in proper relation to him and serve as an encouragement to serve him, rather than have him serve her. Thus, Calvin assists Pentecostal thought in this way.

The other two affinities surround the role of the Spirit in Macchia's proposal concerning justification and the trinitarian nature of justification. In both, the role of the Spirit is writ large in the Pentecostal view compared to Calvin. There is a direct role in justification, according to Macchia, but the Spirit is only involved indirectly for Calvin, creating the conditions for justification. This is exactly reflected in the two accounts of the trinitarian nature of justification. What does this offer Pentecostals?

There is no doubt that the role given the Spirit by Macchia is of a totally different order from that in Calvin. Macchia has drawn the Spirit to a prominence not enjoyed in Calvin—the hypostasis who is self-effacing and secretly acting to create the conditions in which Christ can justify is brought to the center to stand alongside Christ to do some of the heavy lifting involved in justification. There is no common ground, but Macchia at least is not introducing the Spirit to the stage, he is simply shifting the Spirit's mark to one appropriate to a starring role. The Spirit is there in Calvin; Macchia could be said to make use of that to develop a bigger role for him. Thus, where Calvin says that the Spirit creates the union in which Christ can act to justify, Macchia says that is so, but the union is justifying in itself through what it makes possible, so the Spirit is justifying also. It is in this sense a magnifying of the Spirit present in Calvin in this respect, once again a sort of seed for Pentecostals to grasp and develop.

These affinities allow the development of Pentecostal doctrines from Calvin's thought in the ways I have suggested. From Spirit release to doctrines on the assurance of faith, providence and justification, starting points or common touch points can be identified in Calvin from where Pentecostal doctrines concerning pneumatology and the union of Christ and the believer can be developed. This does not require the application of what I term calvinist ideas to Spirit release in order to make use of his thought; new concepts which arise out of the Pentecostal world context and their claim to a direct encounter with God, in which the Spirit is directly apprehended are certainly admissible. The task, after all, is to develop a global *Pentecostal* theology. I have shown how the affinities allow Pentecostals to give witness to their experience by using Calvin's theology to show that their testimony has a base within historical Christian thought and that they can appeal to that for validity as a supplement to their appeal to Scripture. It is not my intent to embark on that development here, but it is appropriate to point out what this offers to Pentecostal thought. That extensions from Calvin's thought in Pentecostal terms are possible means that Pentecostals can look back to Calvin for support in their critical, distinct doctrines and this can be of immense benefit to them.

Pentecostals Looking to Calvin

As I pointed out at the start of this chapter, popular opinion on Calvin means that he is not an immediately obvious source of support for the development of Pentecostal doctrines, but his account of the intimate interest God takes in the life of the elect closely parallels the Pentecostal testimony to the everyday presence of God through the Spirit in the life of the believer, available to guide and direct as his assistance is sought. Even Duffield and Van Cleave's description of life with the Spirit as a "personally conducted tour,"[76] which takes God's interest to an extreme, is closely aligned to Calvin's position. For Calvin, everything which occurs in the believer's life is according to God's purpose, which is akin to the activity of a tour guide although the involvement of the believer needs to be taken into account. From this point of contact many others can be developed in detail, as I have done, demonstrating the richness that is available to Pentecostals in Calvin's thought. This rich-

---

76. Duffield and Van Cleave, *Foundations of Pentecostal Theology*, 285.

ness offers great assistance to Pentecostalism as it works on its own global theology, giving a powerful link to the history of Christian thought to stand alongside Pentecostalism's reading of Scripture.

Historically, the Pentecostal position has been largely defined by the view that all that is needed in the Christian life and witness is the Spirit and Scripture. Hollenweger discusses this, citing P. v. d. Woude; "we cannot go wrong if we keep to the teaching of Jesus and his apostles."[77] He also notes that Scripture is understood as the directly inspired infallible word of God and highlights the rejection of "higher criticism" as undermining faith in the supernatural.[78] This is what underlies Gabriel's description of Pentecostal theology as a 'biblical' theology, tied tightly to Scripture, which he contrasts to the academic discipline of biblical theology.[79] While the church started with the Old Testament and the teaching of Jesus and the apostles, the approach is very limiting, as it firstly refuses to give credence to the reality that in writing such a theology an interpretation of Scripture is offered and it is no longer Spirit and Scripture alone which are in play.[80] Secondly, it attempts to completely ignore the rich history of biblical interpretation and development of theology which has continued since the early church and of which Calvin is a very significant part.[81]

There is great benefit here for Pentecostal theology in the touch points with Calvin from which a deeper engagement with his thought can be entered and, through him, also with the wider history of Christian thought. By adopting such an approach, no longer is Pentecostalism left with its reading of Scripture as the sole basis for its theology in respect of pneumatology and union. Now it can be directly engaged with a major Christian theologian and thus gain greater depth and wider acceptance for its theological positions.

Recognition of the calvinist account of Spirit release and its extension to form a Pentecostal doctrine will also aid in the development of a global doctrine. As I have noted, there is no agreed position on Spirit release, with the occurrence being affirmed, but there being disagreement on its character or content. An example will serve to highlight these differences and how Calvin

77. V. D. Woude, *Pinksterboodschap*, cited in Hollenweger, *The Pentecostals*, 294.
78. Hollenweger, *The Pentecostals*, 291–97.
79. Gabriel, "This Spirit is God," 74–75.
80. This was well illustrated by a charismatic meeting attended by the author in late 2014. The speaker took as his topic the "simple gospel" based on the premise that Scripture was all that was required, as opposed to theology. He then proceeded to embellish the scriptural text he used, thus engaging upon the very thing he was opposing!
81. "Calvin is arguably the most influential theologian of the English-speaking world" according to Zachman, *John Calvin Reconsidered*, 233.

can assist. Classical Pentecostalism asserts that Spirit release occurs with tongues following. That is, that speaking in tongues *always* accompanies Spirit release. This is held so tightly that failure to speak in tongues is accounted as evidence that Spirit release has not occurred. Thus, the content of Spirit release always includes receiving the gift of tongues—it is so closely identified with it that it is part of the event itself. Other Pentecostal expressions, labelled Charismatic and Neocharismatic by Studebaker,[82] do not take this position: Spirit release may occur without tongues following. This is a different happening from that described by Classical Pentecostalism.

However, Spirit release developed in the calvinist form I have outlined can easily accommodate both views. As release is the expression or manifestation of some capacity of the Spirit new to the believer, whether this includes speaking in tongues or not is not definitive of the happening. The new capacity can include tongues, of course, but it need not. All three Pentecostal streams can agree upon the doctrine of Spirit release as the manifestation of a capacity new to the believer, while acknowledging that the actual capacity may, or will, differ between believers.

Calvin can also assist Pentecostals in dealing with the risks associated with isolating the Spirit, which can occur as a result of Pentecostal doctrine on Spirit release focusing on the Spirit coming to empower and equip the believer for Christian witness. This focus on the Spirit leaves out the Father and Christ and can lead to excesses. Take spiritual gifts, for example, which Grudem sums up as *tools* for the work of ministry.[83] Such a definition contains within it the possibility that the believer will understand gifts as being at his disposal, as tools are, and that they can be used for his purposes. Similarly, the activity of the Spirit in Scripture or elsewhere can be studied in order to develop what might be called spiritual principles which apply to the Christian life. While there may be use in identifying such principles *per se*, the invitation they contain is that some outcome can be secured if the principles are followed. That is, that if a believer is obedient to God in following a particular spiritual principle, then God will be obedient to the principle and provide the outcome promised. This can be seen in the Pentecostal figure Derek Prince, who taught that giving financially would see God repay abundantly in the same coin.[84] The logical outcome of this teaching is that a believer can be-

---

82. Studebaker, "The Dynamism of Pentecostal Theology," 21.

83. Grudem, *Systematic Theology*, 1031 (emphasis his).

84. Prince, *Derek Prince*, 242–45. Prince is certainly at what might be called the conservative end of this view, making clear that it is God who gives the abundance in his time and hedging the principle about with conditions to be met by the believer, including faith. Nevertheless, the core of his idea is that giving in God's service *will* result in God providing financial abundance for the giver.

come wealthy by giving to the ministry. The risk is that the recipient minister will demonstrate the truth of the principle by becoming wealthy, while at the same time potentially impoverishing the givers.

The calvinist position on Spirit release I have developed is a powerful corrective for these sort of results, alongside the full content of Spirit release. As I have noted, the early testimonies of Spirit release were intensely trinitarian: while the Spirit was apprehended directly, the encounter was also with the Father and the Son. Those who spoke of the experience spoke of receiving new insight and conviction about God as Father, Son and Spirit. The recovery of this full content will assist in restraining the excesses which can result from isolating the Spirit, and this is materially helped by the calvinist conception. There, Spirit release occurs within the context of the union between the believer and Christ, so can never be separated from Christ. The union is one in which the believer is *in Christ*, so it is from here that Spirit release occurs, Christ is closely associated with the release, as he must be as the one who baptizes with the Spirit. Put another way, the union is between the believer and Christ and the Spirit is released within this new creation formed at conversion. The being of the believer includes the presence of Christ in the union, so the release of the Spirit is into this being which is inclusive of Christ. Thus, Christ moderates Spirit release and must always be considered in the manifestations of the Spirit which result. In this context, looking to use spiritual gifts for the believer's own purposes cannot be sustained as in the union the believer is in Christ so must be involved in his purposes, not her own. Looking from this vantage point further into Calvin's thought, we see that the believer's own purposes can never be godly, so on this ground such activity must be rejected also. The same points can be made concerning giving to adhere to some spiritual principle: such principles must always be moderated by Christ and his presence in the believer and his attitudes to giving and wealth considered.

Conclusion

In each of these ways I have briefly canvassed, there is advantage to Pentecostal thought in looking to Calvin as it grapples with its own theology. After more than a century of existence as a Christian stream, Pentecostalism is beginning its engagement with this task of developing a global theology representative of the stream. This effort is not insubstantial, and its development will take time, but will inevitably mean much consideration of Spirit release and the context it creates for Pentecostal pneumatology and accounts of the union between the believer and Christ. In this respect, Calvin's thought offers touch points and, through them, a rich resource to assist Pentecostalism in its task. As Pentecostalism looks ahead, there is immense benefit in it also looking to its heritage in Christian thought, represented by Calvin.

Bibliography

Acts Churches New Zealand. "Statement of Belief." http://www.actschurches.com/statement-of-belief/.
Badcock, Gary D. *Light of Truth and Fire of Love: A Theology of the Holy Spirit*. Grand Rapids: Eerdmans, 1997.
Barrett, C. K. *The Acts of the Apostles*. The International Critical Commentary. Edinburgh: T. & T. Clark, 1994.
Barth, Karl. *Church Dogmatics II/2*. Edinburgh: T. & T. Clark, 1957.
Billings, J Todd. *Calvin, Participation and the Gift*. Oxford: Oxford University Press, 2007.
Boulton, Matthew Myer. *Life in God: John Calvin, Practical Formation, and the Future of Protestant Theology*. Grand Rapids: Eerdmans, 2011.
Brittenden, Wayne. "Wayne Brittenden's Counterpoint—Calvinism." Radio New Zealand's "Sunday Morning." Radio broadcast. October 12, 2014. https://www.radionz.co.nz/national/programmes/sunday/audio/20153077/wayne-brittenden's-counterpoint-calvinism.
Bruner, Frederick Dale. *A Theology of the Holy Spirit: the Pentecostal Experience and the New Testament Witness*. London: Hodder and Stoughton, 1971.
Burgess, Stanley M. "Implications of Eastern Christian Pneumatology for Western Pentecostal Doctrine and Practice." In *Experiences of the Spirit: Conference on Pentecostal and Charismatic Research in Europe at Utrecht University 1989*, edited by Jan A. B. Jongeneel, 23–34. Frankfurt am Main: Peter Lang, 1991.
Calvin, John. *The Acts of the Apostles*. Edited by David W. Torrance and Thomas F. Torrance. Translated by John W. Fraser and W. J. G. McDonald. 2 vols. Calvin's New Testament Commentaries. Grand Rapids: Eerdmans, 1965.
———. *Against the Fantastic and Furious Sect of the Libertines*. http://solideogloria.ch/reformation/english/libertines.html.
———. *The Epistles of Paul to the Romans and Thessalonians*. Edited by David W. Torrance and Thomas F. Torrance. Translated by R. MacKenzie. Calvin's New Testament Commentaries. Grand Rapids: Eerdmans, 1960.
———. *The First Epistle of Paul to the Corinthians*. Edited by David W. Torrance and Thomas F. Torrance. Translated by R. MacKenzie. Calvin's New Testament Commentaries. Grand Rapids: Eerdmans, 1960.
———. *Galatians, Ephesians, Philippians and Colossians*. Edited by David W. Torrance and Thomas F. Torrance. Translated by T. H. L. Parker. Calvin's New Testament Commentaries. Grand Rapids: Eerdmans, 1965.

———. *Institutes of the Christian Religion.* Edited by John T. McNeill. Translated by Ford Lewis Battles. Louisville: Westminster John Knox, 1960.

———. *The Second Epistle of Paul to the Corinthians, and the Epistles to Timothy, Titus and Philemon.* Edited by David W. Torrance and Thomas F. Torrance. Translated by T. A. Smail. Calvin's New Testament Commentaries. Grand Rapids: Eerdmans, 1964.

Canlis, Julie. "Calvin, Osiander and Participation in God." *International Journal of Systematic Theology* 6/2 (April 2004) 169–84.

Chan, Simon. *Pentecostal Theology and the Christian Spiritual Tradition.* Journal of Pentecostal Theology Supplement Series 21. Sheffield: Sheffield Academic, 2000.

Chapman, Wallace. "Sunday Morning." Radio New Zealand National. Radio broadcast. October 12, 2014. http://www.radionz.co.nz/search/results?utf8=%E2%9C%93&q=calvinist+Dunedin.

Charry, Ellen T. *By the Renewing of Your Minds: The Pastoral Function of Christian Doctrine.* New York: Oxford University Press, 1997.

Cunnington, Ralph. "Calvin's Doctrine of the Lord's Supper: A Blot Upon His Labors as a Public Instructor?" *Westminster Theological Journal* 73 (2011) 215–36.

Dabney, D. Lyle. "Justified by the Spirit: Soteriological Reflections on the Resurrection." *International Journal of Systematic Theology* 3/1 (March 2001) 46–68.

Davidson, Alan. *Christianity in Aotearoa.* Wellington: New Zealand Education for Ministry, 1997.

Douglas, J. D., ed. *The Illustrated Bible Dictionary.* Leicester: InterVarsity, 1980.

Duffield, G. P., and N. M. Van Cleave. *Foundations of Pentecostal Theology.* Los Angeles: L.I.F.E. Bible College, 1983.

Dunn, James D. G. *The Baptism in the Holy Spirit: A Re-examination on the New Testament Teaching on the Gift of the Spirit in Relation to Pentecostalism Today.* London: SCM, 1970.

———. "Towards the Spirit of Christ: The Emergence of the Distinctive Features of Christian Pneumatology." In *The Work of the Spirit: Pneumatology and Pentecostalism,* edited by Michael Welker, 3–26. Kindle ed. Grand Rapids: Eerdmans, 2006.

Dusing, Michael L. "The New Testament Church." In *Systematic Theology,* edited by Stanley M. Horton, 525–65. Springfield, MO: Gospel, 2007.

Edmondson, Stephen. *Calvin's Christology.* Cambridge: Cambridge University Press, 2004.

Elbert, Paul. "Calvin and the Spiritual Gifts." In *An Elaboration of the Theology of Calvin,* edited by Richard C. Gamble, 303–31. Articles on Calvin and Calvinism. New York: Garland, 1992.

Evans, William B. "Calvin's Doctrine of the Lord's Supper and its Relevance for Today." *Foundations* 68 (May 2015) 4–25.

Fee, Gordon D. "Baptism in the Holy Spirit: The Issue of Separability and Subsequence." *Pneuma* 7/2 (Fall 1985) 87–99.

———. *God's Empowering Presence: The Holy Spirit in the Letters of Paul.* Peabody, MA: Hendrickson, 1994.

"From Other Pentecostal Papers." *The Apostolic Faith,* May 1907, 3.

Gabriel, Andrew K. "This Spirit is God: A Pentecostal Perspective on the Doctrine of the Divine Attributes." In *Defining Issues in Pentecostalism: Classical and Emergent,* edited by Steven M. Studebaker, 69–98. McMaster Theological Studies. Eugene, OR: Wipf & Stock, 2008.

Grudem, Wayne. *Systematic Theology: An Introduction to Biblical Doctrine*. Leicester: InterVarsity, 1994.
Helm, Paul. *John Calvin's Ideas*. Oxford: Oxford University Press, 2004.
Higgins, John R. "God's Inspired Word." In *Systematic Theology*, edited by Stanley M. Horton, 61–115. Springfield, MO: Gospel, 2007.
Hobbes, Thomas. *Leviathan*. Kindle ed. Irvine, CA: Xist, 2015.
Hocken, Peter. "Jesus Christ and the Gifts of the Spirit." *Pneuma* 5/1 (Spring 1983) 1–16.
———. "The Meaning and Purpose of 'Baptism in the Spirit.'" *Pneuma* 7/2 (Fall 1985) 125–33.
Hollenweger, Walter J. *The Pentecostals*. Translated by R. A. Wilson. Minneapolis: SCM, 1972.
Horton, Michael. *Christless Christianity*. Grand Rapids: Baker, 2008.
Horton, Stanley M., ed. *Systematic Theology*. Springfield, MO: Gospel, 2007.
"In a Divine Trance." *The Apostolic Faith*, May 1907, 2.
Jenney, Timothy P. "The Holy Spirit and Sanctification." In *Systematic Theology*, edited by Stanley M. Horton, 397–421. Springfield, MO: Gospel, 2007.
Jongeneel, Jan A. B., ed. *Experiences of the Spirit: Conference on Pentecostal and Charismatic Research in Europe at Utrecht University 1989*. Frankfurt am Main: Peter Lang, 1991.
Kärkkäinen, Veli-Matti. *A Constructive Christian Theology for the Pluralistic World*. Vol. 1, *Christ and Reconciliation*. Grand Rapids: Eerdmans, 2013.
———. "Deification View." In *Justification: Five Views*, edited by James K. Beilby and Paul Rhodes Eddy. Downers Grove, IL: InterVarsity, 2011.
Klaus, Byron D. "The Mission of the Church." In *Systematic Theology*, edited by Stanley M. Horton, 567–94. Springfield, MO: Gospel, 2007.
Land, Steven J. *Pentecostal Spirituality: A Passion for the Kingdom*. Journal of Pentecostal Studies Supplement Series 1. Sheffield: Sheffield Academic, 1994.
Lessing, Gotthold Ephraim. *Lessing: Philosophical and Theological Writings*. Edited and translated by H. B. Nisbet. Cambridge: Cambridge University Press, 2005.
Lim, David. "Spiritual Gifts." In *Systematic Theology*, edited by Stanley M. Horton, 457–88. Springfield, MO: Gospel, 2007.
Lossky, Vladimir. "The Procession of the Spirit in Orthodox Trinitarian Doctrine." In *In the Image and Likeness of God*, 71–96. London: Mowbrays, 1975.
Macchia, Frank D. *Baptized in the Spirit: A Global Pentecostal Theology*. Grand Rapids: Zondervan, 2006.
———. "Justification and the Spirit: A Pentecostal Reflection on the Doctrine by Which the Church Stands or Falls." *Pneuma* 22/1 (Spring 2000) 3–21.
———. *Justified in the Spirit: Creation, Redemption, and the Triune God*. Grand Rapids: Eerdmans, 2010.
Macdonald, A. M., ed. *Chambers Twentieth Century Dictionary*. Edinburgh: W & R Chambers, 1972.
Marshall, I. Howard. *Acts*. Tyndale New Testament Commentaries. Grand Rapids: Eerdmans, 1980.
———. *New Testament Theology: Many Witnesses, One Gospel*. Downers Grove, IL: InterVarsity, 2004.
Matera, Frank J. *New Testament Theology: Exploring Diversity and Unity*. Louisville: Westminster John Knox, 2007.

McDonnell, Killian. *John Calvin, the Church, and the Eucharist.* Princeton: Princeton University Press, 1967.

McFarland, Ian A., et al., eds. *The Cambridge Dictionary of Christian Theology.* Cambridge: Cambridge University Press, 2011.

McGee, Gary B. "Historical Background." In *Systematic Theology,* edited by Stanley M. Horton, 9–38. Springfield, MO: Gospel, 2007.

McGrath, Alister. *Christianity's Dangerous New Idea: The Protestant Revolution—A History from the Sixteenth Century to the Twenty-First.* New York: HarperOne, 2007.

———. *Iustitia Dei: A History of the Christian Doctrine of Justification.* 3rd ed. Cambridge: Cambridge University Press, 2005.

McLean, Mark D. "The Holy Spirit." In *Systematic Theology,* edited by Stanley M. Horton, 375–95. Springfield, MO: Gospel, 2007.

McRoberts, Kerry D. "The Holy Trinity." In *Systematic Theology,* edited by Stanley M. Horton, 145–77. Springfield, MO: Gospel, 2007.

Menzies, William W., and Stanley M. Horton. *Bible Doctrines: A Pentecostal Perspective.* Springfield, MO: Gospel, 1993.

Niesel, Wilhelm. *The Theology of Calvin.* Translated by Harold Knight. London: Lutterworth, 1956.

Olsen, Roger E. *Arminian Theology: Myths and Realities.* Downers Grove, IL: InterVarsity, 2006.

Packer, J. I. *Evangelical Influences: Profiles of Figures and Movements Rooted in the Reformation.* Peabody, MA: Hendrickson, 1999.

Parker, T. H. L. *Calvin: An Introduction to His Thought.* Louisville: Westminster/John Knox, 1995.

Pecota, Daniel B. "The Saving Work of Christ." In *Systematic Theology,* edited by Stanley M. Horton, 325–74. Springfield, MO: Gospel, 2007.

Penner, Todd. "Madness in the Method? The Acts of the Apostles in Current Study." *Currents in Biblical Research* 2/2 (2004) 223–93.

Pitkin, Barbara. "Faith and Justification." In *The Calvin Handbook,* edited by Herman J. Selderhuis. Grand Rapids: Eerdmans, 2009.

Prince, Derek. *Derek Prince on Experiencing God's Power.* New Kensington: Whitaker, 1998.

Railey, James H., Jr., and Benny C Aker. "Theological Foundations." In *Systematic Theology,* edited by Stanley M. Horton, 39–60. Springfield, MO: Gospel, 2007.

Redding, Graham. *Prayer and the Priesthood of Christ in the Reformed Tradition.* Edinburgh: T. & T. Clark, 2003.

Ross, Peter. "New Life for Old: A Hint to Pentecostalism from John Calvin." BTheol (Hons) Dissertation, University of Otago, 2009.

Rowe, C. Kavin. *World Upside Down: Reading Acts in the Graeco-Roman Age.* Oxford: Oxford University Press, 2009.

Schnabel, Eckhard J. *Acts.* Exegetical Commentary on the New Testament. Grand Rapids: Zondervan, 2012.

Selderhuis, Herman J., ed. *The Calvin Handbook.* English ed. Grand Rapids: Eerdmans, 2009.

Shepherd, Victor A. *The Nature and Function of Faith in the Theology of John Calvin.* National Association of Baptist Professors of Religion Dissertation Series 2. Macon, GA: Mercer University Press, 1983.

Stanglin, Keith D., and Thomas H. McCall. *Jacob Arminius: Theologian of Grace.* New York: Oxford University Press, 2012.

Strondstad, Roger. "The Charismatic Theology of St Luke Revisited (Special Emphasis Upon Being Baptized in the Holy Spirit.)" In *Defining Issues in Pentecostalism: Classical and Emergent,* edited by Steven M Studebaker, 101–22. McMaster Theological Studies. Eugene, OR: Wipf & Stock, 2008.

Studebaker, Steven M. "Introduction: The Dynamism of Pentecostal Theology." In *Defining Issues in Pentecostalism: Classical and Emergent.* McMaster Theological Studies Series. Eugene, OR: Wipf & Stock, 2008.

———. "Pentecostal Soteriology and Pneumatology." *Journal of Pentecostal Theology* 11/2 (April 2003) 248–70.

Suurmond, Jean-Jaques. "The Meaning and Purpose of Spirit Baptism and the Charisms." In *Experiences of the Spirit: Conference on Pentecostal and Charismatic Research in Europe at Utrecht University 1989,* edited by Jan A. B. Jongeneel, 35–62. Frankfurt am Main: Peter Lang, 1991.

Sweetman, L. "The Gifts of the Spirit: A Study of Calvin's Comments on 1 Corinthians 12:8-10; Romans 12:6-8; Ephesians 4:11." In *Exploring the Heritage of John Calvin,* edited by David F. Holwerda, 273–303. Grand Rapids: Baker, 1976.

Tamburello, Dennis E. *Union with Christ: John Calvin and the Mysticism of St. Bernard.* Columbia Series in Reformed Theology. Louisville: Westminster John Knox, 1994.

Tanner, Kathryn. *Christ the Key.* Kindle ed. Current Issues in Theology. Cambridge: Cambridge University Press, 2010.

———. *Jesus, Humanity and the Trinity: A Brief Systematic Theology.* Minneapolis: Fortress, 2001.

"A Testimony in Tongues." *The Apostolic Faith,* May 1907, 2.

Trebilco, Paul. *The Early Christians in Ephesus From Paul to Ignatius.* Grand Rapids: Eerdmans, 2004.

Van Buren, Paul. *Christ in Our Place: The Substitutionary Character of Calvin's Doctrine of Reconciliation.* Edinburgh: Oliver & Boyd, 1957.

Welker, Michael, ed. *The Work of the Spirit: Pneumatology and Pentecostalism.* Kindle ed. Grand Rapids: Eerdmans, 2006.

Williams, J. Rodman. *Renewal Theology.* 3 vols. Grand Rapids: Zondervan, 1988–92.

Witherington, Ben. "Christ." In *Dictionary of Paul and His Letters,* edited by G. F. Hawthorne et al. Downers Grove, IL: InterVarsity, 1993.

Worsfold, Luke W. "Subsequence, Prophecy and Church Order in the Apostolic Church, New Zealand." PhD diss., Victoria University of Wellington, 2004.

Wyckoff, John W. "The Baptism in the Holy Spirit." In *Systematic Theology,* edited by Stanley M. Horton. Springfield, MO: Gospel, 2007.

"Ye Are My Witnesses." *The Apostolic Faith,* May 1907, 4.

Yong, Amos. *The Spirit Poured Out on All Flesh: Pentecostalism and the Possibility of Global Theology.* Grand Rapids: Baker Academic, 2005.

Zachman, Randall C. *The Assurance of Faith: Conscience in the Theology of Martin Luther and John Calvin.* Louisville: Westminster John Knox, 2005.

———. "Communio cum Christo." In *The Calvin Handbook,* edited by Herman J. Selderhuis. Grand Rapids: Eerdmans, 2009.

———. "'Deny Yourself and Take up Your Cross': John Calvin on the Christian Life." *International Journal of Systematic Theology* 11/4 (October 2009) 466–82.

———. *Image and Word in the Theology of John Calvin*. Notre Dame: University of Notre Dame Press, 2009.

———. *John Calvin as Teacher, Pastor, and Theologian: The Shape of His Writings and Thought*. Grand Rapids: Baker Academic, 2006.

———. *Reconsidering John Calvin*. Current Issues in Theology. Cambridge: Cambridge University Press, 2012.

Zodhiates, Spiros, ed. *The Complete Word Study New Testament*. Chattanooga: AMG, 1991.

www.ingramcontent.com/pod-product-compliance
Lightning Source LLC
Chambersburg PA
CBHW050347230426
43663CB00010B/2017